Out
in the
Workplace

The Pleasures and Perils of

Coming Out on the Job

Richard A. Rasi, D.Min.
Lourdes Rodríguez-Nogués, Ed.D.
Editors

alyson publications, los angeles, calif.

Typeset and printed in the United States of America.

This is a trade paperback original from Alyson Publications, Inc.,
P.O. Box 4371, Los Angeles, California 90078.

First edition, first printing: October 1995

5 4 3 2 1

ISBN 1-55583-251-2

Library of Congress Cataloging-in-Publication Data

Out in the workplace : the pleasures and perils of coming out on
        the job / Richard A. Rasi, Lourdes Rodríguez-Nogués.

     p.   cm.

ISBN 1-55583-251-2 (pbk.)
1. Gays—Employment—United States. 2. Coming out (Sexual
orientation)—United States—Case studies. 3. Sex discrimination
in employment—United States. 4. Gays—United States—
Psychology. 5. Gays—United States—Conduct of life. 6. Gays—
Legal status, laws, etc.—United States.   I. Rasi, Richard A., 1949–
II. Rodríguez-Nogués, Lourdes, 1947–
HD6285.5.U6088 1995
331.5—dc20

95-44790
CIP

Advance praise for *Out in the Workplace:*

"The stories in *Out in the Workplace* are stories of courage and joy. These individuals have chosen to bring all of who they are to all of what they do. If management today wants gays, lesbians, and bisexuals to give all that they have, they need to allow them to be all of who they are in the workplace. This book challenges all of us to live our lives with authenticity."
—*Virginia Apuzzo, commissioner, New York State Civil Service Commission; former executive director, National Gay and Lesbian Task Force*

"*Out in the Workplace* presents poignant testimonials to the power of coming out. The authentic, personal stories in this book shatter stereotypes of gay people for the nongay reader and show gay readers that they are not alone."
—*Tim McFeeley, former executive director, Human Rights Campaign Fund*

"When we tell our stories, as these lesbians and gay men have so boldly done, we put a face on the issue for those who do not understand. The workplace is filled with good people who simply do not understand the pressures faced by gay employees. Everyone who reads this important book has the opportunity to be both enlightened and inspired."
—*Brian McNaught, diversity trainer, author of* Gay Issues in the Workplace

Dedication

To you, men and women,
gay and straight,
who advocate for a just workplace
through your risk-taking, words, and actions:
May you know that it is because of you
that liberty for all
will truly be achieved;
and
to Jeb, my love, who is never afraid
to be who he is, wherever he is.

To all the gay men and lesbian women before me
whose courageous acts of coming out
have made it possible for me to live in freedom;
and
to Diane, who teaches me about courage
every day of our life together.

Table of Contents

Part III   United We Stand: A Group Story

Part   IV   Know   Your   Rights

Part I

Introduction

Prologue

In the spring of 1993, Sasha Alyson approached us with his idea for a book on the subject of being out at work. Sasha was aware that during the previous fall we had, at the invitation of Richard Branson of the Boston Professional Alliance (BPA), conducted a workshop titled "Out at the Workplace."

At first, we found the idea of putting a book together to be daunting, challenging, and exciting. We started talking about it together, at times getting enthused by the possible project and at other times rejecting the idea altogether. How could we think that we had anything unique and insightful to say on this topic? After all, we certainly were not experts on the subject. The more we talked about it, however, the more the idea of a book on the topic of being out in the workplace seemed not only possible but also necessary.

Our experience in doing the workshop and hearing from workshop participants, as well as our own personal experiences and personal stories told to us by our psychotherapy clients and friends, were all, in fact, strong evidence that a book on being out in the workplace was an idea whose time had come. The question then became, What should this book look like?

As we continued our discussions, two things became very clear to us. We reaffirmed that the process of coming out—personally or professionally or both—is a complex one. What coming out is or is not cannot be easily summed up in a paragraph or even a whole book. Even those who have attempted to explain it in psychological or sociological terms using developmental theories on the stages of coming out have been able to offer us nothing more than a model. It becomes obvious then that the process of coming out is very personal to each individual and also very important to the identity development of each gay, lesbian, or bisexual person. The idea, therefore, of writing a book in which only the two of us as "expert authors" wrote about the process of coming out at work was not very appealing.

The second thing that became evident to us was that what had seemed most helpful and healing to our workshop participants, to our clients, and even to ourselves was the telling of our personal stories. And it isn't that the personal story needs to be a dramatic one in order to be told; it's simply that in each telling we come to own more of ourselves and become more empowered and validated. In the words of a workshop participant, "Listening to your experience gives me courage to face my own work situation and helps me feel not only that it is possible to be out at work but also that I am not alone."

It became clear that a book on being out at work had to be told from the perspective of each individual. The telling of our stories is what gives testimony to our lives as gay, lesbian, or bisexual people. It is the only way to capture, even if for only a moment, the complex process of coming out personally and professionally. Thus—an anthology.

Do not think, even for a moment, that the editing of an anthology is an easy and simple task. Anthologies present their own particular challenges. How do you find the contributors? How do you make the stories representative of a larger community? How do you edit each story and yet preserve the personal style of each author?

We started the process of searching for contributors in several ways. We talked about our book and our search for stories with everyone we knew and, frankly, with anyone who would listen. We called our friends and colleagues throughout the country; basically, we sent the word out. We used E-mail, the Internet, posters in Provincetown, Mass., and ads in gay and lesbian newspapers all over the country. We also answered dozens of phone and written inquiries about the book. The stories started coming. We will never forget the excitement of receiving that first story.

The task of finding truly representative stories for an anthology is challenging and maybe impossible. In spite of all our efforts, for example, most of our stories came from white-collar environments. The rich racial and ethnic diversity of our gay, lesbian, and bisexual community is not as evident in the book as we would have liked. We did better at achieving gender parity. At some point we realized that these stories are not so much representative of a whole as they are significant and important parts of a whole. Each of these stories tells of an important experience in the life of someone. Together they are part of the colorful tapestry that is the gay, lesbian, and bisexual community in the United States.

The other challenge for us has been the editing of the stories themselves. The idea was not for each of these stories to look and sound the same. We wanted to preserve the personal style of each individual—to let the reality of each of these authors come alive through the telling of his or her story. The importance of each story lies in the value that the experience has for the individual. Our hope is that each of the experiences shared by these courageous contributors has something to say to you. Read their accounts with respect and appreciation. Each author has allowed us to share a very important moment in his or her life. We thank them all.

The editing of this anthology has been a long process. At times, the excitement of the project saw us through long hours of reading, discussing, and editing. At other times, we felt so consumed by the task at hand that we had to take long breaks and distance ourselves from the project in order to keep our focus and perspective and once again feel refreshed and committed to the book. Sometimes we saw more of each other than we wanted to, as our friends, partners, and jobs clamored for our time. All in all, however, the editing of this book has been a very rewarding experience. We have learned from each other, from every story, and from every author with whom we have worked.

This book would not have been possible without the help of various individuals we would like to acknowledge. We are thankful that Sasha Alyson came to us with the idea, and we are definitely glad we said yes. Our thanks to the staff of Alyson Publications for their excellent work, especially to Alistair Williamson, who saw us through the latter phase of the project. He was always encouraging and challenging.

Some other individuals need to be acknowledged for their valuable assistance: Glory Rasi for the work of inputting text and corrections, Mark Pearson and Gary Pfitzer for help in editing, and the staff of Rasi Associates for putting up with us in an affirming and supportive way during this long process. We want to acknowledge the support of friends, family members, and colleagues, who nudged us along each time they asked, "How is the book coming?"

We are especially thankful to our partners, Jeb Bates and Diane Sidorowicz, who encouraged and supported us every step of the way and were understanding when we were not available. Your loving presence in our lives is sustaining and nurturing.

Our heartfelt gratitude again to each contributor. Thanks for being patient and persistent through this process and for continuing to "work hard" through every rewrite. The book would not have been possible without your willingness to share your very personal stories with us and every reader. Thank you for your honesty and for the truth with which you live your lives. You make the world a better and safer place for gays, lesbians, and bisexuals. You have touched us all.

Richard A. Rasi
Lourdes Rodríguez-Nogués
Boston, Mass.
February 1995

Dis-Integration
Richard A. Rasi

I was seven years old and in the first grade at Our Lady of Lourdes School in Utica, N.Y. Sister Colette, my teacher, towered over me like the Statue of Liberty (though she was probably only five foot three inches tall). I remember looking up at her kind and always smiling face and hearing myself say, "Sister, someday I'm going to be a priest."

Looking down at me, she smiled, put her hand on my head, and simply said, "That's nice, dear."

Of course she would say that! Many Catholic boys in Catholic schools in the mid 1950s wanted to be Catholic priests. The difference with me is that I never lost the desire.

At the early age of three, before the institution of the Church could taint me with its theocratic bullshit, I had a religious experience of a God who loves and heals and accepts. I was not only captivated by the basic Christian message of love and service, I was also on the receiving end. I have never experienced God differently even when the institution has tried to convince me otherwise, especially around accepting myself as a gay man.

This sense of acceptance, however, occurred for me purely on an internal level. Swirling around me were the forces set in motion by the Catholic Church's phobic obsession with sex and the black-and-white thinking that accompanies that obsession. That is, sex—gay, straight, or otherwise—is wrong, except between two heterosexual persons who are married; and if you are Catholic, you need to be married in the Church, period. It was not easy living in the midst of this pathology, yet the three-year-old within me never lost that initial sense of a loving God.

I entered the seminary on September 13, 1967. I was seventeen years old and light-years from realizing my gayness. It was in the seminary some years later, with another seminarian, that I had my first sexual experience.

The phobia I saw in gay seminarians and priests that anyone might find out cemented a growing fear in me that survival in this "workplace" would come only if I kept my sexuality tightly hidden. In fact, my gay brethren were bigger homophobes than my straight brethren. I believed that I could still be truly happy as a Catholic priest because of my desire and ability to be there for people across the spectrum of life, from birth to death and the myriad places in between. This belief kept me going in the presence of mounting anxiety and confusion, born of trying to integrate a budding gay sexuality and a budding religious vocation. In retrospect I can see that what really happened was that I managed to deal with the personal and the vocational by splitting them off from each other. This was my way of life for eight years in the seminary.

My lifelong dream was realized on May 18, 1975, when I became a Catholic priest. It was one of the most wonderful days of my life. A week later I returned to my hometown and to Our Lady of Lourdes to celebrate my first mass. Shortly after, I saw Sister Colette for the first time since grammar school days and reminded her of my "prophecy."

My workplace was my life. I ate, slept, prayed, and worked all in the same basic environment. I was surrounded by and interacted with many people whom I grew to love, yet I was lonely for the connection with my gay self that seemed to exist at that time only in visits to the bars and in relationships with just a few longtime gay friends. These friends helped me keep the secret of my priesthood well hidden in gay circles and the secret of my gayness almost totally hidden in vocational circles. Not only was it the ultimate splitting of the personal and professional, it was the ultimate splitting of myself. The "healthy me" knew that I could not last this way. Integration needed to happen. Herein lies the reason, therefore, for my interest in and work on gay and lesbian issues in the workplace.

I went back to school on my day off and with my savings, which were meager at the time, put myself through a doctoral program in psychology designed for people in the ministry. I began to push against the system, which didn't know what to do with me for a while. I graduated, however, was hired as a staff psychologist for the University Counseling Services at Boston College (a Catholic college run by the Jesuits), and while there became fully licensed as a psychologist. My bishop was content, though not happy, that I was tucked away working in a Catholic College. His "problem" with me was gone—at least for a while.

It was toward the end of my first year at B.C. that I discovered Dignity, a gay, lesbian, and bisexual Catholic community. After worshiping there for a time, I offered to say mass for the group. Some of my gay priest friends went crazy. After all, there had been recognized spies from the cardinal's office seen in the congregation. What if the word got back? I could be defrocked!

Simultaneously, two of the women chaplains at work whom I had told of my new Dignity ministry began to do outreach to the gay and lesbian students. They invited me to address the group at one of their first meetings. They were very clear that I could make the decision whether or not to come out to the students.

I knew I could lose my job just for addressing the group, let alone coming out. But I was so very tired of living with the constant threats of doom I had experienced all my life: "I won't love you if you're gay"; "I'll take away your priesthood if you're gay"; "I can't be your friend if you're gay"; "I'll fire you if you're gay." With my gut churning, knowing that I had to do it for myself and for them, I came out to this very small gathering of students. The heavens did not cease to exist, the walls did not come tumbling down, and no one left the room screaming. I left the meeting feeling good about what I had done and scared because I knew it was another step out of the workplace closet.

Beginning with Dignity and then coming out to these students, integration, as in most cases, happened little by little. I started talking about the needs of gay and lesbian students at staff meetings and with other counselors in my department and admitted to being gay myself, though only to a select few with whom I felt safe.

Then the realization hit me in a very big way that while I was changing, the world around me was not. I was called to a meeting with the director of Counseling Services, who talked to me about a former counselor in the department, also a priest, who had started advocating for gay and lesbian students long before my tenure at the college. He added that this man had "caused a lot of trouble" for the department and the college, but he couldn't really explain why. He issued a directive to me that I was no longer to talk about gay and lesbian issues publicly at the college, nor was I to bring them up in staff meetings.

However, it was too late. The word had gotten around, and many of the gay students had started to seek me out. (I found out some time later that I was known as the "gay counselor" on campus.) I felt that to cease addressing these issues would be regressive on a very personal level. The gap between my personal and professional lives was starting to close, and for me there was no going back.

Boston College in May 1984 decided not to renew my contract. The director and my supervisors claimed that I was not displaying professional conduct and that my clinical skills needed vast improvement, though no one could give me any specific examples. All they kept saying was, "You just don't get it," as if there were something wrong with me. I was outraged.

Under the circumstances, I knew this was all happening because I was gay. That is when I began to realize that I could not have it both ways. I was losing the protection of this position within a Catholic college, and I knew I could not go back into the closet of the institutional Church, where my only option was to be a parish priest.

I was hurting enough to not want to carry around the stigma that I had been fired from my job and thus ruin future job possibilities. So, in order to protect myself professionally, I decided to resign my position at the college rather than be fired.

I was frightened, sad, angry, and lonely. I could not get beyond feeling the shame. I felt there must be something wrong with me because I couldn't do what I believed so many other priests were doing—leading a double life split right down the middle. I was being forced to make a choice between the two things I loved most in life at the time: being gay and being a priest.

At the end of all the sadness, anger, depression, anxiety, hiding, sidestepping, and lying, however, I realized that I was tired of trying to fit in at a place where integration just wasn't going to happen. My decision to put myself in a place where I could do what I do well, be a self-accepting and out gay man, and not compromise my life led to a course that I did not intend to take. After years of struggle, I decided not to go back to the "active" ministry and instead began my own private practice as an openly gay therapist.

Through therapy, a supportive love relationship, wonderful family and friends, and a loving and supportive spiritual community, I am now able to own the fact that I had to leave the priesthood because the institution was unable (and still would be) to support who I am as a gay man and as a Catholic priest.

I'm gay, and I'm "normal." I no longer have to convince anyone that I am worthy of their acceptance. My self-image and self-esteem as a man who happens to be gay are no longer dependent on the opinions and biblical interpretations of other humans who think that they speak for God. Rather, they are dependent on the way I face my own fear and integrate every part of my life—including my work.

Claiming ourselves as "normal" means going beyond being out in our personal lives. When we can talk to our colleagues about our personal lives in the same way everyone else does, put up pictures of our gay families in our work space, talk with coworkers about what we *really* did on the weekend without being vague, use our partner's name without skipping a beat, grieve when a friend dies of AIDS as everyone else does when someone close to them dies, share our joy when we celebrate our commitment to our partner or have children, then we will be the "normal" people that we really are.

Our quest for freedom as gay, lesbian, or bisexual people has taken many forms. However, I believe that today, more than ever, our efforts need to be focused on legislative change that will ensure the preservation of our rights. I agree with one of our contributors, who states that "the *real* change is going to come where people work. Attitudes change in the workplace. Segregation changed in the workplace, and when companies started to do the right thing, society changed."

We did not have a choice in deciding our sexual orientation. We do, however, have a choice in how we decide to live our lives as gay, lesbian, or bisexual people. The choices we make dictate the life we lead. "To thine own self be true."

I Shall Not Be Silent
Lourdes Rodríguez-Nogués

I will never forget the day. On a cold Monday morning in November 1993, several of my gay and lesbian colleagues from Simmons College and I gathered at the president's office at her request. The five of us joined President Dowdall, the director of human resources, and the administrative vice president at the round table. We were there because the president wanted to announce to us that she had just approved spousal-equivalent benefits and wished to have us look at the policy and give her our feedback on its details. I cannot capture in a sentence, or even a paragraph, the emotion of that day. Some of us responded with nervous laughter, and some of us with tears. President Dowdall was gracious and said, "We are doing this because it is the right thing to do." For us it was probably more than that. This act, which made things equitable and just for the gay and lesbian employees at Simmons College, was, to me, a gift. A gift because the approval of those benefits (benefits that I did not need for my partner) helped me feel not merely accepted or tolerated but valued. I do not know if President Dowdall, who just wanted to do the right thing, ever knew the impact of that moment in my life as an out lesbian at work.

The victory of that day was, for us at Simmons, a moment to savor. It was a victory that had come after a few years of organizing, strategizing, lobbying. We had accomplished something important, and we had done it by taking risks, by speaking out, by being more and more out. We had moved from fear into action, and we had a victory. We had a reason to celebrate.

Several days after this victorious day, however, I started feeling sad. At first I did not comprehend my odd emotions. I had been so moved, and I had felt such joy. Eventually, I understood my reaction. I felt sad realizing how pathetic it was that I could feel such gratitude for something that I should have had all along. Why did I feel like I had received a gift? Why did I feel so valued just for being acknowledged for who I really am?

The whole situation reminded me of that Thursday night some years back when many of us, while watching television, witnessed that now-famous *L.A. Law* lesbian kiss. My phone rang constantly that night: "Did you see that?!" My excitement was out of control for hours and even days afterward. The intensity of my reaction (and that of many of my friends) made me realize how deprived we feel as gays and lesbians that we have to react so strongly to a ten-second lesbian kiss on television because it is such an atypical occurrence.

The lack of role models, the lack of laws protecting our civil rights and of policies at work safeguarding our security, and the lack of validation—religious or civil—for our love relationships renders us invisible and thus powerless. That invisibility and sense of powerlessness, which many of us have felt in both our private/personal lives and in our public/professional lives, has an impact on the quality of our daily life—at work and outside of work. Sometimes our invisibility is so automatic and so much a part of us that we do everything we can to preserve it, even at our own risk. With every pronoun we edit in talking about our partners, with every story about our lives that we fail to share, with every homophobic remark that we choose not to confront, a part of us dies. I used to think constantly about the risks of coming out. What price am I going to pay? Am I going to be rejected by friends and family? Could I lose my job? I have now begun to think about it differently. What price am I going to pay if I do not come out? There really are consequences either way, aren't there?

Some years ago, probably in 1983 or so, after I had been working at the Simmons College Counseling Center for about four years, the dean of students, Charlotte Morocco, made a request of our staff. In a conversation with us about how to best serve a diverse population, she expressed concern about the needs of our gay and lesbian students. She did not know whom to talk to about it because she didn't know any faculty or staff member at Simmons who was out. "Please spread the word that I want to speak in confidence with any gay or lesbian employee who would be willing to help me with this issue," she said. I knew at that moment that I could not be silent and that, afraid or not, I had to respond to her request. I was not out beyond my own department, and the thought of coming out to the person who had hired me felt like a risk. But I also felt that keeping silent was a greater risk. Perpetuating my invisibility by not speaking out felt to me like an assault on the self. I faced up then to the realization that there could be consequences for me either way.

Several days after the request was made, I went to meet with Dean Morocco. "I am here because you said that you needed to talk with a lesbian or gay employee. I am a lesbian. How can I help you?" Dean Morocco was respectful and supportive (and not very surprised, I might add), and we had a very productive conversation. At the end of our talk, I asked her to give me a sense of how safe it would be for me at Simmons if I chose to be more out. This was before we had protective laws in Boston or in Massachusetts and before Simmons as an institution had an antidiscrimination statement that included sexual orientation. Her response was simple, but not what I wanted to hear. She said something like "I do not know if it is safe. I will always support you, but I cannot protect you."

I was appreciative of her honesty and felt afraid for a moment. The reality is, however, that that was the beginning of my opening the "work closet." For some reason, her statement jolted me and broke the wall of denial that had me thinking that the only way I could risk coming out was if someone could give me a foolproof guarantee. I recall saying to myself, "Guarantees are never possible, Rodríguez, so which is the greater risk?" Once again I knew that for me the greater risk was to be silent.

The road between 1983 and 1993 was not always easy or straightforward (no pun intended). More and more of us gays and lesbians at Simmons identified ourselves to each other, networked, went to dinner, and had long conversations. We always ended with the same questions: "Why aren't we all out and more visible?" "What is it about this place?" "What are we really afraid of?" And off we would go with our philosophical, psychological, and social discussions of the reasons. I wouldn't have had the courage or strength to be out if I had thought I was out there all by myself. I probably would not have had the energy either to combat the system and work to implement change without the power of a group. The conversations were helpful as we all moved more and more into visibility. Together, we worked with the administration to obtain more money for gay and lesbian programming, the addition of sexual orientation to the antidiscrimination policy (which we obtained even before it became law in Massachusetts), and the spousal-equivalent benefits policy. I am grateful for the presence and support of all my gay and lesbian colleagues at Simmons. The strength of our working together has profoundly affected how I see my responsibility to be an out lesbian at our college.

During this whole time I was also going through changes in my personal life. I found myself becoming more outspoken about gay and lesbian issues and more visible and out. A good friend of mine has always said that coming out is "just correcting the wrong assumptions that people make about you every day." This definition has influenced me greatly. I started being more true to myself in my life and taking what I would call a "spontaneous" approach to coming out. I took advantage, as much as possible, of those opportunities offered to me when anyone would make a statement that wrongly placed me in the heterosexual world. After all, wouldn't I correct people if they mistook me for Italian or Portuguese? I would be quick to say, "No, I'm Latina." And not because it is bad to be Italian or Portuguese, but just because that is not what or who I am.

One of my tactics became that of revealing my lesbianism through casual conversation. For example, I used "she" in talking about my partner and introduced her as such, and I became more daring in my public displays of affection. I became more visible and out with my siblings, friends, and neighbors and more involved in gay and lesbian organizations. I was getting to be known as an out lesbian therapist and participated in the gay and lesbian caucuses and committees of my professional organizations.

One of the things that propelled my "outness" in my personal life was my involvement with Dignity/Boston, an organization of gay, lesbian, and bisexual Catholics. During the years between 1982 and 1991, I served on the board and as vice president or president on several occasions. It is hard to be a gay or lesbian activist and not be out. My involvement with Dignity made me very visible. I appeared in *Bay Windows, The Boston Globe, The Tab,* and *People Are Talking,* to name a few. My name and face were definitely "out" there.

The more out I became in my personal life, the harder it was to stay hidden in my place of employment. At first I thought I could find a compromise by never mentioning Simmons College in these public forums. I thought that maybe this way I could be protected. But who and what was I protecting? How could I really believe that I could be that out in my personal life and not at Simmons? Who was I fooling? And really, did I truly need to be so careful? The wall of denial came tumbling down one day when a colleague at Simmons said, "I read about you in *The Tab.*" I thought to myself, *Well, at least you are a lesbian and knew all about me already anyway; my cover is protected.* I then had to laugh at myself for the naïveté that had led me to believe, if only for a couple of moments, that probably no one else at Simmons had read the article. Wake up, Rodríguez, the word is out!

The more out I became in my personal and so-called private life, the harder it became to keep my life hidden at work. The gap was narrowing, and it would have taken an inordinate amount of energy to keep the two worlds separate. And at what price to my sanity? I wanted to make my life congruent and be myself more of the time. I wanted to be a more integrated, happy, and productive human being. Since I was not willing to move into the closet in my personal life, the only alternative now was to move out of the closet at work. And that is what I have done.

Sometimes I hear folks say, "I keep my homosexuality hidden at work because it is nobody's business." Comments such as that bother me a great deal. I feel a combination of sadness and anger on hearing them. What kind of internalized homophobia are we buying into when we think that way? Of course, there are personal things about me that I keep to myself and do not share with people at work, or maybe not even with friends. We all do that. But my identity as a lesbian is not one of those things. It cannot be because being a lesbian permeates everything I do—the way I look at the world, the way I perform my job, the way I interact with people. Being a lesbian is not only about what I do in bed; it is about who I am. And what I am, I am twenty-four hours a day. And no, I am not keeping that to myself.

It is very clear to me that heterosexuals do not keep their sexual orientation to themselves. They "come out" around us all the time. I walk into a colleague's office, and her wedding picture is on her desk. As we are going to begin a meeting, someone comments, "My boyfriend and I went to a wonderful restaurant this weekend." I hear my worried-looking colleague state, "My husband has to have surgery." A teary-eyed coworker shares that he and his wife are getting divorced. We really do not expect them to keep all of this to themselves, do we?

Editing this book has underscored for me how complex the process of coming out is. As one of our contributors wrote for her title, "once is not enough." No kidding!

I have often been puzzled by that popular question that gays and lesbians are always asking of each other: "When did you come out?" That question always makes it sound as if for every one of us there was only that one day....Was it the day that you first paid attention to someone of your same sex and felt curious or excited or shocked? Was it the day when you looked at yourself in the mirror and said, "Guess what, you're gay"? Perhaps it was that day when you first acknowledged your sexual orientation to someone else. Could it have been the first time you kissed that special someone? The truth is that, for most of us, the day we came out is a collection of moments imprinted in our memories. I have come to prefer the question "How did you come out?" Or better still, "How do you come out?" Questions phrased in this manner better capture for me the notion that coming out is definitely a process and that, indeed, "once is not enough."

Owning up to the fact that coming out is a process helps me have compassion for myself and for others when acts of being out become difficult or tiring. But seeing it as a never-ending process also gives me energy and motivation to continue putting myself out there over and over again. Knowing that coming out is a process that as gays and lesbians we all have to go through helps me feel that I am not alone. When I am feeling isolated or overburdened, I can ask a gay brother or a lesbian sister to share a story of a coming-out moment with me. That experience helps me feel connected to the larger movement toward gay liberation as well as giving me inspiration and courage. The coming-out stories in this book do that for me. Each and every one of them is a piece of our history, to be remembered and cherished and to be passed on to future generations.

Another thing that has struck me in the editing of this book is how different all of our experiences of coming out at work are from one another. Not only are our work situations and circumstances different, but so are our styles of becoming visible and the challenges and consequences that we each have had to face. For some, it was important to make themselves known in the job interview, risking the possibility of not getting a job. Others have had to deal with the reality of having the choice taken out of their hands by being outed at work. For some the decision to come out had to do with finding the gap between the personal and the professional grow so wide that it became unmanageable. For still others the choice has been between a real self and a false self, with the consequences of silence ultimately being too much for their souls to bear. Then there are those who have come face-to-face with injustice and unequal work situations that they can't help but challenge with their coming-out. And for some the search for an identity has brought them, inevitably, to a coming-out moment. The common theme in all of these stories is that they are all examples of courageous risk-taking. The life of each of these individuals was never to be the same again after their experiences of coming out at work. And they have each certainly convinced me that they would not have had it any other way.

The stories of coming out at work told by each of these men and women have touched me deeply. I am thankful that they have allowed me to be a witness to their moments of courage. Their stories are a gift to all of us, and their decision to be out is a contribution to our life in freedom.

Part II

The Stories

Ask/Tell
John Dibelka

*Magazine columnist and editor John Dibelka manages
an industrial safety office for the California State Department
of Transportation (Caltrans) in his native San Diego. Although
Dibelka used the pen name Jay Shaffer to begin his publishing
career writing gay men's porn during his tour of duty in the
U.S. Navy, he tells in this essay how he came out in other ways
to his officers and shipmates and what advantages he finds
in being honest with his coworkers and himself.*

We called him the Munchkin: a squat Navy Reserve Nurse Corps
lieutenant commander with a serious overbite and bulging eyes,
a scruffy beard, a shiny bald head, and a taste for more jewelry
than the regular Navy or good patient care would allow. He wore
summer white uniforms so starched they squeaked and told, whenever possible, vicious, condescending jokes. He was my patient-care instructor at the
Naval School of Health Sciences, and for ten weeks he spent part of every
business day peering over the edge of a lectern at me and more than thirty
other sailors who thought we wanted to be hospital corpsmen.

I don't give him much credit for the fact that most of us succeeded.

But I do have to thank him for bringing me out at work.

"Duh-BILL-kuh," he barked at me one afternoon, from somewhere in the
middle of an especially tedious lecture. He never did learn to pronounce my
name right.

"Sir?" I responded, sitting at attention and suddenly feeling my mind go
completely blank.

"Perhaps you'd like to tell the class—"

"Sir?"

"Are you a spitter or a swallower?"

Every man in the room turned around and stared straight at me. I didn't
think. I answered. Fast. And honestly.

"I swallow, sir," I shot back, clearly. In the spring of 1980 no one knew we
weren't supposed to—yet.

One man gasped. Another snorted. Someone to my right said, "Shit." Even the Munchkin looked stunned.

"But I try not to swish too much first."

I love having fun with the truth.

Ironically, I'd only known the answer to that question for a little bit more than a week when he asked. I married young, divorced soon after, joined the Navy late, and began to start my life over, but before I enlisted I'd never had sex with a man. My first was another of the school's instructors, a funny and physically imposing man who leaned across a table in an on-base bar one night and said, "You know, only half of all gay men start out that way, don't you? The rest just get kind of sucked into it."

I was twenty-three years old.

I thought I had fallen in love. I knew I loved the sex. I had just barely learned what it meant to say "So-and-So had brought me out," and suddenly the Munchkin's snipe had made the whole thing public. I don't know how many of my classmates took my answer seriously, but the fact that I could get them to laugh with me over it made a big impression on me.

I quickly discovered I liked living life—even Navy life—in the open. I could see the toll their hiding took on people like the Munchkin, bitter, stunted men and women who appeared to hate themselves as much as they told me they hated the rest of the world and who almost always drank too much. I decided I deserved much better and determined I'd secure it for myself. I particularly liked the power I got from talking honestly to people who didn't believe what I had to say or, if they did, didn't care.

My coworkers knew—or suspected they knew. The ones who asked me one-on-one, I told. I figured the question took some courage to pose, and the people who asked it honestly deserved my honest answer. As a policy, this gained me many more friends than it lost. One of them looked at me, shook her head, touched my hand, and told me sadly, "What a waste. For me, I mean." Another one punched out a beer-drinking buddy of his when the man called me a "queer."

· All my first-line superiors knew I was gay. When they asked, I told them, but I also made it a point to explain that I intended to do my job well and keep everything else to myself and my partners. They seemed to respect that. No one I worked for directly ever made an issue of my sexuality or told me it made me unsuitable for military service. Every one of them seemed to feel honored. All of them thanked me and said they'd help me in whatever way they could. For the rest of my time in the Navy, they did.

By earning me allies, my honesty helped keep me safe.

Only the Naval Investigative Service seemed to care much how I spent my off-base time. The NIS let me know it was keeping close tabs on me four different times in the six years that made up my Navy career, going so far during one shakedown cruise as to have someone tail me into bars on my nights off. I decided early on I'd fight to stay in if the NIS ever forced the issue.

They never did. Scuttlebutt told me I had a whole fan club of agents watching where I went and whom I went with, and I heard a lot of pointed tales about the kinds of things that happened to a certain breed of sailors out on liberty in certain ports. It quickly became clear, as innuendo came and went but legal action didn't, that NIS officers couldn't do anything to me but threaten to expose me to the world, sit back, and wait for me to beg for a discharge.

In the eyes of the NIS, this course of action made perfect sense. The record of outstanding service I'd built didn't matter much to them, they told me. The commendations I had gathered meant, they said, a little less. Any good man could go bad, they reminded me obliquely, and in the eyes of the Navy my homosexuality made me an obvious target for blackmail. Before the "Evil Empire" got the chance to use my deep, dark secret to coerce me into bringing on the fall of Western civilization, the officers at NIS felt it was in their own best interest to use exactly the same tactics to intimidate me into leaving the playing of war games to "better adjusted," or just "better," men.

It might have worked, I guess, if I had felt the need to lie to anyone regarding my sex life or anything else.

I came out to my parents over the phone. After some awkward and expensive pauses, the three of us had a good laugh at the logic of spies. They both told me they'd "suspected things" but felt relieved and honored that I'd finally chosen to tell them. I told them I'd only just figured it out for myself.

I would have preferred to go home to tell them in person, but I couldn't afford the plane fare at the time, and I wanted to make sure they heard it from me before the Navy told them or I needed money for a lawyer or my face, like that of Leonard Matlovitch not so very long before, wound up on the cover of *Newsweek*.

Once they knew, anybody could tell anyone for all I cared.

I left the service at the end of my enlistment with an honorable discharge, a good-conduct medal, and an offer to sign up again. Instead, I started working for the State of California. I have worked in three different state agencies since, under six different supervisors. I've come out to them all and to most of the people I've supervised. It has never occurred to me not to.

On the other hand, by law, this state must advertise itself as "An affirmative action employer—equal opportunity to all regardless of race, color, creed, national origin, ancestry, sex, marital status, disability, religious or political affiliation, age, or sexual orientation." While I don't expect to ever file a suit invoking status as a member of a protected minority, it comforts me to know I can.

I started in the Department of Social Services, helping disability evaluation analysts in Oakland determine which applicants qualified for state payment of their medical bills because they were too sick to work. I lived in San

Francisco, showed up for work in leather, compared notes on our boyfriends with female coworkers, and helped define the relatively gay-specific terms (like *poppers* and *fisting*) that showed up in medical records from time to time. I earned a promotion to supervisor, introduced my new lover, Robert, around, and started socializing more with work friends after work. I took a six-month leave of absence to care for a friend while he died, and came back, drained, to flowers and cards and good wishes. I felt special and cared for, accepted and loved; not in spite but because of all of who I was.

I used my boss's shoulder for a good cry every time I learned another friend had heard his AIDS diagnosis by reading the news in his case file before I had a chance to get it through the grapevine. She'd also nursed a good friend while he died. We still talk on the phone and still comfort each other.

We decided to leave San Francisco the day Robert got his diagnosis, so I transferred back to San Diego, to an office of the state attorney general. Even in such a conservative atmosphere, I chose to hide nothing. Literally. When nude photographs of me appeared in *Playgirl* and some other publications, I heard some rumblings from the state law enforcement machinery that reminded me of the NIS, but, like the NIS, nothing further came of them. When Robert filed an AIDS antidiscrimination suit against a local chiropractor, however, I called a meeting with the staff I supervised and came out to them as a group, much as I had come out to my parents, for much the same reason and with similar results.

Since then I have taken another promotion and moved to the Department of Transportation (Caltrans). I manage a three-person office now, working for an engineer twenty years older than I am and with a field safety officer closer to my age who is also a former military medic. They're both male, both straight, both divorced. We each know the others' regular dates by first name. We talk about our sex lives sometimes. More often we talk about work. When Robert died, I took three days' bereavement leave without any questions from anyone, beyond asking what they could do to help.

On the whole, however, Caltrans is a tradition-bound organization, full of engineers and bureaucrats more comfortable with equations than with people and notably politically conservative. I know of only two other openly gay or lesbian employees among the almost fifteen hundred that make up the district I work in. Some people tell me they feel their lives would be in danger if they were out to their coworkers in the field, building or maintaining highways, where everyone's safety depends on clear communication and mutual respect.

I disagree. By helping show my coworkers that I trust and count on them as much as they can trust and count on me, being out at work has not only kept me safe, it has provided me nothing but benefits. Then again, I'm convinced that my attitude determines how I'm treated. I provide and expect respect. I try to treat people compassionately and find they do the same for me. I make it clear that I want to do the best job I can, I need help to do it, and plan to help others to do their best too.

Most of all, I stress communication, with an emphasis on honesty. Part of my job is to ensure that every Caltrans work space in my district has a poster that reads

No job is so important nor a service so
urgent that it requires you to perform your
job in an unsafe manner.

I believe very strongly in this credo as it stands. Still, sometimes when I read it I mentally substitute the word *dishonest* for the word *unsafe*. Ever since I met the Munchkin and his unhappily closeted cohorts, these words have seemed to me to mean about the same thing.

I have come out to fundamentalist Christians, members of various ethnic groups, closeted gay men, and militant feminist lesbians and continued to work with them all. Many of these people have become my friends. After I've made it a point to present myself as a capable, well-rounded person with a sense of humor—but without any tolerance for bigotry—my sexuality has generally ceased to be an issue. Those who can't get over it learn to ignore it when I consciously, consistently refocus their attention on the quality and quantity of the work I do.

As an openly gay man, I have had the chance to clear up misunderstandings and misconceptions, to act as a sounding board, to stand up for my rights, and to offer closeted employees proof that they're not alone.

As a person publicly living with AIDS, I have had people from throughout the department ask me questions about everything from transmission to treatment and have been able to direct them to authoritative sources. As co-facilitator of department's sexual-harassment prevention workshops, I have helped spread the word that discrimination is intolerable, no matter who the intended victim is, or why. As editor of a monthly safety newsletter, I have been able to put information on AIDS education in print for people who very likely wouldn't get it any other place.

As an honest human being, I know my friends love me for who I really am. I can sleep at night and look at myself in the mirror each morning.

I honestly can't imagine working—or living—any other way.

Fiction Into Fact
Terri de la Peña

Terri de la Peña is the author of two novels, Margins
and Latin Satins, *and is an academic-affairs assistant
at UCLA. Her fiction about Chicana lesbians has been
included in the curricula of Chicano studies, women's
studies, and lesbian and gay studies courses in the
University of California system and in universities
across the United States. In this story Terri speaks about
how her coming-out process on the job occurred in tandem
with her becoming a published writer.*

"**S**he makes me feel really uncomfortable," my coworker confid-
ed when the ophthalmology department's computer trouble-
shooter had left our office. Without meeting her gaze, I kept
filing medical reports. "Why?"

"Well...I know Laura's a friend of yours," Beth said. She moved away from
her computer and glanced over, as if expecting me to fill in the details. "I've
heard from the clinic staff that she's a lesbian."

I faced Beth with some defiance. "I don't understand why anything like
that would bother you."

"You *know* what I mean."

The telephone's insistent buzz interrupted us. I escaped by carrying a
hefty armload of medical files to the departmental storage room. Safe from
prying questions, I proceeded to alphabetize the files and stayed there
longer than necessary. When I returned half an hour later, Beth was still on
the phone, engrossed in booking the operating room for emergency
surgery.

Together we put in long hours providing secretarial assistance to the chief
of pediatric ophthalmology, a temperamental workaholic and world-
renowned surgeon. With our heavy workloads, Beth and I were much too
busy to become distracted over fragmented conversations. Although I did
not forget her introducing the subject of lesbianism, I wondered when she
would attempt it again.

Next time I had lunch with Laura, I mentioned Beth's comments.

She seemed amused. "Terri, if someone asks point-blank if I'm a dyke, I won't deny it. The point is, Beth won't ask *me*. She's more curious about you. She's already met your lover. Don't tell me Beth hasn't figured it out by now."

"As if I didn't have enough to deal with already. Now *I'm* the one who's uncomfortable," I admitted.

After that conversation with Laura, I felt even more stifled in that medical secretary position. Having experienced the surgeon's daily doses of racism and sexism during working hours, I had no desire to confront homophobia as well; I was more determined than ever to keep my personal life private. I would have preferred working elsewhere on the UCLA campus, yet in 1982 I had accepted that job because it had been the only one available.

The medical center's pecking order had quickly become apparent: white male physicians at the top, women and all people of color at the bottom. The legendary staff attrition rate was caused in large part by high stress levels arising from racism and sexism, impossible workloads, little chance for advancement, and personality clashes with physicians. The administration was seen to favor the doctors and overlook staff grievances. From the staff's perspective, the Powers That Be in the medical center chose to ignore the University of California's antidiscrimination policies in order to maintain the status quo. I hated the injustice prevalent there but was not eager to challenge those ingrained attitudes formally. I knew leaving would be the most realistic solution to insure my mental health and self-esteem. Unfortunately, obtaining a transfer to another campus department proved a difficult task.

Meanwhile, in 1983, I began the equally difficult process of coming out to my family, at the same time as I was building a relationship, attending evening college classes, and attempting to find time to write fiction. I found myself caught between my Chicano-Catholic family and my closeted white lover. My family preferred to continue thinking of me as their celibate and unmarried daughter, not as sexual, certainly not as lesbian. My lover questioned my desire to maintain a close relationship with my parents and siblings; she had moved across the country to be away from hers. Exhausted from these conflicts, not to mention my long hours of work and school, I had little time to write fiction and even less to ponder the feasibility of being out in the workplace. On that point I agreed with my family and my lover: in the already stressful environment of the medical center, I would not be safe being out.

My friend Laura eventually resigned her position when she was accepted into medical school; my coworker Beth became pregnant and took maternity leave. Without Laura I felt more vulnerable because I knew of no other lesbians in the department. During Beth's absence, other coworkers, including one of the medical residents, often insinuated the topic of homosexuality into conversations. I never took their bait and, surprisingly, no one forced the subject; they already knew my outspokenness about racism and sexism and perhaps had a grudging respect for my privacy.

Their curiosity about me became moot in the spring of 1986. That April my long-awaited transfer came through, and a few days later I won a fiction award in the Twelfth Annual Chicano Literary Contest. "A Saturday in August," a story I had written in 1983, featured a Chicana feminist's encounter with a Chicana lesbian. That story symbolized my own continuing struggle to evolve from Chicana feminist to Chicana *lesbian* feminist, from office worker to published writer. While I could hide neither my gender nor my ethnicity, I had managed for four tedious years to keep the most intimate details of my life—my creativity and my lesbianism—a secret in the workplace. No wonder I felt euphoric that achieving recognition as a writer coincided with my leaving the medical center's secretarial ranks.

I had always longed to work in the north campus. In contrast to the medical center with its brick-and-concrete institutional facade, the north campus boasted verdant quads, eucalyptus groves, a sculpture garden, and stately buildings housing the humanities and social-sciences departments. The north campus was not Utopia, yet its sprawling grounds seemed more compatible with my interests and temperament.

When I began work as an academic-affairs assistant in the Office of the Provost and Deans of the UCLA College of Letters and Science, I immediately identified myself as a writer. Embracing that identity seemed natural since winning the fiction prize had bolstered my self-esteem and self-confidence. My new coworkers readily accepted my creative side as well as my gender and ethnicity; I did not press my luck by revealing my sexual orientation. Although I was a bit leery about being one of the few people of color and probably the only lesbian in the office, I was too relieved to have escaped the medical center to complain. I was determined to function in this less stressful environment. I concentrated on learning the campus academic personnel policies and realized I did not miss the secretarial field one bit.

Compared with the medical center's steamroller approach to its employees, the Office of the Provost and Deans regarded its staff as individuals with individual needs, not merely as extensions of typewriters or computers. This humanistic attitude was attributable to Willa Sisson, the down-to-earth Letters and Science personnel director. A former teacher, Willa had a knack for bringing out the best in people, myself included. She had taken a chance on hiring me: I had no previous personnel experience, but she recognized I was willing and eager to learn. I was grateful for her patience, her readiness to listen and be of help. During my first six months under her supervision, I experienced the trauma of my father's death from pancreatic cancer and a childhood friend's death from AIDS complications. Willa and my coworkers were exceptionally understanding and supportive during my times of grief.

One in particular cheered me with silly jokes and Gary Larson cartoons. Hopelessly heterosexual, Gail also amused me with stories of her gay men friends, and I wondered if she suspected my lesbianism. My lover, who was also closeted in her teaching job and already leery of my burgeoning writing career, cautioned me not to reveal myself. Since Gail and I took breaks and often lunched together, I found it impossible to keep the truth from her for long. When I came out to her, she laughed and said, "I wondered when you'd get around to telling me."

Carolyn, another coworker, had been three grades behind me in parochial school, though we had not been friends then. Finding her in the dean's office was an added treat. Once she casually asked whether I dated anyone. While Gail giggled, I blurted out, "I'm in a relationship—with a woman." Carolyn took that news in stride. After that, we often discussed relationships, theirs with the men in their lives, mine with my lover.

While I grew comfortable being out to selected people in the office, my lover did not appreciate my gradual emergence from the closet. She spent her days among teenage students at a private school and was envious, if not threatened, by my increasing openness, especially whenever I mentioned my interest in writing about lesbians. While I was adamant about writing under my own name, she insisted that I use a pseudonym, and I resented her attempts to censor me. We began to quarrel over this and related issues. In September 1987, less than a year after my father's death, she ended our relationship.

I turned often to Gail and Carolyn for emotional support; together they bolstered me through the blues and the sudden loneliness. By then I had become a book reviewer for the Los Angeles-based *Lesbian News* and thought about reviving my own unfinished manuscript about a Chicana lesbian coming out to her family. By mid October I began filling my empty evenings with uninterrupted creative time, devoted to completing my novel.

The prize-winning story "A Saturday in August" appeared in print the following year. Willa brought French pastry into the office to celebrate my being a published writer. Shortly after that, more of my fiction was anthologized, as was my coming-out story. Some of the stories focused on Chicana issues only; others contained lesbian erotica. Still wary about being out to everyone in the office, I informed my coworkers only when the Chicana-themed stories went into print. My identity as a writer had been hard-earned, and I was unwilling to jeopardize it by revealing anything else. Although I often felt hypocritical about focusing only on my Chicana stories, I realized that if my novel were published I would have no choice but to be out to everyone I knew. Most of my coworkers probably imagined me to be a shy celibate, too dedicated to my craft to have much of a personal life; those who thought so were not far off the track. I dated infrequently and spent evenings and weekends concentrating on the novel. It became the cen-

ter of my existence, and I was very protective of it. Rarely did anyone in the
office ask for details about the manuscript's characters and plot. If anyone
expressed interest, I said that the novel in progress had a Chicana coming-
of-age theme—which was true, though not entirely descriptive. That answer
seemed to satisfy everyone, myself included.

Meanwhile, I attended writers' workshops during vacations, particularly
three consecutive summers at the Flight of the Mind Women Writers'
Workshop in Oregon. There I pored over various drafts of *Margins,* the novel
in progress, networked with other lesbian writers, and made my first contact
with the Seal Press. As my stories continued to be published, I gave readings
in local bookstores, at community events, and even on the UCLA campus;
some of my coworkers attended the latter. I read a Christmas story at the
Latino Faculty and Staff Association's holiday party and an excerpt from the
novel at a Gay and Lesbian Staff and Faculty Network potluck. Through the
Network I met lesbians and gays in other departments on campus.

My coworkers considered me an office team player who also happened to
be a Chicana fiction writer. In southern California, most people in the arts
moonlight, so my situation was not unusual. I felt wary, however, whenever
my readings were publicized in the *Los Angeles Times* book review section;
I hoped curious coworkers would not show up at gay bookstores or lesbian
events. Except for Carolyn, Gail, and a few others, I still had not revealed the
increasing lesbian slant in my fiction. As time went on, however, Chicana and
Latina professors and women's studies instructors on campus began to
invite me to speak to their classes. Willa allowed me time away from my job
for this.

Although I often felt split about being a Chicana employee and a lesbian
writer, my shyness began to evaporate as I grew more confident about presenting and discussing my work. In 1989 I gave a reading at the June L.
Mazer Lesbian Collection in West Hollywood. It was there, after two years of
productive solitude, that I met Gloria, an adorable woman of Sicilian-
Croatian descent who would become my lover.

At first I was reluctant to get too involved. My writing had taken center
stage, and I hesitated to focus my attention on a flesh-and-blood woman
rather than on fictional characters. Both Carolyn and Gail encouraged me to
take the chance of beginning a new relationship, and eventually I did.
Somehow I managed to divide my priorities and continued reshaping
Margins, while Gloria worked as a secretary and attended evening classes.

Gloria remained closeted in her workplace, an insurance company, yet
unlike my previous lover she had no qualms about my being out to some
people or about my being a writer. She often remarked how lucky I was to
work on a campus that had a lesbian and gay network of staff, faculty, and
students. While this was true, I still opted for being out only to a select group

of coworkers, mainly as a means of self-protection. As I would tell Gloria, "Once you say those words, you can't take them back." I let my intuition guide me; if anyone in the office seemed the slightest bit intolerant, I took note for future reference.

Our relationship flourished. Gloria and I hiked and went on camping trips, often with other lesbians and gays. She was much more sociable than me and often succeeded in drawing me out of my shell. This caused problems at times, because I had to choose between having fun with her or working on the novel. Although I did not want my writing to take a backseat, I found myself getting stressed over the diminishing amount of creative time. At that point, my campus job had become the least troublesome part of my life.

My writing career continued to offer opportunities. Sometimes I said yes to these without fully considering the consequences. For example, I agreed to teach "Writing After Five O'Clock," a short-fiction class in the UCLA Extension Writers' Program, before realizing how time-consuming an evening class would be. One thing I did know: I would have to come out to the class of twenty students the first evening, because they would no doubt ask about my own fiction. Despite the January chill, I was drenched with perspiration when I told them: "I am a Chicana lesbian, and that's what I write about." There were several women of color and some lesbians present; in fact, many of them had taken the class because they had read my work. The heterosexuals in the class were nonconfrontational, though one later wrote in his evaluation that I "had a particular bent which...limited [my] scope." Another mentioned that "as a white male, [he] sometimes took offense to [my] political views of literature." Admittedly nervous, I did not doubt I could have handled that class better, but it ended on a positive note when the Seal Press accepted *Margins* for publication. One student added to his evaluation, "Knowing her novel will be published is a real boost of inspiration."

A year later, I carried an armful of copies of *Margins* into the office and stacked them beside my desk. Sharing my excitement, most of my coworkers, even the deans, bought books from me. When I proudly but anxiously watched them flip the novel over to read "*Margins* gives us a memorably real portrait of the Chicana lesbian as daughter, sister, aunt, friend, writer, and lover," I knew I could not have planned my official coming-out any better. That line summed up my novel, and my life as well. If anyone there had a negative reaction, I have yet to hear about it.

With *Margins* in hand, I have not only come out to longtime acquaintances in the office, many of whom never suspected my sexual orientation, but also to Chicana and Chicano students in classes, to complete strangers in bookstores. I have received touching letters from readers as far away as Portugal. And when readers reach out to me, sharing their own stories and experiences, I realize again how fulfilling it is to be out.

As for my coworkers, I believe they have come to see me in a wholly different light. In the past, they felt free to ask my opinion about Chicana/Chicano issues such as bilingualism and immigration, and now they know they can discuss lesbian/gay issues with me as well. To some this might be threatening, but to others I think it has opened the lines of communication. I must admit to being apologetic about having been closeted to some office friends, especially if any of them were hurt by my lack of trust; that was never my intention. For my own well-being, however, I do not regret waiting until *Margins'* publication date to come out to all my coworkers at once. I had sensed that the novel would answer everyone's questions—and it has, many times over.

Being out in the workplace can be stressful, however, even tokenizing. As an out Chicana lesbian, I am expected to have opinions on a variety of gay and Chicana-related issues. As a fiction writer, I am more accustomed to speaking through the words of my characters, which allows me greater freedom to voice a variety of views. In the office, however, while I would prefer to discuss racism and sexism because I believe they affect me more than does homophobia, my coworkers seem more likely to talk about the gays-in-the-military controversy or other gay and lesbian rights issues. Ironically, after the 1992 civil disturbances in Los Angeles, gay issues probably appear less provocative to them than racism and sexism do.

Outside my office, this is not always the case. For example, the campus human resources office asked a gay Japanese-American colleague and me to help conduct a homophobia workshop in a situation in which lesbians and gays of color were being discriminated against by heterosexual people of color. The stereotypical questions we were asked ("Do you want to be a man?") illustrated the lack of awareness and understanding there is about us among people of color. That experience was a demoralizing one, yet it reemphasized my goal to continue exploring such issues in fiction.

A decade after Beth's comment that Laura made her feel uncomfortable, I know I unintentionally may have the same effect on others. Still, I prefer that to the alternative of returning to the isolation and suffocation of the closet. Although it has taken a decade to accomplish, I am proud to be continuing to transform my fiction into fact.

Yeah. So What?

Barney Frank

*Barney Frank is a United States congressman from the
Commonwealth of Massachusetts. The story of his
coming-out is the story of his effort to make politics a
substitute for a satisfying personal life and of his recognition
that a political career could not substitute for an emotionally
healthy private life. As long as he did not have the latter,
he could not begin to realize his potential in the former. This
is also the story of reactions from voters and political colleagues
that were far better than he had expected them to be.*

In the spring of 1987, I decided to acknowledge, publicly and voluntarily, that I am gay. Once I definitely decided that I should come out, I had to deal with the question of how. As a member of the U.S. House of Representatives, I recognized that my sexuality would be a matter of some public interest, with a potentially significant impact on my own political career and, to a lesser degree, on public discussion of homosexuality. I sounded out several people whose judgment I respected, reflected on what I'd learned in four years of college, five years in a Ph.D. program, and three years of law school, thought about the lessons of twenty years of active political work, and drew heavily on my lifelong study of political rhetoric to conclude that what I wanted was for a reporter to ask me if I were gay and for me to answer, "Yeah. So what?" That is what happened—in part. Kay Longcope of *The Boston Globe* asked, and I responded with that answer.

From the perspective of 1995, several elements of this strategy now seem unduly defensive. I had expected the results to be a trade-off in which enormous gains in my personal life would outweigh setbacks in my standing with the voters and my ability to influence congressional colleagues. Happily, I was wrong. Not only were the gains in my personal life much greater than I would have predicted—meeting my lover, Herb Moses, being the most profound—but the negative effect on the political side was close to nonexistent.

I can say in defense of my having miscalculated so much on the pessimistic side that I did not make this mistake alone. A large number of friends with whom I discussed my coming out urged me not to do so, predicting political consequences ranging from mildly discomforting all the way to dire. While their counsel did not ultimately dissuade me, it did lead me to be much more careful about coming out than I have been about anything else I have ever done.

I realized that I was gay when I was thirteen: that is, I recognized a fact over which I had absolutely no control and about which I was decidedly unhappy. (I find it hard to believe that anyone would really think that a thirteen-year-old kid living in New Jersey in 1953 would have decided that spending the rest of his life as a homosexual was a really neat idea.) For the next twenty years, I lived in terror that anybody else would find out, and I had little occasion to meet other gay people in normal social or professional settings.

In May 1972, I decided to run for a Massachusetts State House seat that was being vacated in the Beacon Hill and Back Bay sections of Boston. This opportunity required me to decide how to deal with being gay. Coming out was unthinkable—and not simply because it would have meant I couldn't win. The notion of going from being completely closeted to being one of America's most public homosexuals—the consequence of running as a gay legislative candidate in 1972—was far beyond my emotional capacity. At the same time, I was by then already angry at the world and at myself because I was suppressing so vital a part of my personality. I decided that I would run and that I would stay closeted but that I would be a strong, unyielding supporter of gay rights. I would vindicate through my public work what I so fiercely kept hidden in my private life.

I did not think there were many gay men and lesbians living in my future district, partly because there were fewer than now live there, but even more because despite the nascent gay rights political movement then present in Boston, most of us were still keeping our closet doors tightly shut. Thus I was not pressured into taking an aggressive pro-gay and pro-lesbian position; the generally sophisticated attitudes prevalent in those neighborhoods, however, produced a range of reactions to my gay rights advocacy from tolerance to admiration. I worked with new gay and lesbian friends on various issues. For example, after the election I filed two gay rights bills. One would have repealed the law against private consensual sex between adults, and another would have banned any discrimination against people based on their sexual preference. Neither bill went very far legislatively, but they did begin the public discussion of gay rights in Massachusetts.

The antidiscrimination bill I had filed was the first to be given a hearing. I clearly remember how nervous I was. This was the first time in my life I would be discussing gay rights in a forum composed primarily of straight people, most of whom I assumed would be either indifferent or hostile. I was at the time an unmarried thirty-three-year-old man, appearing in public as the first legislator in Massachusetts history to offer and push for a bill to end discrimination against gay people. I worried that I would be asked if I were gay, and I was so unsettled by the possibility that I couldn't even calmly think of a good way to respond. I also worried about the possibility that many people would read or hear about my work on the bill and simply assume I was gay. And short of paying a woman to interrupt my testimony by serving me with papers for a paternity suit, I couldn't think of anything I could do to counter that assumption.

It turned out that the consensual sex bill, which would have repealed the sodomy law, created the bigger stir. It was defeated by a vote of approximately 210 to 11. But before voting it down, dozens of legislators pushed the "yes" switch on their desks, temporarily giving the bill an overwhelming majority on the board. They then uproariously switched to "no." I was not offended, but the next day Carol Liston of *The Boston Globe* wrote an eloquent, blistering attack on my colleagues for not simply killing the bill, but instead making a joke out of something so important to so many citizens. The column rang true, and several colleagues apologized to me after reading it. It was the *Globe*'s lead op-ed piece for that day, an important mark of respect for our cause from mainstream society.

The concrete result of all this was nothing much, but for me it was a very important nothing. No matter what various people may have thought, nobody asked, said, or did anything about my sexuality. Consequently, I felt confirmed in my view that I could maintain a bifurcated existence—remaining totally closeted while playing an active public role as a leader in the gay rights fight.

And I did, for the next seven years, despite an event that, logically, should have persuaded me that I could come out and still remain in the legislature. In 1974, Elaine Noble ran for a new seat in the House. The seat had been created after redistricting and was made up to a great degree of areas that had been in my district when I won in 1972. Elaine was open about her lesbianism. While this was an issue used against her, she defeated a credible neighborhood activist in the primary and a well-financed independent candidate in November.

Why did this event have so little impact on my opening the door of the closet? After all, Noble's victory undermined my stated reason for being so resolutely secretive about my homosexuality: namely, to preserve the option of a political career. At that point, I still considered myself lucky to have won a State House seat in my unusually cosmopolitan, sophisticated district. As a Jewish, closeted gay man from New Jersey who spoke with a noticeable non-Massachusetts accent and was fifty pounds overweight, I thought I was much too unconventional a candidate to ever win a larger constituency. My long-standing insecurity about being gay and an attendant fear of rejection led me to rationalize, however, that while Elaine could pull it off, I could not. I continued to be as active in the fight against homophobia as any politician in America, but I continued to convince myself that coming out would jeopardize my career.

By 1979, events were again converging to make me think about publicly acknowledging my gayness. First and most powerfully, I was increasingly realizing—and regretting—the harm I was doing myself by trying to suppress all evidence of so important a part of me. I was more and more jealous of my gay and lesbian friends with whom I was socializing, whose social and physical intimacies I envied. And while I did not realize it very clearly yet, this unhappiness with my life was having a negative effect on the way I was doing my job. While being totally closeted had probably helped advance my career at first, since it meant I had few social distractions to take me away from work, the corrosive effect this way of living had on my self-esteem and my emotional balance by now definitely detracted from my work.

Another reason I wanted more and more to acknowledge my gayness publicly was that I now knew many other homosexuals and saw how they could live strong, healthy, normal lives. The notion of telling other people that I was gay no longer seemed such a terrible leap. In fact, while I was still paradoxically convinced that, unlike Elaine Noble, I could not come out of the closet and stay in the House, that no longer seemed to me such a bad deal.

So I started to come out.

For me, approaching the age of forty in late 1979, the only possible way to do this was to come out to one close friend or relative at a time, with intervals of a few weeks to recharge my emotional batteries sufficiently to empower the next confession—since, alas, that is what it still felt like to me. Everyone took it very well, with the gay people I told expressing a great deal less surprise than the straight ones.

I had barely reached double numbers when politics and the pope intervened dramatically. Pope John Paul II ordered Father Robert Drinan from the adjoining district not to run for reelection to the U.S. Congress. My subsequent decision to run for Drinan's seat required a number of choices, but one option no longer seemed open—acknowledging my sexuality. In fact, I told my sister and brother-in-law, Doris and Jim Breay, about my running for Congress in a phone call that I began by saying, "You are about to hear a closet door slamming shut." I was very worried about the possibility that I would be "accused" of homosexuality during that campaign, and I still did not know how to respond.

My support of gay rights was used against me in the campaign along with a number of other issues that were tied together with some success to portray me as an alien, valueless big-city type poaching on a suburban and semirural district. I won, but only narrowly, in both the primary and the final election.

When I got to Washington after the November 1980 election, I gave a great deal of thought to how to deal with being gay. I was not remotely ready to come out publicly, but neither was I prepared to re-create the hermetically sealed private life from which I had just begun to emerge.

My initial response to this dilemma is very relevant to contemporary discussions about how we gay men and lesbians should live our lives, because I tried hard for the next six years to live the way many straight people tell us we should live. Their question is essentially "It's okay for you to be gay, but why do you have to make a big deal of it? Can't you just do what you want to without telling everybody?" The position urged on us by this attitude is literally impossible to maintain. No one can get through a week's interaction with other human beings without revealing his or her sexual orientation except by either lying outright or refusing to answer the normal civil questions that make up much casual conversation: "What did you do last weekend?" "Where will you spend the holidays?" "Are you married?" "Do you want to bring a date to the party?"

My most compelling evidence that this is an impossible way to live without a great deal of evasion, double-talk, and outright dishonesty is my attempt to do so from 1981 to mid 1987. It did not work. From the time I arrived in Washington, I was out to other gay men and lesbians but not to the public. In effect, I tried to live a dual life. With straight people, I ignored my sexuality and made no references to it. Privately, I spent much of my time socializing with other gay people, with no effort to hide my identity. This mode of life became more and more difficult. I was uncomfortable once again with dissembling before straight people. The fact that I was a member of Congress, whose comings and goings were of some relevance to the media, exacerbated the problem, since it meant I had less privacy than most other people do.

What I learned was that, once again, Abraham Lincoln was right. I could not spend half my time as a gay man in private while enslaving myself to anti-gay prejudice the other half of the time. Asking others to share my life at that point means asking them to follow a very peculiar set of rules about when to acknowledge gayness and when implicitly to deny it—or at least avoid it in ways that could lead to awkwardness at best and de facto hypocrisy at worst. As it became increasingly clear to me that this solution was not working either, my emotional state worsened to the point of a stupid involvement with a hustler which was later to cause me significant embarrassment. I became involved with this individual in 1985, at the same time as I was still trying to coexist as half gay and half none of the above.

At any rate, by 1986 I was determined to complete the process of coming out. This determination was not motivated, however, by mounting fears of exposure. Neither the closeted gay reporters nor the openly straight ones ever so much as suggested that they would make a public issue of my sexuality until and unless I chose to.

Confirmation that the press would not break the story against my will came in the summer of 1986, when I was outed in the autobiography of former Congressman Robert Bauman, a Republican who had lost his seat in 1980 after himself being outed. The press declined to publicize my outing to any great degree. One magazine printed the excerpt of the book relevant to me, but with my name deleted.

This incident did serve, however, as sort of trial coming-out for me. When I learned that some newspapers might publicize Bauman's comments, I thought it best to prepare some of my colleagues for the revelation that might be coming. The most interesting reaction I received came from Tip O'Neill. At first he assured me that no one would accept what Bauman had said. I replied that while I was not volunteering the information, it was, in fact, true. His reaction was troubling, not because of any negative feeling by him, but as a reading of the effect this revelation would have on my general political standing. The thrust of his remarks was that I had damaged my career and that any chance I might have had to be in the House leadership no longer existed.

At first this reply bothered me and caused me to feel a little sorry for myself. I reminded myself that I was already enjoying the great privilege of serving Congress, where I felt free to pursue issues according to what I saw was right, with few political constraints, and that I had tried every possible variant of dealing with being gay short of simple candor—without finding a satisfactory alternative. To start backsliding because it might hinder an already extremely slender chance to join the House leadership was not sensible. I thus felt free to resume my slow march toward "outness."

By the summer of 1986, the fact that I was gay and might be planning to talk about it was not one of Washington's better-kept secrets. Some of my straight, liberal House colleagues discussed this with me, and, overwhelmingly, their view was that I should not make any public statement. To do so, they said, would be to risk "marginalizing" myself. My views on every other issue would be discounted, and I would be recast as a single-issue congressman. Their arguments were flattering—couched in terms of not wanting to lose my advocacy for other major issues—but also, of course, a little depressing.

All of us at that point assumed that I would pay some price in diminished influence on some issues for being candid about my sexuality. Unlike my gay and lesbian friends, straight people tended to see little reason to pay that price. Generally, they underestimated the importance to me personally of dropping all pretense and equally underestimated the public importance of my making a simple statement that I am gay.

The very fact that so many decent, wholly well-intentioned political leaders—themselves strong and effective opponents of homophobia—understood so little why coming out was important made it even more clear to me just how important it really was. Even my closest political allies saw the semicloset in which I was living as a perfectly reasonable way to deal with prejudice. They urged me to continue living a life that was costing me a great deal emotionally, thus demonstrating to me that we would not be successful in abolishing homophobia without doing a better job of telling the straight majority exactly what it is all about.

Thus paradoxically but profoundly, the advice I got not to come out strengthened my resolve to do so. But it simultaneously strengthened my conviction that this was something to be approached very carefully, so that I could do it in a way that minimized the political damage almost everyone foresaw. My solution was to accelerate a process I came to think of as "leaking out." By the mid 1980s enough people had figured out that I was gay that I could joke about it with both straight and gay friends. I was even enjoying the fact that I could finally make light of being gay, after years of schlepping it around as if it were the world's heaviest burden. This in itself was a very important sign to me that self-hatred was rapidly disappearing from my psychological makeup. Directing humor at myself had, I believe, a disarming quality and made it less likely that my gayness would be used as a weapon against me.

As it turned out, when I did finally give Kay Longcope the answer I had told her she could elicit, and *The Boston Globe* printed it on June 1, 1987, the consequences were far better than I had anticipated. Politically, it had no negative effect either on my ability to win reelection to the House or on my ability to function within that institution.

I have run for reelection three times since coming out. An estimate from a 1987 poll that I might lose about two or three percentage points turned out to be accurate, but even so I was reelected in 1988 by a margin of 70 percent to 30 percent. Two years later, I won 66 percent to 34 percent, in what was generally a bad year for Democratic congressional candidates. In 1992, I received 68 percent of the vote as compared to 26 percent for the Republican candidate and 5 percent for the Ross Perot candidate. In 1994, I ran unopposed.

Also subsequent to my announcement I was asked by the House leadership to run for the Budget Committee, and I was appointed in 1993 to the speaker's leadership advisory group. The two most respected evaluators of congressional reputation, the *Almanac of American Politics,* published by the *National Journal,* and *Politics of America,* published by *Congressional Quarterly,* explicitly asserted that coming out did no damage whatsoever to my standing in the House. In fact, being out has clearly enhanced my effectiveness as a member of Congress, precisely because it has benefited me so much personally.

Since November 1994 I have been working with the Democratic House leadership in its opposition to the conservative Republican House majority. Early efforts by the Republicans to delegitimize me by stressing my sexual orientation backfired, and I do not believe many people think that my being gay in any way detracts from my participation in the leadership effort.

The personal consequences of my public coming-out have been extraordinarily favorable. The most important of these was meeting my lover, Herb Moses, in August 1987. He has transformed my personal life and is the major reason, I think, that I am in a frame of mind to do my job more effectively. My relationship with Herb has since led to a second coming-out, this time as one half of a gay couple.

Herb and I decided early on that we would do things as a couple just as other couples do them. We do these things not to make a statement but simply because they are the kinds of things couples naturally want to do together. The fact that we are together in a wide variety of environments and circumstances in which gay or lesbian couples have not previously been visible helps the fight against homophobia.

In the end, any assessment of my coming-out decision ultimately boils down to a good news/bad news analysis.

The good news is that coming out brought none of the negative consequences I anticipated. But the fact that I did find myself anticipating them is bad news and the very fact that I had to come out at all, even worse. In a rational and unprejudiced world, I would have let people know I was gay as soon as I found out, just as I have with every other important aspect of my life, without worrying a great deal about the consequences.

Analogously, regarding homophobia in general the good news is that there is a lot less of it than there used to be, the bad news is that it ever existed in the first place, and the worse news is that it remains far stronger than is healthy for a society dedicated in theory to equality under the law.

Remembering how far we've come toward the goal of equality, as well as how far we have to go to reach it, are both essential if we are to get there.

Once Is Not Enough
Bianca Cody Murphy

*Bianca Cody Murphy is an associate professor of psychology
at Wheaton College, Norton, Mass. Before going to Wheaton,
she had been a lesbian-identified psychologist for many years—
writing, speaking, and even appearing on television to talk
about gay and lesbian issues. She tells the story of being out
as an untenured faculty member and the issues it raised for
her as she found herself coming out again and again—
finally by writing an article in the college magazine
the summer before her tenure hearing.*

"I'm sure you understand women loving women, don't you? I
know I've always been close to and loved my women friends. It's
probably just hard to imagine what two women do sexually with
each other." That's what I told a group of women, all "medical
student wives," as we had dinner while our husbands studied for final exams.
One of the women had just made a negative comment about lesbians. I was
distressed by her comment. I really did understand women loving women,
and a couple of years later, the first time I was with a woman, I knew exactly what lesbians did sexually with each other. I remember feeling, "This isn't
strange. It feels so right, like coming home."

Discovering my lesbian identity felt wonderful. Affirming it publicly was
easy. I felt good about myself and felt that being a lesbian was simply a part
of who I am. It was sad and painful to leave the man I married, but I knew I
was doing the right thing.

At the time I came out in the mid 1970s, I was in graduate school in Boston
getting my masters degree in counseling psychology. It was "easy" to be a
lesbian in the feminist community of Cambridge and Boston at that time. I
never had any thoughts about hiding my identity. To the contrary, I believed
that it was important to educate others about gay and lesbian issues.

Entering academia

By the time I interviewed for a tenure-track position at Wheaton College in

1986, I had published articles about lesbian couples and had given lectures and led in-service training about gay and lesbian issues at mental health centers and college campuses around the country. I had even been on television as a lesbian. I was out to all my family and very committed to "being myself"—that is, affirming my identity in all arenas of my life.

When I decided to apply for tenure-track academic positions, I knew that I might be in for a difficult time. I had recently read an article about the negative effects on academic careers of being out, and I had held a one-year appointment at a Catholic college where I was advised informally that my being lesbian would probably make it very difficult for me to get tenure.

My lesbianism is all over my résumé—publications, papers, and presentations. I had also done research on environmentally contaminated families. Would potential employers think that it meant I was a member of a family exposed to environmental toxins? Would they know I was a lesbian?

I wanted to make my lesbianism clear in my interview at Wheaton without making it an announcement or a statement that would demand some sort of response. The faculty didn't announce their sexual orientations to me, but they did mention husbands, wives, and children in our social interactions as I walked from one interview to another. I disclosed my orientation in my usual style, which I call the "my partner, she" method. One of the faculty members with whom I was interviewing had worked at Boston State Hospital at the same time as my partner, Sandy, so I was easily able to slip "my partner, she" into the conversation. That together with a judicious use of "we"—as in "We live in Newton" and "We're going to spend the holidays with family"—made it pretty clear without making a response demand.

I know that not everyone accepts or approves of lesbianism and that some people find it shocking, sick, or immoral—even in the "liberal" atmosphere of a New England college. Using the "my partner, she" strategy I am creating a context that says, "This is no big deal." By assuming a normalness, I also demand it.

Since both areas of my research could be viewed as controversial, and since my research was clinical and qualitative (which is sometimes not as valued as quantitative research), I made a point of asking the provost during my interview if she felt I would have any problems pursuing those lines of scholarship at Wheaton. Her answer was affirming: "Absolutely not. We welcome those topics." I then asked what she felt the atmosphere would be like for an out lesbian faculty member on campus. "It should be just fine," she told me.

When I was offered the job I continued the "my partner, she" style of disclosure and assumed that everyone would take it in stride. Sandy came to the annual party for faculty and their families at the provost's house at the beginning of the semester, and I introduced her to everyone as my partner.

The provost's warm welcome helped set a tone of acceptance. I quickly learned, however, that there were no other lesbian or gay faculty who were out on campus. For my first two years there, I was the only out lesbian or gay person on campus. I refer to these as "my lone(ly) lesbian years."

The lone(ly) lesbian years

When I arrived on campus, I was relieved not to be asked to be the adviser to the Lesbian Alliance. This group already had an adviser—a straight man. I didn't want to be known solely as *"the lesbian faculty member."* I also liked the idea that there was at least one other faculty member who was identified as being sensitive to lesbian and gay issues. (The Lesbian Alliance was renamed the Lesbian, Gay, and Bisexual Alliance [LGBA] after Wheaton went coed.)

At the beginning of each year, one of the deans hosts a dinner for lesbian (now lesbian, gay, and bisexual) students "and their friends." A number of faculty and staff attend. During the dinner my first year, I made sure that I said the phrase "As a lesbian..." so that there was no doubt in the students' minds that I was a lesbian and willing to identify myself publicly as such. However, a couple of months later, some antigay incidents occurred on campus, and a meeting of "all interested people" was called to discuss them. There were about eight students present, along with a number of student-affairs staff, the dean of students, and a couple of faculty. I noticed that none of the students spoke as an identified lesbian. They clearly felt uncomfortable being public, and to my dismay, I noted that they weren't sure they could refer to me as lesbian. I quickly began by saying, "As a lesbian member of the college community, I feel..." and heard their sigh of relief. They later said that they weren't sure if I was out only to the lesbian students or to everyone.

I was shocked to discover that the Lesbian Alliance did not advertise its meetings. I expressed my concern and asked how students who wanted to attend would know where they were meeting. The students said that they felt if was unsafe for the location of their meetings to be made public. They feared that other students would stand outside and note who went to the meetings. I felt their fear, but I was stunned.

These students were clearly having a hard time being out. I kept wondering what I could do to help them. Some of them were unclear about their sexual orientation, and the atmosphere on campus was one of uncertainty and fear, not activism and pride. I felt that if they had more models of gay men and lesbian women, they might feel more comfortable in affirming themselves. I decided, therefore, to invite other gays and lesbians to campus as speakers in my psychology course in human sexuality. I decided to make it an "open class" so that any students interested in the topic could come. I felt a little nervous about posting signs all around campus, but I felt it was an important issue. I invited speakers from the local gay and lesbian speakers bureau. One of my psychology colleagues brought his class, and many of the lesbian students also attended. A number of them commented to me about how important it was that there was this public event on campus.

Wheaton has a tradition of listing the names of all spouses in the campus phone book. I actually think it is a nice idea, allowing people to address invitations to events correctly, for example, "Derek and Sue Price" or "Kathleen Morgan and Warren Miller." So my other minor piece of activism that first year was listing "Sandy Albright" as my partner in that phone book. I was surprised at how many people noticed and commented on it. I later realized that since Sandy could be a man's name, I had her listed the next year as Sandra so that it was very clear that my partner is a woman.

I knew that there were other lesbian women faculty and staff at Wheaton, and slowly, one by one, they came out to me. Disclosure was often preceded by an invitation to lunch off campus—an unusual event on a campus where everyone eats in the faculty dining room. I conveyed to each of the women my respect for her decision but also asked her about it. At times I felt that some of the lesbian faculty and staff avoided being seen with me because of fear of guilt by association. However, one of my favorite experiences occurred at a faculty meeting during my second year on campus. As I sat in my seat, I realized I was surrounded by lesbians. There was one on either side of me, one in front of me, and one behind me—almost the entire lesbian contingent on campus, *a phalanx of lesbians*. What a great feeling! Unfortunately, no one else, including them, realized it.

I was amazed and saddened by how scared all the lesbians (and gay men, if there were any on campus) felt. Wheaton has a very affirming administration and what I believe is one of the best statements on sexual orientation of any college in the country. This statement on sexual orientation has appeared in Wheaton's student handbook since 1986:

The Wheaton College community has long held and continues to hold the position that basic rights, including the right to sexual preference, must and will be extended to all members of the community. The issue for the college is not that gays and lesbians are part of the community, but rather that they may choose to become a visible and vocal part of the community. Sexual preference is a private matter and not an issue unless other people make it one. Acting upon this position involved eradicating certain misconceptions as well as espousing certain assertions.

First, the Wheaton community and those concerned with its welfare must not confuse the demand of lesbians and gays for their human rights with proselytizing and sexual aggression. The college has a responsibility to protect students from all forms of sexual aggression, both heterosexual and homosexual; it also has a responsibility to respond positively when members of the community request to participate fully and openly in the life of the community.

Second, requests that lesbians and gays be recognized as complete human beings cannot be equated with advocacy that everyone should be gay or lesbian. The confusion of these two very different ideas often leads to an unnecessary defensiveness on the part of heterosexuals.

Third, the visibility of gay and lesbian staff, faculty, and students also raises the important issue of role modeling and professional competence. Role modeling and professional competence are not affected by sexual preference any more than they are by any other personal characteristic such as race, sex, or handicap. Rather, the chance for students to get to know adults who are handling difficult jobs effectively and fairly, as well as other students like themselves, can be an important part of the educational process.

Fourth, the college asserts that a person's sexual preference should not be a criterion in employment decisions; rather, demonstrated competence must be the major criterion.

Fifth, the college asserts that lesbian and gay students and staff are entitled to an environment which is non-oppressive. Harassment based on sexual preference is not acceptable and will be addressed through appropriate administrative action as well as educational programming.

The college's support of gay and lesbian students and staff reflects its belief that Wheaton must accept and integrate the world's diverse population into its educational community in ways that are responsible both to the college and to the world.

Despite the existence of this statement, the students and faculty still felt frightened—and so did I. Why?

Being out doesn't mean that you're safe from gay jokes or from threatening moves. Shortly after I arrived at Wheaton, for example, a colleague was in my office when a student came in. She was late in registering for my class and asked for the course syllabus. As I handed it to her, I pointed to a reading and said that she needed to do it for the next class. I touched her arm as I showed her the reading. When she left, my colleague asked me, "What do you think about sexual harassment laws?" I said, "I think they are important." He said he thought they were overused and asked me whether I agreed that they could be more trouble than they were worth. I said, "No." He then said, "For example, that woman could have felt that your touching her arm was sexual harassment and reported it." My heart started pounding. I told him what I truly believe: "That's why sexual harassment laws are important. If that student felt at all uncomfortable with my behavior, it would be important for her to know that there is a place where she can go to talk about it. No student should feel harassed or threatened." When he left, I felt scared.

Another day at lunch, I shared a table in the faculty dining room with a number of colleagues, one of whom told a gay joke. I remember noticing the discomfort of two others at the table, who looked over at me when it happened. Neither of them made a comment about it. I knew I didn't want to let it pass, and at the same time I didn't want to make it a big issue. I simply looked at the person who told the joke and said, "Hey, remember who you are sitting with." He apologized. I was glad I said something, but I still felt bad that the gay joke was made and that I had no one to talk to about it.

Building community

After two years in which I was the only identified lesbian at Wheaton, the college hired a new woman to join the student-affairs staff. Ann knew I was out and quickly informed me that she was lesbian and also willing to be out. What a relief! We had lunch together in public on campus. It was wonderful to have a lesbian colleague.

Part of Ann's job was to do outreach to the lesbian and gay students. One of her first projects was creating a pamphlet called "You Are Not Alone." The pamphlet, which is placed in every student's mailbox at the beginning of the academic year, lists all the gay and lesbian resources in the area. It also lists those faculty and staff who are available as resources for lesbian, gay, and bisexual students. The pamphlet is a wonderful idea. It not only makes the lesbian and gay students feel recognized but also sends a message to everyone that there are gay and lesbian students on campus—an important piece of visibility for this invisible minority.

That year, as part of a film series on human sexuality, we showed *Pink Triangles.* We always have discussions after each film in the series. Ann and I facilitated this one. After the discussion, a few of the lesbian students stayed behind and told us about some homophobic graffiti in the library. Since the conversation after the film had been about homophobia, we asked the students why they didn't mention it in the larger group. They said that they were uncomfortable, afraid that people would know they were lesbian. Both Ann and I went home saddened by the thought that even in a discussion about homophobia, the lesbian and gay students felt uncomfortable speaking openly. We each felt that we should do something about the graffiti. It was gay and lesbian awareness week, and as usual the LGBA had put pins with a pink triangle in everyone's mailbox. Both Ann and I were wearing our pink triangles as we walked into the library and asked about the graffiti. We felt like the "lesbian police" with our badges on. The staff informed us that they had already painted over the offending graffiti and thanked us for our concern. I was pleased to see how quickly they had responded.

I started a tradition of inviting the lesbian, gay, and bisexual students to my home for dinner each year. They were excited to see a committed lesbian couple with a house in the suburbs, a dog, and a station wagon—a lifestyle to which these predominantly white, middle-class lesbian women and gay men aspired. I am painfully aware, however, that students need other models: they need to see lesbian and gay people of color, lesbian and gay people with disabilities, lesbian and gay parents, lesbian women and gay men who are single, and others.

One day I received a call: the English department was interviewing an out lesbian for a tenure-track position. I was asked to advise her about where to live if she came to Wheaton. I liked the idea that they really wanted her to come to Wheaton and that they felt having her talk to another out lesbian might help.

Good things were happening everywhere. The counseling center wanted to hire a new counselor and was hoping to find someone who could work with the lesbian and gay students. They asked me if I could suggest where in addition to the traditional sources they might advertise and involved me in the interview process. Because I am a clinician, this seemed to make sense. They ultimately hired another out lesbian!

There were finally enough of us for a meeting. I invited all the lesbian and gay colleagues that I knew, those who were out and those who weren't, to my house for dinner. People were very anxious about attending. They asked who was coming, but of course I couldn't say whom I had invited, because that would disclose their identity to others. We joked about how nervous people were. I said that they could wear brown bags over their heads when they came. A couple of people actually made brown bags for everyone to wear. We kidded about having our picture in the college paper.

From that dinner two groups emerged. The Caucus was the public group. There were seven of us who agreed that we would be willing to have meetings and lunches on campus and to advertise those meetings so that there would be a visible lesbian and gay faculty and staff presence. The other, more private, group agreed to get together for lunch off campus on a monthly basis for informal socialization and support.

Things were going quite well. I felt we had made a lot of progress. The counseling center was running a support group for lesbian, gay, and bisexual students. The Caucus was having meetings. A group of gay and lesbian faculty and staff were having lunch. And I was coming up for tenure.

An unexpected crisis

The spring before my tenure decision, I was asked to write an article for the *Wheaton Quarterly*, the college magazine that is sent to every member of the college community: students, parents, alumnae, faculty, and board members. Over the years I had been asked to contribute to the magazine on a couple of occasions. Each time I felt that the topic they wanted me to write about wasn't one I felt particularly knowledgeable about or committed to. This time, however, I was invited to contribute a faculty member's perspective to a special edition on gay and lesbian issues. I was delighted—and I was frightened.

I was surprised that I felt nervous about writing the article. I had been out for years, and I felt good about my previous publications and scholarship on lesbian and gay issues. Why was I scared? Was it the upcoming tenure decision? Probably. Everyone worries about tenure. I was no exception. I felt that my scholarship, teaching, and community service were all quite "tenure-able." I did not worry about whether anyone would be uncomfortable because some of my scholarship was on lesbian issues. I knew that my articles were published in some of the journals in my discipline. But now I was being asked to write an article that would go to all parents and alumnae. Would this put my tenure decision at risk?

I had to decide if I would come out in the article. Would I use the phrase "as a lesbian"? I thought about writing the article without actually saying I was a lesbian. I even talked to other out lesbian friends to get their "permission" to not come out. They assured me that it was reasonable to be fearful, especially since the magazine would be in everyone's mailbox right before my tenure hearing. I was still surprised at the degree of anxiety I felt about it. I have always said that coming out is an ongoing process, one that a person makes again and again in each new social situation. I had been coming out for years—usually with very little difficulty on my part—even when the reactions of others had been negative. I was surprised that I was so scared this time.

My article was called "Everywhere, Invisible." In it I addressed the fact that gay men and lesbian women are everywhere—in big cities and small towns, on the farm and in the boardroom, and on college campuses as students, faculty, administrators, and staff. I noted that gay men and lesbian women are often invisible—invisible because sexual orientation is not obvious and invisible because many choose to keep their sexual orientation hidden for fear of discrimination or violence.

Would I come out in my article? I was in a dilemma. I said such things as "Having an open identity as a gay man or lesbian woman in the home, family, workplace, and community fosters a cohesive self-identity, builds self-esteem, and enhances overall psychological adjustment." And "Coming out and affirming a homosexual identity affects the well-being of us all.... Learning about and coming to accept 'difference' fosters a healthy pluralistic society, when stereotypes break down and we grow beyond our various definitions, categories, and biases."

Of course I came out: I inserted it in my usual style, saying "As a psychologist working with lesbian women and gay men, and as a lesbian woman myself, I have seen the effects of heterosexism and homophobia."

The article inspired many letters to the editor; in fact, the issue generated more response than any other. Some of the letters were quite angry and hateful, but there were some that made me cry. One alumna wrote, "As a lesbian who finally came out to herself almost fifteen years ago—twelve years after graduating—I admit that I am somewhat envious of the supportive atmosphere Wheaton is attempting to provide....I remember 'suspecting' that some of the professors and administrators were lesbians, but it would have been a boon to know. Role models would have helped me and the other lesbian students accept our sexual preference earlier in life and feel better about ourselves. I thank Wheaton for trying to improve the attitude of the college's current population for all lesbian women, gay men, and heterosexuals."

I am happy to report that I got tenure and am now teaching the first gay and lesbian studies course at Wheaton College.

Seamlessness

John-Manuel Andriote

*John-Manuel Andriote is a thirty-six-year-old freelance
journalist and AIDS educator in Washington, D.C. He is
currently writing a book about the gay community's response
to the AIDS epidemic, to be published in 1997. He describes
how he came to appreciate the importance of being openly
gay and dealing with AIDS issues in his work as the result
of a hostile, probably homophobic legal confrontation
with his first Washington employer.*

At this stage of my career, I believe I enjoy a kind of seamlessness
between my professional and personal lives in that I am the same person at work as I am at home. This is what being out as a gay man
means to me: to be as consistent and comfortable with myself among
professional colleagues as I am among personal friends. It doesn't mean I immediately tell everyone I meet that I'm gay, which strikes me as exhibitionistic.

It *does* mean that I feel at home within my skin, that I enjoy being who and
what I am—which happens to be a man with a variety of interests and aptitudes. It also means that as a professional, I expect to be evaluated by my
associates on the quality of my work and not on my sexual orientation.
Fortunately, I have chosen work in which my sexual orientation is in many
ways an asset. My work also stimulates my intellect and nourishes my gay
spirit, which pushes me beyond the level needed simply to "do my job."

Arriving at this stage in my personal and career development has been a
metamorphosis of sorts, with small triumphs and pitfalls along the way. The
sense of cohesion I feel between my professional and personal lives is a result
of both age—it has become better in my thirties—and the choices I have had
to make along the way. My work experiences, in particular, have taught me to
pursue honesty and integrity as a gay professional rather than dissemble and
hide behind a false mask of either asexuality or heterosexuality.

I was until recently the AIDS training coordinator for the American
Psychiatric Association. Many of the doctors with whom I worked to set up
AIDS education conferences across the country are themselves gay or lesbian, and the rapport I enjoyed with them because we "speak a common language" contributed in no small way to our professional collaboration. Of

course, the other side of being a gay man who works in AIDS education is that I must deal with many personal feelings—including rage, sorrow, and frustration—to my work that a nongay person might not comprehend or share.

The comfort I enjoy nowadays as a gay professional has come only after hard, even bitter lessons. The hardest and bitterest lesson came as part of my first job in Washington, D.C., where I moved after finishing a master's degree in journalism at Northwestern University in 1986. I wanted to move back to the East because it's where I grew up and also where I'd met a wonderful man while doing a reporting internship in Washington in 1985. But neither my academic training nor love would shield me against what lay in store for me a year after I arrived in town.

My first job in D.C. was with a trade association, where I worked as the editor of its eight newsletters. I was hired at a low salary and learned subsequently that my employers would have been happy to have paid an even paltrier salary to a younger, less educated schmuck if they could only get rid of me. Regardless, six months after I was hired, I received the $1,000 pay raise that we'd agreed upon when I came onboard: everyone seemed pleased with my work. In fact, the trade association entered one of the newsletters I edited in a national competition for association publications, and it won a gold award for general excellence.

While working for this association, I was also moonlighting as a freelance journalist. I wrote fairly often for the *Washington City Paper,* a weekly alternative that covers the offbeat side of life in the nation's capital, and sometimes for our local gay paper, *The Washington Blade.* Mostly I wrote about gay political issues and AIDS, with a couple of my cover stories being displayed in the newspaper dispensers around town. I showed copies of my articles to one or two people in the office with whom I'd become friendly and didn't think much more of it.

I didn't know at the time, however, that my boss was apparently thinking about it quite a lot. But I found out once the association had hired a man a few years older than I to become the director of communications and my immediate supervisor. This man turned out to be gay, like me. But unlike me, he was very closeted and furtive about his orientation. He only revealed to me that he was gay one night over after-work beers. He also revealed to me that my boss had told him that I was gay and that I wrote about gay issues for the newspapers.

That bit of confidence turned into overconfidence on my new supervisor's part when he began to harass me sexually. In the mornings he'd come into my office, stand in front of my desk, and position himself so that his crotch was prominently displayed before me; sometimes he'd touch himself suggestively and offer to provide services in the men's room. I laughed it off at first, though I added, only half jokingly, that he might want to think about the risk he was taking that I'd sue him for sexual harassment. He, of course, laughed that one off.

All of our laughter turned to anger and anguish a couple of months after these shenanigans started. One day I was summoned into the office of the association president, where he and my boss asked me to sign a letter of resignation that they'd already drafted. They said that my work hadn't measured up to their expectations. I thought to myself, *What about that salary increase? What about that gold award?* I refused to sign the letter and told them instead that I wanted to confer with an attorney first. Another gay man in the association with whom I was friendly had been asked to resign two weeks before, and I knew he had retained a well-known attorney to represent him in a wrongful discharge suit against the association.

I spent the Memorial Day weekend of 1987 summing up in a memo for this lawyer what had been happening in the office. He agreed to represent me in a three-pronged suit: wrongful discharge, discrimination on the basis of sexual orientation—which has been illegal in the District of Columbia since the early 1970s—and sexual harassment. The association placed me on administrative leave, so that I still received my salary without going to the office every day.

After what seemed an interminably long period, depositions were taken from the association president and my boss. Sitting in the wood-paneled boardroom of my attorney's firm, with a court reporter recording all that was said, was a harrowing experience. I wanted to shout at and push the bastards who had been my employers as they bloodlessly recited their litany of lies about how I'd let them down—despite the raise, despite the award for excellence. The fact that my sexual orientation was a major subtext and that an allegation of sexual harassment against another gay man also figured in my suit made this whole procedure extremely discomforting, to say the very least. Actually, it was humiliating and awful.

I was hurt and angry, felt as if I'd been rejected and turned out, and I didn't know but that this employer might blackball me and ruin my career. I'm sure this would be a very upsetting situation for anyone, but I think it was particularly so for someone new to Washington and just starting a career. I believed most of all, however, in my professional ability, and, certain that I was being done a grave injustice, I decided I was not going to allow these people to force me into a closet of shame. I'd been putting my name out there in the press writing about gay issues, and I wouldn't let myself fail this test of my own "outness." I told myself that if these people thought they were going to embarrass me into keeping quiet and slipping out the back door with my tail between my legs, they were messing with the wrong faggot!

If I sound like I was a crusader, then I've conveyed the wrong impression—because I really wasn't. I was embarrassed at having to talk so candidly about my sexual orientation and a man's coming on to me and at speaking the slang terms that were used in doing so. I was embarrassed at having to have a lawyer defend my honor. But I realized even at the time that this experience was not only a test of my self-confidence as a professional, it was also a test of how sincerely I myself believed what I wrote in newspaper and magazine articles about "gay clout." I had the District's antidiscrimination and sexual harassment laws on my side, and I had a lawyer who believed me when I said I'd been wronged and that the laws had been violated.

A week before my gay former colleague was to give his deposition, the association's outside counsel called my attorney with an offer to settle the case out of court for a lump sum of money. I agreed, feeling vindicated and glad to close the book on this painful chapter of my life.

I learned through this ordeal just how much I value honesty and integrity and standing up for principles, even when it causes me embarrassment to talk about things I would prefer to keep private. I also learned the necessity and appropriateness of playing hardball when people do things that hurt you and can potentially damage your livelihood.

This ordeal was a tough but extremely important turning point in my growth as a gay person. I learned, for example, how important it is to me not to fear that who I am as a gay man may be held against me professionally. I also learned how important it is to me to do work that is personally meaningful and makes me feel that I am contributing something to others, particularly to gay people.

Today, my personal experience as a gay man who has dealt with the illness and death of friends and lovers strongly motivates the work I do. In addition to my AIDS educational work for the American Psychiatric Association, I continue to write newspaper and magazine articles that deal with AIDS or gay life or both. I feel that the choices I have made, to be open about my gayness and to work in the area of AIDS, are the right ones for me. Losing people I love has motivated me to learn and to educate others about AIDS. As a journalist with a profound curiosity about the world around me, I take enormous interest in the ways in which individuals and society deal with AIDS. And as a gay man with my particular skills, it has been extremely rewarding to contribute in a way that benefits my community.

I accept the fact that the choices I have made in my professional life preclude making certain other choices. My résumé has *AIDS* all over it. My portfolio includes articles that deal with homosexuality and AIDS—articles that I am very proud to have written but that in some areas of this country would be tossed out by a prospective employer. Yet I have chosen not to live in such places or work for such employers. I am enjoying my life and my work tremendously, and I believe that enjoyment has everything to do with knowing who I am and what I need and getting it for myself.

I believe that following the road that I have chosen—to be honest and out as a gay professional—has, as Robert Frost put it, "made all the difference."

On Visibility

Ruthann Rudel

*Ruthann Rudel is an environmental health scientist whose
coming-out-at-work story takes place in a research
laboratory and an environmental consulting firm. She
has struggled to learn how to be out at work without
feeling that she is making too much of being gay and
without feeling that she is hiding parts of her life that
straight people typically make visible. Her story describes
her search for a middle ground.*

The struggle for gay liberation—the freedom to be openly gay without apology or shame—is one that each of us fights on a personal level. We are not marginalized from society as a visibly identifiable group whose skin color, for instance, makes us easy to target as different. We do not grow up in all-gay families, with gay parents and siblings, in gay neighborhoods. Rather, we are individuals scattered throughout the general population. Because of this, we are well positioned to educate and influence people with whom we come into contact. But doing so requires that we come out. Each of us faces the daily task of defining ourselves to ourselves and to those around us. This process—this constant series of interactions during which we reveal ourselves—is about negotiating our own visibility. By coming out, we allow others to see us, to understand us, and to empathize with us. We move away from the feeling of alienation and invisibility that most of us are so familiar with and toward the small but significant level of openness with our peers that most straight people take for granted.

Beginnings

I am a thirty-one-year-old white woman born to a Jewish father and a Catholic mother. I think one of the greatest lessons they taught me, by example, was that you have to trust your own instincts about what or who makes you happy, regardless of what anybody thinks. Although my parents broke the rules when they married, their families have adjusted well over time. One Christmas, I remember sitting in my grandparents' kitchen and asking my mother (before I came out to her) what I would have to do to upset her as much as she upset her parents by marrying a Jewish man. She said, "I don't know, I guess if you married a woman...." *Oh, boy,* I thought to myself, *she's hit the nail on the head.*

Although it made me nervous that she had identified this as something that would be very upsetting to her, it was reassuring to know that however upsetting it might be, she put it in the same category as something she had done herself. Her parents had come to love my father, and he them, as they moved past their initial fear of this untraditional arrangement. My parents would do the same for me. Tolerance, I had learned, does not mean never being upset and scared by the unfamiliar. It means being willing to move past the fear, to question learned prejudices, and finally to trust your own judgment about right and wrong, regardless of what the neighbors might think.

I don't know where else my perspective and self-confidence came from, but luckily I believed that I was okay as I was, and I sensed that my feelings about myself were more important, ultimately, than my standing in the public-opinion polls—even if I wished many times to be more popular or more "normal." I now credit this early sense of self-acceptance as essential to my ability to come out as easily as I have. I consider myself fortunate. I am keenly aware that there are many gay people for whom the feeling of being different, abnormal, odd, despised, or alienated is intolerable.

My experiences at work

Despite my core sense of my gayness as being okay, I have struggled with the issue of how to be out at work—and have felt very much alone in this endeavor. I am struck by the absence of role models, instruction books, or other resources for figuring out how to manage the process. As a result, many of my day-to-day encounters have been extremely clumsy.

I studied chemistry and neuroscience at Oberlin College (a gay mecca and generally a wonderful place) in Ohio and then moved to Boston, where I began working in a neuroscience research lab at Tufts Medical School. While working in the lab, I went to school part-time, finally receiving a master's degree in environmental management and policy. I spent the next four years working as an environmental toxicologist with Gradient Corporation, a consulting firm in Cambridge, Mass. I am currently on the staff of the Silent Spring Institute, a research group studying potential environmental impacts on women's health.

Don't ask, don't tell—self-imposed

My job at the neuroscience research laboratory was particularly pleasant, largely because of the fact that the three professors in the department were women and that most of the students and staff in the lab were women.

Despite the fact that my coworkers were nice, I typically did not bring up the fact that I am gay in general conversation. For example, when I moved in with my lover, I simply noted that I was moving and, if asked, gave her name without describing her as either a friend or a lover. While my coworkers did things outside of work with boyfriends or husbands or friends, I always did things with "friends." And while they talked about new love interests or a hot date or the painful end of a relationship, I was silent about my romantic pursuits. As a result of my reluctance to bring up gay-related parts of my life, I ended up censoring a lot about my life outside of work.

It is interesting that, in spite of all the censoring I did, I probably would still have characterized myself as being out. I knew that if asked directly, I would tell the truth. And I would not do anything to try to prevent people from figuring it out, such as make up boyfriends. I thought that on some level my coworkers knew that I was gay.

I have come to accept the fact that being out is a continuum along which we move as new situations come up. In fact, I find that I move up and down the continuum from moment to moment, my level of "outness" determined by my internal courage barometer and the perceived threat of the particular situation. In general, at this job I considered myself out because I would not lie. However, I did not talk with most of my coworkers about aspects of my life that had anything to do with being gay. There seemed to be an unspoken agreement between us not to talk about it.

Although this method of being out at work is popular, I never felt satisfied with it. I felt frustrated that I couldn't discuss anything about my life—from the mundane to the intense—with my coworkers. I felt disconnected, alienated, and awkward, as if I were only half there. It may seem like a trivial complaint to be unable to talk about my personal life at work, but as I thought about it, I realized that straight people enjoy an openness with one another that is fundamental to any relationship. I was feeling dissatisfied because I couldn't have that too.

My personal life is not strictly personal

On a very basic level, our ability to sketch out the vague outlines of our lives provides one another with information we rely on for even the most superficial relationships. My casually mentioning my husband identifies me as one person. My mentioning my roommate identifies me as a different person. But if my roommate is my life partner, with whom I have taken an oath to "love, honor, and cherish," I am really more the person with the husband than the person with the roommate.

I find myself faced with the problem of not having an easy way to provide this very basic information about myself—information that most straight people transmit within the first five minutes of meeting someone new—

unless I come out. And coming out can seem like a very big deal when measured against the straight person's casual reference to a husband. Nevertheless, I can't count the number of times I've heard people say "I don't advertise my heterosexuality; why do you have to make such a big deal of your homosexuality?"

When I don't come out, I am typically assumed to be single, straight, and looking for an opposite-sex partner. Being characterized this way is not bad, it's just not necessarily me, and being mischaracterized can feel very alienating. For years before I came out to my parents, they thought that I had never been in an intimate relationship with anyone, when in fact I had been in a couple of fairly serious, long-term relationships. In fact, one of my "friends" came on an extended family vacation with me during which we slipped off whenever possible for passionate moments alone. However, my parents' perception of me as someone who had not experienced intimacy was hard to live with and made me feel very alienated—an asexual spinster "not interested in boys" or who "can't get a guy." The fact that they never saw me as being attractive to someone or loved by anyone made me feel unattractive and unlovable.

Likewise, I now believe that on a professional level it can be important to establish some sort of personal connection with your coworkers and supervisors. I don't mean they have to know everything about you, but they need to have a sense of you—to know what "makes you tick"—in order to develop trust in you.

I can't explain

I don't know how the agreement not to talk about my personal life fell into place during my years at Tufts, but I suspect my coworkers were picking up on the fact that I was ashamed of being gay. It might have been okay with them. They might even have been curious about it. But I didn't know how to present my life and my concerns in a way that I thought any straight people would want to understand or relate to. And they didn't bring it up. I don't want to suggest that I was completely antisocial; I was friendly and interactive and participated in activities. I just did not share much about my life that in any way related to my being gay. If someone asked what I did over the weekend, I said I had a friend over for dinner, rather than saying I had a date.

During the time I worked in the lab, I met a woman who worked on the same floor, and we started seeing each other. Toward the end of my tenure there, we decided to have a commitment ceremony. I know that on a personal level, I was feeling happy with my gay identity. Nevertheless, I only told a few of my coworkers about the relationship and the ceremony, and I called the honeymoon a vacation. If I had been straight, I'm sure that everyone in the department would have known that I was getting married and how many bridesmaids we were having and where we were going on our honeymoon and what our parents thought of this and what china pattern we had picked out and a million other details. But the process of explaining to everyone at work that I was in a serious relationship with a woman and we were "getting married"—and that it basically meant the same thing to me as it did to most straight people—didn't seem possible at the time.

There were a few people at work whom I did tell about the wedding. One woman (who had some other gay friends) left a wedding gift on my desk when I came back from my honeymoon, and another, who was a fabulous baker, actually made a beautiful tiered wedding cake for the ceremony. I was touched by her gift, and I remember feeling somewhat awkward when we went over to her house to pick up the cake and came face-to-face with the fact that we hadn't invited her to the ceremony. She reassured me that it was okay, but I felt stupid for acting like such an alienated, unfriendly individual when these people were trying to make me feel understood.

I am struck by how I made my life much more invisible than I had to in the workplace. I felt so self-conscious about bringing it up. I would always feel a little insecure or nervous when I was talking with a straight person about my being gay.

Monkey see, monkey do

Just before I left that job, I promised myself that in my next workplace I would be different. My guiding principle was going to be that I would be just as out about my sexual orientation as straight people were about theirs. I wanted to be myself, sharing what I would have shared had I been straight. For example, in my new job at Gradient, I would use "we" all the time or say "Lisa did" this or "Lisa said" that without explaining who my partner Lisa was—just the way straight people did in referring to their spouses, who didn't require explanation. And I vowed to bring Lisa to holiday parties.

On the other hand, I didn't want to be accused of making a big deal out of being gay. I was going to navigate the process of coming out guided by the basic principle that I would strive to parallel the behavior of straight people with regard to their sexual orientation. I would characterize myself as married and refer to my partner when they referred to their spouses. I would use their behavior as a measure for my own, to make sure that I wasn't talking about it too much or keeping too much to myself.

I've tried to abide by this guiding principle since I started work at Gradient in 1991. I've gotten a lot of blank looks, and it hasn't been smooth sailing. I've had to deal with my own shame about being gay. I've also realized that "just being myself" is really difficult, because it requires that I deliberately bring up the fact that I am gay (since it affects so much of my life) in order to build the foundation of understanding among my coworkers that allows anything related to my being gay to be a topic of conversation.

Thus it didn't take long after I started my new job to realize that just mimicking the behavior of my straight peers was not necessarily going to achieve what I desired. One day, a few months after I started work at Gradient, I was having a conversation with a woman who was managing a project I was working on. Our talk somehow drifted to marital status, and she asked me whether I was married. (I wore a somewhat ambiguous ring on the ring finger of my left hand.) I felt myself blush, my face get hot, my stomach get queasy, my breath get short. Familiar symptoms. "Yes," I replied. "I've been married about a year and a half." *This is working okay,* I thought to myself. *Just like a straight person. Parallel lives.* I paused, waiting for her to ask my husband's name or what he did or something that would allow me to come out by gently correcting her. Then maybe she would be embarrassed instead of me. Unfortunately, no such question was forthcoming. I sat there for a while, trying to think of how straight people might casually bring up their partners' gender. It seemed too awkward to bring it up deliberately now. What should I say? "I know what you're thinking—you're thinking that I'm married to a man. Well, I'm not." I couldn't do it, and we were interrupted soon after that. I was very concerned about what, in fact, I had led this woman to believe.

I soon began to realize that it was impossible for me to be out in the way I intended. I had thought that if I paralleled the way straight people were "out," it would come naturally. Instead, whenever I did come out, it inevitably felt awkward. "What are you doing for the holidays?" a casual acquaintance at work asked (he couldn't have picked a more loaded question). "I'm visiting my family in Washington, D.C." Deep breath. "My partner, Lisa, is staying here to be with her family." There, I had said it. But it felt so uncomfortable—like I should have left off the part about Lisa. She wasn't even coming with me, so why mention it? When I didn't come out, opting for silence instead, I felt that I was being too closeted (straight people always mention their significant others when discussing holidays). The situation rarely seemed "ripe" for the revelation.

Perhaps this feeling of awkwardness is due to the widespread and often unconscious social expectation that gay people ought to "keep it to themselves." When my lover and I walk down the street holding hands, we are automatically making a statement. Straight people don't even think twice about it. We disrupt the world view that doesn't include us when we force ourselves into the picture. And behaving with the expectation that we have the same social rights as straight people feels about as awkward as forcing ourselves into a photo in which we are not wanted. I cannot be myself without making a statement, because being myself means coming out, and coming out means defying the social order to be straight or be quiet. And so I began to accept that I would often feel as if I was making a statement, and that the price I would pay for not making myself bring up the issue was continued invisibility.

Pushing forward

I eventually found out that once I did come out to my work mates and share a little of my life with them, it became very natural to "be myself." I can now talk about the political candidate with the best record on gay rights or the end of my marriage or the reasons that I won't live in Colorado or how I feel about being gay or the fact that I am writing this story. The dynamic has finally evolved into what I originally hoped for: With a number of my coworkers, I can now regularly and casually discuss life outside work. But breaking down the original presumption of heterosexuality and then continuing to introduce gay issues into conversations until people became comfortable discussing them required a huge effort.

There have been a number of exchanges with my straight coworkers that I can now fondly recall as the payoff for my continuous efforts to bring my gay life to light. These represent what I am aiming for—situations in which I can easily be myself. One night after work, for example, about ten of my fellow employees and I gathered in a conference room to have our colors done—where someone drapes colored fabrics on you and determines whether you are a summer, autumn, winter, or spring, and thus what colors you should be wearing. We were quite lighthearted about the event, anticipating that our money would be well spent just based on the entertainment value of the evening. When it was my turn, the woman providing this service became perplexed, finding that she couldn't decide whether I was a summer or an autumn. She finally gave up, somewhat flustered, and told me I was a good candidate for a "personalized palette." I smiled and joked to the group that this wouldn't be the first time I found myself not fitting neatly into the established categories. I felt good about having created an environment in which I could make that joke and most people would get it, laughing with me. I imagined my self-conscious silence had I not been feeling strong and happy and had I been barely out rather than comfortably out.

Another day, most of the staff attended a meeting about the new health insurance plan that would be replacing our existing plan. During the meeting I took a deep breath, tried to calm the butterflies in my stomach, and asked whether the plan would provide family coverage to same-sex partners of employees and their children. The answer was "only if required by law." I think I knew the answer, but I wanted all my coworkers to hear it too.

In any case, after the meeting I asked a coworker about some birth control aspect of the health plan. She said that she didn't know, and I gave her a quizzical look, since she was married with two children and I was puzzled about why she wouldn't have had to deal with the issue. She explained, blushing, that she hadn't needed anything new since her previous job, which had different health insurance. Then it was her turn to look at me quizzically, wondering why *I* cared. I smiled and explained my theory about considering it to be an indicator of company attitude. It was just a minor interaction, but it made me feel good because it all felt so natural. No lies, no awkward silence, and for once I didn't feel like a completely asexual person. I was surprised at how good it felt to have my sexuality be acknowledged and realized that as gay people we typically only get this from other gay people.

As I mentioned earlier, being out at work is a continuum, not an either/or proposition. And it's a continuum along which I seem to move up and down from one second to the next. I can still go rapidly from feeling strong, confident, and proud to feeling self-conscious, speechless, and humiliated for no apparent reason. One day, feeling fine, I put on my running clothes with a T-shirt that says I CAN'T EVEN THINK STRAIGHT and headed through the office on my way out for a midday run. All of a sudden I got hit by an attack of insecurity. I felt very self-conscious wearing the shirt and very confused about why I was feeling so bad, since I had worn it previously without incident. I stood in the lunchroom for a drink of water and ran into a fairly senior coworker whom I had never explicitly come out to (though he had certainly had many opportunities to figure it out). He looked at the shirt, reading it out loud and looking at me quizzically. I shriveled up inside, wishing I could disappear. I quickly changed the subject, starting a conversation about something else. I then went back to my office, thinking that maybe the shirt was inappropriate for work or that I was making a big deal out of being gay. I moved my National Coming Out Day postcard to a less prominent spot on my bulletin board. The whole event left me feeling drained and horrible.

Why was this so hard? I somehow felt that by wearing the shirt I had put myself in a position where I couldn't defend my behavior as being appropriate. I had lost my confidence in my own ability to explain, if asked. In a calmer moment, I know that if that happens again, I have to smile, look him or her in the eye, and, if necessary, explain the shirt.

Playing teacher

Most straight people don't really know very much about our lives. Despite our substantial numbers, we remain largely invisible, and our straight peers remain ignorant. Exasperated and angry, I often find myself thinking, after coming out to someone and being told "You could get a boyfriend if you wanted," that they just don't get it. I've found that even straight people with gay friends are hesitant to ask questions. Part of what we need to do when we come out, therefore, is to play the role of educator to our straight coworkers, friends, or family.

As an example, I brought my (former) partner to holiday parties and other events and referred to her in conversation as others refer to their significant others. But many times I have felt that something specific to our experience as a *gay* couple was appropriate in the conversation. For example, while discussing holiday plans with a coworker, the individual brought up a problem relationship with an in-law. At that point, I explained my own problematic relationship with my in-laws, which was due entirely to my being gay. I described how intolerant they were and how their hatred had a major impact on my life with my partner. It was probably the first time my coworker had thought about homophobia and how it could affect a life and a relationship.

A few years ago I would not have shared this information with a coworker. I just wouldn't have felt comfortable bringing the subject into the discussion. Bringing it up is like opening a curtain and letting someone have a look at a world that they have never seen before, with you as their guide. The dynamic that results can seem a lot like teaching the course "Gay Life 101" to your colleague, who may be a peer or a supervisor or even the company president. It feels awkward, and I feel self-conscious as I start to guide them through my world. Yes, I say, in response to their surprise, it is true that we can legally be fired from our jobs simply for being gay and yes, it is true that my neighbors greeted me and my roommates by shouting "Dykes!" down the street when we left the house or came home, and yes, my former partner's family really did refuse to let me in their house. These have been routine, albeit painful, events in my life, but they come as a jolt to most straight people. And there is no easy way to bring them up in conversation.

I think educating our peers is necessary, though I can't see any way around the awkwardness we feel as we start to reveal what has traditionally been kept so secret. I try to remember that "they" won't get it as long as the basic information about what it is like to be gay in this society is kept from them. As difficult or awkward as it might be at times, we need to lift the curtain and lead our peers through the tragic, painful, funny, unique, and alternative landscape of our lives.

When I am feeling frustrated or discouraged by how hard it is to "be myself" in the basic ways I see my peers being themselves, I remind myself that the task at hand is enormous. Most people are completely ignorant about the lives of gay people, and our oppression is a result of that ignorance. The act of coming out is a powerful way to educate individuals in our lives and thus to break the cycle of ignorance and oppression. We have been invisible for too long.

Wait! There's a Child Under Those Bricks!

John Menichello

*At the time of this writing, John Menichello is employed as
a staff member at Northeastern University's counseling
center in Boston. In addition to providing both individual
and group treatment for students and staff, he specializes
in outreach to Northeastern's gay, lesbian, and bisexual
students. John's professional endeavors span a variety of
settings, including a corporate conglomerate, community
agencies, and educational institutions.*

I believe, through experience, that we are destined to repeat what we don't allow ourselves to address and understand from our childhood. A child needs first to feel loved by others before developing the capacity for self-love. I grew up in rural northeastern Pennsylvania as a "misfit" with strong awareness of my "difference." Despite a loving family, both my religious and my cultural influences hindered my ability to seek externally the validation for this difference and thus discover it internally. Characteristic behaviors I had developed to protect myself in my earliest "influential years" continued as I grew toward adulthood, embarking on a career within the American Telephone & Telegraph Corp. (AT&T).

It is coincidental that as I write these words, I celebrate my ten-year anniversary as a member of the workplace. Writing this story has helped me reflect on a decade that held significant transitions, amid both painful pitfalls and empowering ascensions. During this decade, I found myself in the crux of two inseparable developmental stages: a struggle from adolescence toward adulthood as well as from being closeted toward a healthy sexual-identity integration. What is the meaning of acknowledging and integrating sexual identity? To me, *acknowledging* means coming out, which occurs on a variety of levels. And *integrating* means incorporating the results of coming out, positive or negative, into a personal framework for living and continued decision making. I would define *coming out* as the lifelong practice of authenticity—of being true to oneself—and of measuring both internal and external validation levels, that is, self- and societal acceptance. I refer to the process as a practice because, in our world, I believe it involves the repetition and refinement of a skill of predicting what the consequences of this authenticity may be beforehand and then making a conscious choice between authenticity or facade. Consequences of my comings out over the years have ranged from ostracism to genuine acceptance. In the workplace, however, the choice was always mine, and regardless of the consequence, each time I chose authenticity, my capacity for self-awareness became greater.

Let me start by first explaining how it was I chose "big business" for my venture into my workplace decade. It was 1979. My collegiate course of study was developed by a shy young man determined to play out the only vision he could foresee for himself at that point in his gay identity: remaining anonymous and lonely, an invalidated facade. Where best to do this, to bear proof of all those past "most likely to succeed" awards? Well, why not in a quiet corner office of a big high-rise in a large city, where no one would ever notice or harass me again and where I could conceal my identity and avoid the questions about girlfriends and sports involvement that had plagued my high school years? I made myself believe that my various mental pains could be both hidden among the ranks of corporate America and eased by the security and pleasure of financial success. Since I knew of no better way to conceal my own inner feelings of inadequacy, I would do what I had always done. Hide. Although I had a genuine interest in human-service professions at that time, Dad's comment, "Why would you want to study those...they're girl's professions!" further confirmed to me the dangers of being true to myself in my largely blue-collar environment. I was tired of being called "faggot" and would steer away from giving anyone *any* inclination to use such a term on me again. I was going to follow what were proposed as "proper roles for young males" of my time.

Wisely opting for safety versus disclosing my identity in hopes of support, I buried my pains and suicidal ideations in a study frenzy and completed my college degree both early and with high honors. My initial coming-out occurred during these years via a discreet bus trip to Provincetown. But although I had made some genuinely supportive contacts since, all were long-distance and thus "safe." My life revolved around rural Pennsylvania, embedded in a facade. And while my sister was happily and well into planning her sanctioned and abundantly supported vision of engagement and marriage, I was unfortunately off to embark on my own sole vision of anonymity within the corporate ranks. A new life in a new world, but I carried the old pains within me—still a child, never having allowed myself to feel truly loved, and thus incapable of loving himself.

My vision was quickly the reality. AT&T could provide all the anonymity I could ever want. But did I really want it, particularly at age twenty-two? I remained intensely lonely, and my "metro New York" office was actually a stale uppity suburb in rural New Jersey. I was attracted to another quiet, shy newcomer in an office nearby. One night, I saw him at the grocery store. My heart leaped. Could this be fate? Would the natural adolescence I was denied in earlier years now begin? Could I really love or be loved? But I had no dating skills—just one body whose lack of confidence was filled by fear. I had no experience in what I'd learned was the cruising game, which seemed so odd to me anyway. And what if he saw me looking at him? Would he start a work rumor? Would the snickers and jeers of earlier years in the school yard begin all over again? So now, though I was granted the anonymity I had envisioned, I continued to exist as I did through my childhood and teen years, creating my own romantic fantasies to avoid the fear of looking either inside or out for love and acceptance...to ease the pain.

In 1984, I did not perceive AT&T's good-old-boy network as a safe place to come out. Early on, like others in the pool of rookies, I was assigned a mentor. Unlike the newcomer in the office nearby, this sly male, who had learned to play within the corporate system, was far from attractive, especially on the inside. Instead of providing training on the computer system to which I was assigned, he spent most of his time behind his own closed door with an office mate. I would hear their constant laughter and banging noises continuously through the thin partition. I sat, again lonely and confused, as I waited for my mentor. Finally I decided to teach myself the system rather than speak my frustration and make waves. Waves could blow the cover off my anonymity. And I feared his power over my difference again, like the boys in my childhood school yard.

Weeks later, that same sensitivity for which I had in earlier years been ostracized had led me toward support. It was Susan, a coworker, to whom I told in confidence my mentor's behavior. Susan was Latina and shared her office with another "woman of difference." Both seemed cut off from the good-old-boy network. Our marginalized status created our sensitivities, which in turn created both our bond *and* our justified skepticism and paranoia. I was attracted to Susan's professional strength and confidence, which she maintained despite her status. At the time, I wondered why I hadn't these same healthy attributes. I now realize one reason to have been the support she received from blood family, relatives, and friends while growing up in a largely Hispanic neighborhood. Although she hadn't the option to hide at work, for me that option, which may appear to some as a benefit, had come at great cost. But what choice did I have? As a dependent child, I naturally abandoned myself rather than run away from my family or commit a sin, and my resulting adult attributes were shame and lack of self-worth, again reinforced by early religion and culture.

I eventually came out to Susan, and fortunately our friendship only became stronger. My authenticity here thus prevailed, and our work days together were much less stressful with both of us knowing we had genuine support just a few doors down the corridor. Sad to say, but I was also fortunate in that she provided a good cover. The rumor mill at work seemed pervasive, and we would both often field subtle inquisitions from coworkers regarding our relationship, later laughing together at their curiosity and ignorance.

Fortunately, I was often able to isolate myself from most other coworkers and maintain that anonymity I thought I wanted. At lunch time I would frequently just walk around at the mall. Sometimes Susan and I would have lunch together and pour out our similar situations. Inevitably, however, to promote a supportive work environment, the staff would plan luncheons, which I dreaded. At five minutes to noon, the pains in my stomach were similar to those I'd had as a child on my way to the dentist. Will Susan be coming along? Since I had come out to her, her presence was like an incredible pillar of support. If she didn't attend, I'd take a seat at the far end of the table, minimizing the necessity of nervously maneuvering my way around the questioning. "What did you do over the weekend?" "Oh, nothing much." "So, what's going on between you and Susan?" Talk of dates and spouses occurred while walking to the ice cream store afterward. If Susan was not there, I'd either walk far ahead or behind, my posture indicating the bricks of pain on my shoulders.

Fate, I believe, had placed Susan in my life. For the first time in the workplace, I had consciously chosen to be real, and the result was positive. A first but significant brick among the many I carried had been lifted. And I had thus been empowered to look for more support.

After several months I located and began attending weekly meetings of the Gay Activist Alliance in New Jersey. As I made friends, life became a little easier: half a lie (the workday) instead of one big one. Some of these friends even worked at other AT&T locations nearby! But now, attempts to remain hidden led to increased paranoia and confusion as I tried to play the "switch personal pronouns" game at work, replacing "he" and "him" with "she" and "her" when I spoke on the phone with members of my newly acquired support system. Most gays, like me, were still largely in corporate closets. Perhaps at the same time, however, my coming out to Susan had me feeling a little more comfortable with myself.

This may have been a first recognition that I might not, after all, have had to lead a corporate life of complete anonymity. I made *some* sort of statement by volunteering as the only male on a team of nine formed to collect toys for disadvantaged children. Was this human-service interest a "faggot-like" thing to pursue, while peers were joining the corporate ball teams and going out afterward for a brew? Though still confusing sex-role stereotypes with sexuality, I didn't care as much anymore. I now had Susan.

Gaining a level of confidence from my slowly growing after-hours gay social support network, I decided to seek a transfer out of what I felt was a uniform environment of despair. I was successful in obtaining a management position at another location. Susan left the company altogether.

My next three years within the corporate conglomerate were the most productive and enjoyable, both professionally and personally. Under the supervision of Sandy, I was responsible for writing and producing a variety of texts to accompany AT&T's computer products. Sandy's management style of "take the ball and roll with it" worked fine by me, and professional success was soon forthcoming as I received awards such as Product Team Most Valuable Player. Work was never too grueling to keep me from taking advantage of exploring gay life in the many major cities to which I began traveling. In particular, during my frequent trips to a vendor in Atlanta, I acquired a group of Southern friends with whom I would hang out after hours. Many of these acquaintances were much more at ease with their sexuality than I. This became less surprising to me as I realized it seemed not such a problem in their work environments: restaurants, small travel agencies. However, most gay corporate peers with whom I'd come in contact chose to remain closeted during the workday. Although the "two lives" game just wasn't coming as easy for me anymore, I placed my trust in the opinions of these older and wiser mentors regarding job security. At times I felt as if I were performing a balancing act on a tightrope. The positive feelings and self-awareness on one side of the rope would increase through continued gain of support and knowing I was no longer alone. Concurrently, however, increasing self-awareness also brought along an increase of negative feelings on the other side of the rope, for as I became more aware, I also became more angry about denying my personhood in new corporate contacts. Inner pains grew as I was still largely inhibited from living one life by risking coming out and seeking corporate acceptance and support.

Sandy and I had developed a mutual fondness, yet I continued to uphold that personal line which neither she nor other coworkers in this significantly friendlier environment would be allowed to cross. And Sandy would be the first to admit her "curiosity" about other people's personal lives. Although I enjoyed her company, it was such a drag to have her travel with me on occasion. I recall that while dining out in Atlanta, we ran into a new acquaintance of mine. As I received a big Southern "Hi" and a hug, my paranoia would set in as I looked at the face at the opposite end of the table. But Sandy never said a word. And neither did I.

It was always hard later on in the evening to ask for the rental-car keys to "go out for a little while." Would Sandy ask to join me? If so, what would I say? She's a nice person, and I don't want to hurt her feelings. More importantly, she was my boss, and I'd *better not* hurt her feelings—especially in this political climate. And what if she found out? To me, Sandy represented both kindness and evil, warmth and cold, success and failure. You're a friend for life, or you're dead with one wrong move. But again, Sandy would say nothing as she handed over the keys before turning in.

For a brief time in 1986, I dated someone I had known since my high school days in Pennsylvania. When the short-lived affair ended, I was distraught. Responding "Nothing is wrong" to Sandy's continual inquiries, I tried to keep my grief hidden to forestall further questioning. I must have looked haggard: at one point, Sandy insisted I go for a physical. When the results reported my tip-top shape, I recall Sandy stopping in my office, politely asking my office mate to leave, then slamming the door and demanding, "I want to know what's going on with you!" Here was that moment of encountering, hopefully, a warm and trusting heart or, at worst, corporate doom. Would she really be on my side? Or would she blackmail me to get what she might need someday in the workplace? Horror stories raced through my brain, and I gulped and choked as I shared both my identity and my acute pain. Sandy didn't snicker. Sandy didn't throw stones. "You think *that's* bad!" she lamented, "I've been dating a black man for years, and my parents *still* refuse to acknowledge him." Sandy not only showed her sensitivity. In fact, she had been fearing *my* reaction to *her* life situation as well. Her responses fluctuated during that meeting: humor about my perceiving this as a big deal; warmth for my struggle between fear and forthright honesty; compassion for my grief over a lost love; and lastly, nonchalantness in going forward with a typical workday. As we often continued sharing our struggles, our relationship deepened over time. Sandy's professionalism as my manager remained both disciplined and consistently fair, and this coming-out experience fostered my most significant growth within AT&T. Once again, authenticity prevailed. Sandy continued to serve as a source of personal empowerment, encouraging my creativity in managing. She even empowered me to come out to an additional select few, and this group became for one another a family of support through the years of layoffs ahead. I went on to become accomplished both as a manager and as a technical writer. In fact, my self-confidence increased so much that after hours I eventually managed a successful part-time modeling career. Not only did additional external bricks lift off my shoulders at work, I believe Sandy was instrumental in many ways in helping me to begin the painful process of questioning my *internal* validation—looking at the love I'd failed to give to myself—though this problem would still remain largely on the shelf for a few years.

In one way, it was easy to remain anonymous at AT&T, for reorganization became a daily friend after the famous breakup of the Bell System. During my six-year career, I survived fourteen supervisors and at least fifteen reorganizations. After one reorganization, I was promoted, and unfortunately, Sandy and I were not to work together again.

Now, as product manager, I was responsible for managing a staff to lead new products to successful market introduction. Although I played the game to succeed in this culture, it was too difficult to tolerate the male coworker to my left nudging me at a meeting and stating, "Hey, John, check out the set of knockers on the girl across the table!" Once a boss even told me that I should try sleeping with the woman in public relations to gain her cooperation. *Sorry, these things don't work for me,* I thought. *And by the way, with people like you around, I'm* glad *I'm me.* In times like these, I was happy to have been marginalized. In such an environment, I was relieved that Sandy and other coworkers had kept my personal disclosure confidential. Justifiably, blackmail was still often on my mind.

Despite professional success, my search for personal meaning through human-service endeavors continued, and I volunteered in a weekend recreation program for children with cerebral palsy. However, this balance between an acceptable corporate life and volunteer efforts provided enough comfort only for a short time. I soon tired of the goings-on in the most recent corporate environment and decided to give AT&T one last chance to retain a dedicated, but getting frustrated, employee. I became certified as a sales/systems consultant, and transferred into sales—finally making it to Manhattan.

I was hired on to a national account, selling and servicing AT&T's products primarily in the customer's Wall Street locations, in particular at the stock exchange. Since we were on the verge of winning a bid worth more than twenty million dollars, AT&T was optimistically expanding staff to assist in the configuration and installation of the voice and data systems that were already perceived as sold. I thought for sure I'd find a more cultured, progressive staff in the city. And personally, I assumed the environment would be more open to the many facets of life and lifestyles. Now, though I wasn't open about my personal life at the workplace, I wasn't hidden either. My past positive coming-out experiences had had a significant influence on both my attitude and my achievements. Additionally, outside *this* office door an array of healthy options existed for young gay men. I shared freely with new inquiring staff members my interest in after-hours volunteer efforts for such organizations as the Gay Men's Health Crisis (GMHC).

When I was just a few weeks into the job, we lost the bid on the account, and the millions went to a competitor. The staff then dwindled from twenty-four people to four, and I was among those retained. I was left with a few unlucky others to clean up the messes of those who were now assigned to new positions. Before fleeing herself, the account manager who had originally hired me called me into her office to tell me that I wasn't pulling my weight on the account and being fair to the other employees. What did this mean? I didn't understand since, as a newcomer, I had been away for weeks of training. My intuition sensed harassment: after all, my new after-work involvements had leaked through the workplace, and I felt this individually absorbed manager would blame anyone else to save her face.

Through the next several months, a coworker and I did our best to maintain the systems for our clients. I held a brief additional responsibility of
soliciting for charitable contributions, and I was touched when a fellow consultant donated money to GMHC, confiding to me his loss of a friend to the
AIDS epidemic. I was volunteering as a buddy at GMHC, providing crisis
management and help in daily living for people with AIDS. These efforts had
never interfered with work responsibilities. Out of professional courtesy, I
informed our new account manager a week in advance of a necessary noon-
time doctor's appointment to which I would be escorting a GMHC client.
She approved my request for an additional thirty minutes at lunch to do so.
However, the day following the appointment, I was called into her office.
"Where were you yesterday?" She ignored the fact of my previously inform-
ing her and documented the incident in my records. My dispute and efforts
to meet with our upper management proved futile, for once again, we were
recently reorganized.

In my volunteer efforts, as AIDS clients died, slices of my self-identification
died as well; fortunately, those slices held little value when measured against
authenticity. Nearly extinguished was the huge slice that once believed money
and corporate success could alleviate the pain of difference, half-time
anonymity, and internal invalidation. It was the turbulence of a partner's on-
again, off-again pranks at this time that completed the draining of whatever
satisfaction remained in my now-dog-eat-dog corporate environment.

Hitting an existential crisis, I found myself skipping client luncheons and
instead feeding pigeons in Battery Park. At GMHC, I was confronting the
deaths of my gay brothers, which caused me to reassess the quality of my own
life. Turning my back on my sexuality, invalidating myself personally and professionally, was turning away from a basic aspect of my personhood, and turning away, I felt, from a community that desperately needed my help. Through
the past corporate comings-out, fortunately, plenty of bricks had been lifted off
my shoulders. With these recent life calamities, I could now painfully see the
walls behind the bricks that emerged from the weak foundation sadly laid out
during childhood without the necessary ingredient of internal validation. How
could I have loved myself as a little boy when I never felt safe enough to allow
anyone else to love the real me? I had gone on as an adult to construct my now
obviously inadequately supported walls. Although I'd gained *external* support
in my practice of authenticity, in coming out at the workplace, my inner walls
were cracking, lacking that internal validation in the foundation as a necessary
basis to self-love and acceptance.

During the next four months, I drew deep inside my well of existential
pain to rethink my long-lost goal of pursuing a career in a human-service
field. I realized that the career choices I'd made were not really *my* choices,

since they had been chosen by a child who, again, had opted for safety over authenticity. In December 1989, therefore, I put a halt to nearly six years of a promising corporate climb. Handing in my letter of resignation signified the bulldozing of an inadequate construction.

How and where would I begin to reconstruct my walls? Although I had saved enough money to pursue some schooling, I could no longer afford to live in the city. I chose to return to my rural roots in Pennsylvania—at least temporarily—in order to take prerequisite courses for a graduate program. I promised my authentically achieved support system of friends I'd be back to study in the city at some point, and I left both their physical proximity and some flourishing freelance modeling and technical writing opportunities behind.

Though spiritually broken, a flicker of empowerment remained somewhere inside. I just needed some time to find and rekindle it. My year and a half in Pennsylvania proved indeed to be a return to health—or possibly toward mental health for the first time. Although I had come out to most blood family members years ago, I now had the opportunity to live with them authentically.

During this time, while attending school, I also obtained a new corporate position: writing and editing educational texts for the National Education Corporation. The regional "blue-collar" views, which emphasized traditional gender roles of husband and wife only, not surprisingly seemed to permeate this workplace. Although I enjoyed my work with a motherlike mentor, she would sometimes cross professional boundaries, inquiring about personal interests and attempting harmlessly to fix me up with women whom she considered suitable. This time, however, because of my prior positive experiences of workplace authenticity and my own increased personal comfort, I felt less intimidated. Eventually I came out to a select few coworkers. Surprisingly, all were incredibly supportive and, to my knowledge, respected my privacy. One coworker's comments were most interesting: "I knew you were gay the first day I met you. No straight man would ever hold the door open for me, as you did." Another time, however, though she may have been joking, she told me that "one night with me, and you wouldn't be gay anymore." I also discovered a gay coworker, with whom I would share my break-time walk around the building. In this new environment, I neither freely disclosed my sexuality nor kept it rigidly hidden. I simply let myself be.

Largely because of the accumulated positive experiences of coming out at workplaces, I was ready to begin a full-time graduate program in the fall of 1991. Although my first choice had been to return to New York as planned, financial constraints led me to a psychology program in Boston. Since that time, I have completed a master's degree, and for the past two years I have been practicing psychotherapy as an openly gay therapist at Northeastern

University, specializing in outreach to the gay, lesbian, and bisexual student population.

Had I not chosen to come out at work, to gauge and then risk the consequences of authenticity, I would never have had the opportunity to rebuild my life. Each coming out, whether positive or negative, increased my self-awareness. It was painful to view the inadequate foundation and cracked walls, but there was no turning back to a facade. My coming-out decisions gave me the chance to reconstruct a person who had once purposely trained his mind to operate on denial and to accept loneliness, anonymity, and internal invalidation as the only options for life's duration. Self-acceptance and the resulting honesty and self-confidence have opened many doors for me. My fears of rejection by my family and in the workplace have never come to pass.

Currently, I try each day to see my life and choices made as new paths of exploration, paths now undertaken by a person with both a less-clouded mind and the ability most often to be true to himself. At present, my self-view is still on occasion surprisingly somewhat defined by my perceptions of both current and past societal views. Issues and feelings I would hope to have resolved both do and will continue to flare up on occasion. Perhaps there will always be bullies somewhere in a school yard. However, I become less defensive, less paranoid, and more open and trusting each time I experience love and acceptance resulting from sharing my personhood. I will continue in my work to overcome hurts both innate and fueled by a prejudiced and fearful world. My advice to others is to examine the internal consequences of life without authenticity and then choose your confidants with a bit of wisdom. Always remember that one's experiences of the mysteries behind life's pains and pleasures never end.

Truth and Consequences
Carla Lupi

*Carla Lupi is a thirty-six-year-old obstetrician-gynecologist
living in Miami, Fla., with her life partner, Raquel Matas,
and their two cats, Frida and Amelia. She recounts the first
time she came out in a job interview and the emotional and
professional consequences of her worst fears realized.*

I was a few months into my fourth and last year of an ob/gyn residency—the time to get serious about the next rung on the employment
ladder. After months of fits and starts in trying to decide what scenario
would best fulfill my hierarchy of needs, I had finally reached some
conclusions.

First and foremost, residency had whittled at every level of my being, and
I knew that I didn't have the emotional energy to uproot my girlfriend or
myself. I decided, therefore, not to pursue an academic fellowship. My next
option would have been employment with a reputable HMO system such as
the nonprofit Kaiser chain, for which many of my lesbian friends in California were doctoring in apparent bliss. Miami offered no such opportunity.
I could only fantasize about an "alternative" type of position, such as being a
full-time medical director of a Planned Parenthood operation or a school clinic. Such jobs, unfortunately, were rare in Miami, a city located in a state with
no income tax and only a minuscule array of inventive public-service organizations and positions.

These conditions left private practice as my only workable option. I wondered whether my lesbianism would work against me, but I preferred not
to dwell on that possibility. As determined as I was, I had never yet been
stonewalled in matters relating to my medical career. Coming from a working-class community, I had earned the generous scholarships available at
that time from the State of California and graduated with distinction from
Stanford University. I attended the fourth-ranked medical school in the
country and was considered among the best residents in a group that the
attending physicians considered one of the finest they had ushered
through. As icing on the cake, I spoke Spanish in a county that is 50 percent Hispanic and was a woman in a specialty in which women doctors
were few and in demand. Onlookers who were unaware of my lesbianism

often said that I could write my own ticket.

Reinforcing my hope for fair play was the fact that I had, in metered steps, come out during my third year of residency. During my first two years I had shrouded myself in the closet, having decided that my colleagues and superiors should first judge me on my performance as a doctor before any of their prejudices might twist their perceptions. I still debate the merits of that strategy.

At the end of my residency, I received a call from a woman physician (Dr. W), who wanted to interview me as a potential fifth member of an ob/gyn group with three men. After four years, she was still the most junior member of a group that projected a young and supposedly progressive image. Dr. W had come from the same residency program as I had and was well regarded. The doctors in this practice had also been talking to a male candidate from another part of the country. While the male doctors had let him know the job would probably be his, I sensed that Dr. W had held out to lobby for me.

I had a couple of meetings with Dr. W, during which I told her about the more recent events within the residency program. She talked broadly about being in private practice, about her partnership deal with this particular ob/gyn group, and about the experience of being in practice with three men. Dr. W noted that patients tended to save more of their questions for her and expected more attention from her, which they got. When Dr. W asked me why I had left California, I told her that I had fallen in love. She asked me whether I was married and what *he* did. Without using pronouns, I said no to the marriage question and told her that my partner was a lawyer. From that point Dr. W, and later her associates, referred to my partner as my "fiancé." It was clear that I needed to decide whether to keep silent, letting them think what they wanted to think, or to come out to my prospective colleagues.

I began seriously to consider coming out. I consulted with friends and even called Dr. Patricia Robertson, whom I had met during my fourth year of medical school at the first national convention of lesbian physicians. She was in private practice, after having done a residency in San Francisco. A star of sorts, both intellectually and professionally, she had come out to faculty members and helped to found a health clinic for lesbians without damage to her reputation. She insisted that coming out was the only sane option. Referring to the demands of group practice, she told me, "You'll spend more time with them than you will with your girlfriend. And to be comfortable with the lesbians you will bring into the practice, they have to be comfortable with you." She agreed to talk to my prospective employers to calm any fears they might have that a lesbian doctor might scare away patients.

The next decision was how to make my announcement. Should I speak with Dr. W first in order to get her advice on how the others might react, to allow her to prepare to lobby for me more effectively, and to spare her any embarrassment? Or should I come out to all of them at once as a mark of respect for the entire group?

The second scenario felt more honest, so I scheduled a meeting with all the partners. On the appointed day I escaped clinic a bit early to get home and dress myself up. Besides doing my makeup and putting on nylons, heels, my classy red silk suit, and matching jewelry, I made an atypically successful effort at styling my hair. After arriving at their office at the end of their daily hours, I waited a few minutes in the waiting room before being ushered into the office of the most senior physician of the practice, Dr. S. I sat at the end of a couch opposite his desk. An unopened deli platter of fruit was at the corner of his desk—something, I thought hopefully, to celebrate the impending offer of a contract.

Pleasantries were begun, during which the second-ranking member of the group, Dr. T, entered the room and positioned himself in a chair next to Dr. S. Then the third-ranking associate, Dr. U, came in and sat on the other side of the couch. I was first asked about my migration to Miami, and I once again told them that love was the reason, and that no, I was not married. One of the doctors told me that he hadn't expected to like me so much, that I had a nice smile, and that my verbal recommendations were stellar. I showed them my written evaluation from my third year, which included an A+ for my oral examination grade and glowing reviews for my intelligence, hard work, and dedication—all this signed by someone who rations compliments the way famine workers do food. They all glanced at it, appearing duly impressed.

Dr. S mentioned that the other candidate, after learning by phone a few days earlier that there was another serious prospect, had developed some second thoughts about the job. Dr. S then alluded to how we might all go out, they and their wives, the woman doctor and her husband, and I and my fiancé, should everything work out. So, I smiled to myself: Dr. S had already put the other candidate on notice and had begun thinking in terms of "we."

I chose this moment to tell them that my partner was a woman and that I needed to know if any of them had a problem with that. It was at this point that Dr. W arrived and, entirely unaware of my revelation, mentioned that she had many homosexual patients. Were we rehearsing a sitcom? Dr. S brought her up to date on the meeting's progress. I will always be able to remember each person's reactions at this point.

Dr. S had silently but quite visibly panicked during my declaration. The cordiality drained from his face, and his body became tense. I mentioned my conversation with Dr. Robertson and her willingness to talk to them. I also told them that I knew of lesbians in very successful private practices. Then Dr. S made the statement that he would repeat like a mantra through the remainder of the meeting, in uneasy attempts to convince himself of his lack of prejudice: "Carla, it's not *you* we have a problem with; it is how everyone else will receive this."

He was clearly afraid of losing patients: "What if there are visible lesbians in the waiting room?" Apparently, he had forgotten that "all those lesbian" patients of Dr. W had already been gracing his waiting room.

Dr. W, in her major supportive comment of the day, asked, "So what if we lose a few immature patients?" Not sure why, I felt compelled to add that I had been in relationships with men before and had had to deal with the same issues of sex and birth control that straight women do. Nonsensically, out of nervousness probably, I mentioned that I do aerobics too.

"What if everyone finds out, and the nurses on the labor floor start talking?" Dr. S worried aloud.

"I do not come out to all my patients," I replied. "I respect the boundaries of the patient-provider relationship, which include not discussing my personal life with patients."

In order not to back him into a corner, and perhaps out of my own internalized homophobia, I conceded that my being gay might be a problem in our sometimes conservative community. I pointed out that the contract was only for a year and that they could always simply not renew it. The possibility of my sexual attraction and/or attractiveness to patients came up, but they agreed that conceptually the issue is the same between straight male doctors and their female patients.

Initially, Dr. T was calm and seemed to remain friendly, agreeing with the notion that losing a few "immature" patients would not be a tragedy. As Dr. S's discomfort increased, however, Dr. T alluded to the fact that as Dr. S was the engineer of their economic prowess, his stance deserved special weight.

Dr. U was my only clear ally among the men. I know that he has at least one openly gay friend, living proof of the research that shows this to be a determining factor in people's level of acceptance of gay people in general. He told his associates that they all should value my honesty and that my coming out to them had probably not been easy for me. Years later, I thanked Dr. U for his support.

We did discuss a few other things besides my lesbianism. Dr. S was interested in how hard I wanted to work. I mentioned my interest in the quality of my life but also my well-proven ability and willingness to do my part. Dr. W pointed out that for someone who graduated from our residency program, "working a bit less" would still translate into a significant contribution. In retrospect, however, I'm sure I jeopardized my candidacy by mentioning that in the distant future, I might want to have a child and that perhaps a part-time arrangement would be necessary at that time.

Dr. S finally moved toward wrapping up. He said they would really have to think about this, again mentioning that it had nothing to do with *me* but with everybody else. "Dr. T will call you with our decision early next week," he concluded.

The meeting ended. I felt sure that I would not get the job and felt profoundly wounded after confronting the veiled but nonetheless brutal bigotry expressed during the interview. I went home and called my partner at her office. She came straight home and listened and consoled me as I expressed my anger and frustration through tears. Although these feelings hardly disappeared that night, I began to notice a sense of freedom. Never before had I so directly confronted virtual strangers with my lesbianism. For once I had not been weighed down by self-imposed secrecy and pronoun dances. The anxiety of dealing with questions about personal life had not damaged my interactions or distanced me from either myself or the others. This new and powerful feeling of pride came out of a sense that I completely own who I am without any apology.

Dr. T did not do me the courtesy of calling as promised, so I called Dr. W, who was embarrassed at her associate's "forgetfulness." Dr. T called me back within minutes, apologized for not getting back to me, and told me that the other candidate had accepted their offer.

I was surprised at the amount of anger that swallowed me over subsequent months. I daydreamed of renting a billboard proclaiming the doctors' bigotry so that lesbians would leave the practice in droves. In spite of my anger, I felt lucky that while this lucrative job was denied me, a decent living would always be within my grasp. I cannot imagine the rage of people who have few or no other opportunities available to them after a potential employer's prejudice cuts off their hopes.

Sometimes the universe—or just time—works things out. I did ultimately find a job in a practice with two other women, a straight Jew and a straight African-American. I am out to everyone at the office, and my practice with both lesbian and straight women is flourishing.

I have been thrilled to participate openly in the mini-lesbian baby boom that has recently visited our city. Seeing so many lesbians who have avoided the medical-care system and ended up with sadly delayed diagnoses, I am reminded over and over that our health care will remain piecemeal and substandard until we feel comfortable coming out to our providers. Helping to fill this gap in my community has probably served as the best healer of my wounds of rejection.

Resurrection
Les Wright

*Les Wright is a humanities professor at Mount Ida College,
a small technical/vocational college located in a western
suburb of Boston.*

When I first decided to declare myself totally out, I did not realize that coming out is a lifelong process. This insight came only after many years of working on myself internally and after plenty of rude shocks dealing with the outside world. It's difficult now for me to draw a line between a time when I was in the closet and a time when I was out.

How I came to teaching college-level humanities and landing a full-time tenure-track job in academe is a long story filled with many detours, some utterly unexpected, some quite horrifying, but all of them spiritual lessons in life. I successfully mastered my alcohol and drug addiction through the twelve-step recovery program long before it became socially popular or politically correct; I am dealing with HIV as a long-term survivor (more than fourteen years as I write today); and I have faced class issues (a blue-collar background that did not in any way prepare me for the pitfalls of the professional classes or the academic work environment).

My earliest childhood memories are of feeling totally overwhelmed at the sight of other males. I remember watching three of my older male cousins walk across the side yard of our family house in East Syracuse, N.Y. I couldn't have been more than three. I remember a mixture of terror and ecstasy, being filled with incredibly delicious feelings at the sight of these males. Years and years later it dawned on me that these were sexual feelings. I had a lot of sex beginning about the age of eight, when a teenage male cousin forced me to service him sexually on a regular basis.

When my family moved to the country, I was ten. And I immediately went about finding male sexual partners. It wasn't until my mid teens that I grew more self-conscious about what I had always intuitively known to keep secret. What I did went by a very ugly name.

Being sexual was never a problem. Accepting the social identity that went with such behavior was a different matter. I appreciate today the distinction between "homosexual" (sexual behavior) and "gay" (social identity). At first, I was not able to reconcile my attraction to men with what I had seen as iden-tifiably homosexual (that is, effeminate) behavior. I was sure I *was* a sissy, but I could not reconcile the social condemnation of effeminate behavior with homosexual activity. I knew society said there was something wrong with me, but whatever that was, it was *not* my attraction to men.

I had a steady girlfriend in high school, though we never engaged in sex. I fled my parental home at age seventeen, going to Germany and, among other things, practicing complete sexual abstinence for a year. When I returned, I began my studies at the State University of New York at Albany and "came out" as a heterosexual man. After a year of heterosexual sex, how-ever, I realized that the pain of living this lie was far greater than the conse-quences of being labeled a homosexual. During my freshman year I was on the editorial board of the campus literary magazine, and we shared our office space with the then-brand-new Gay Liberation Front, the campus's first gay activist group. The Stonewall riots had occurred only two years ear-lier. While I was terrified of being publicly revealed by this tribe, I secretly admired everything I saw them do.

At a campus activities fair in the spring of 1972 I saw two gay men embrace and kiss each other right in front of me. Nothing happened to them. No one screamed at them or threatened them—and they were glowing with some inner energy. I decided then and there that I would come out publicly.

Over the next two years, I joined a fraternity and started going out to the gay bars in downtown Albany. However, I spent a great deal of time being confused and consuming mass quantities of mind-altering chemicals. I hap-hazardly pursued my major in comparative literature, which meant a lot of classes in German and Russian. I decided to go back to Germany for my senior year—a panacea in my eyes, if there ever was one. It would be good career preparation, get me away from drugs, and afford me the opportunity to come out totally—in effect, to start over with a clean slate.

I spent the year I turned twenty-one at the University of Würzburg. I arrived "out" and met my first lover. From Würzburg we relocated to Tübingen, where my lover taught in the American studies department and I began my postbaccalaureate studies. I enjoyed a very special position as a gay faculty spouse—my lover the token homosexual in his department—and also as a nonmilitary American in Germany for whom the local rules did not apply so stringently. Being openly gay Americans in a prosperous nation still occupied by American military forces and saddled with an unparalleled col-lective guilt was something that did not go unnoticed or unexploited.

After six years in Germany, with great expectations of finishing my academ-ic preparations at the University of California at Berkeley, I moved to San Francisco in 1979 and lived in that exciting experiment in gay community called

Castro Street. The Castro, as it is called, was at its pre-AIDS peak, a street party that went on seven days a week. I reveled in being gay: the only time I needed to leave my all-gay environment was to go to work (when I *had* work).

In 1981 I was finally ready to pursue a doctoral degree at Berkeley. It was a watershed year for me: I got sober, returned to graduate school, and was infected with the still-unknown HIV. By that time I had grown so accustomed to being totally out, at least within a strictly gay universe, that I had little sense of heterosexual society's boundaries.

I love teaching, but my reasons for pursuing a career in academia had more to do with my survival instincts. I anticipated being denied employment in most other fields because of my gayness. An academic career, by contrast, would allow me to drink and cavort freely. All I had to do was show up in time to teach my classes. Furthermore, in a university setting, I thought, I would be "safe" by teaching adults—I still clung to old fears about homosexual teachers being falsely accused of child molestation.

I ultimately decided to be more discreet about my gayness on campus, admittedly something of a step back into the closet. On the outside, however, I looked like I had just walked out of a Folsom Street bar. The director of the language program tried to have me discharged from my teaching post on the grounds that a known homosexual was unsuitable as a classroom teacher. He attempted to mount a case against me and spread rumors among the teaching faculty, citing my homosexuality as grounds to have me dismissed. The fact that he said such things to openly gay faculty (through whom I eventually learned of the extent of his campaign) struck me as the height of irony.

Openly gay faculty members advised me confidentially to downplay my homosexuality. Prominent gay scholars suggested that I follow their path and remain silent until after I had tenure and a healthy list of publications under my belt. Meanwhile, the director wrote me up on a minor infraction of his rules.

In the end, I threatened to file a counter letter, challenging his. He backed down in the face of my challenge. This episode, though widely known, went largely unrecognized. I realized that my mistake had been to be equivocal about my gayness. I realized also that I would receive no support from any quarter. Gay faculty had shown their cowardice, and fellow graduate students all feared jeopardizing their own budding careers.

Through all this I maintained an interest in gay history and what has subsequently become known as gay studies. Because of the situation in Berkeley, I turned to the gay community in San Francisco in a new way. I became a founding member of the San Francisco Bay Area Gay and Lesbian Historical Society, working as its founding newsletter editor, serving in various positions on its board, and expanding my own knowledge of gay history. I joined the San Francisco Lesbian and Gay History Project, an informal group of academics and amateurs who met monthly to discuss either a member's current research or a recently published book. It was here that I connected my ivory-tower Berkeley and grassroots San Francisco experiences. I was more and more like Indiana Jones: mild-mannered college professor by day, reckless adventurer by night.

As I expanded my gay studies interest during the course of my doctoral studies, I sought to explore, through my work, the phenomenon of AIDS. It was a way, I thought, to keep AIDS at arm's length. I was HIV-positive, and people in San Francisco had started dropping like flies. Faculty in my department suggested I approach a junior faculty member (of the rhetoric department) who was building a career for himself in this emerging field. I thought he would be just the person to help me develop a dissertation topic.

While taking a course that he taught, I discovered that he had lifted the syllabus directly from his dissertation director at Princeton—a fact that I pointed out in my course evaluation. It was another lesson that the pursuit of truth does not include honest appraisal of colleagues. I made several appointments to see him during scheduled office hours, but he was somehow not available. I do recall meeting with him in his office once. I had passed a dissertation proposal on AIDS to him for feedback. He told me, with a great deal of anger in his voice, that it was garbage and that I had nothing to say. He sneered at my ideas, dismissing them as typical of what I and my "San Francisco friends" would come up with.

The incidents, both big and small, accumulated. I wasted a great deal of time kicking around other ideas for a dissertation. In the end, I chose to stick with my original concept, addressing the evolution of post-Stonewall gay male literature, the interplay between politics and the printed word, and the impact AIDS had had on it all.

By the end of my doctoral studies, I was a complete wreck. I ended up first on general assistance, then on social security. I was living rent-free when my housemate suddenly died of lung cancer. I was also ill for the first time with an HIV-related condition, was briefly homeless, then was taken in by another friend. As I finished my dissertation the one thing left in my life, a lover whom I had thought to be the love of my life, left me. Despite the nervous breakdown this triggered, I somehow managed to stay alive and finish the dissertation. In the end, the rage at all I had gone through, been put through, and had allowed others to put me through sustained me. Suddenly I was *the* gay scholar in my department.

I now teach film, literature, and writing courses at Mount Ida College, a small, technical/vocational college once hailed as the leading model for combining hands-on technical training with elements of a traditional liberal-arts education. Mount Ida is hardly the place I expected to end up, and it's light-years away from what I trained to do academically. When the call came, a full year had elapsed from the time I had received my Ph.D. and had first interviewed for the post at Mount Ida. I had resigned myself to never finding a teaching job or even to working full-time again. I went into my interview with nothing left to lose and everything to gain.

During the interview I was completely honest about my teaching and academic interests, and my desire to be at a small school rather than an Ivy League university. I explained that although my training had been in German, Russian, and literary theory, my real interests were sociology and history, gay studies, and film. I was ready to work with working-class students who had real-world expectations in an environment where I would be free to pursue my true academic interests. I interviewed as an openly gay man and as a grassroots gay scholar.

I was somewhat nervous about all this, and since getting the job I have grown somewhat hesitant about revealing my HIV status, because now I have something to lose again. While health issues did not arise during the interview, my personal connection with AIDS was explicit in the published writing samples I submitted. Much to my surprise, relief, and joy, I have found a disarming warmth and acceptance among my colleagues. True, the homophobes distanced themselves at first and closeted members are in evidence, but I feel myself valued in this community for my teaching ability and enthusiasm, for my budding administrative talents, and for my collegiality. At the end of my first semester at Mount Ida, I was awarded a research grant in support of an analysis of "AIDS and its impact on the gay community." In that semester I met with more open support than in my ten years at Berkeley.

All is certainly not rosy, and there may well be land mines farther up the road. Having been completely open about being gay, however, I have also been able to be myself. This has been a tremendous boost to my self-esteem, self-acceptance, and professional proficiency. It also obviates my ancient worry about legal difficulties. I was stupefied by the realization that I had been hired with the college's *expectation* that I would engage in gay research and publish in gay studies at a small, vocationally oriented, conservative, private New England college.

My approach has been to open myself up gradually, talking freely but privately with some colleagues, coming out about my HIV status on an individual basis, while bringing a gay point of view to committee meetings and faculty workshops. I collaborated on a gay and lesbian reading list when the library solicited my suggestions on that and on AIDS topics. I was also the featured faculty member for the winter, with my work displayed in the library's main entrance.

Of course, I still have much ground to cover in educating many of my colleagues; the biggest challenge, however, lies in enlightening the students. I approach my students in the guise of Auntie Mame, seeking to open their eyes to all the wondrous things in the world just waiting for them. Some of them "get it," and some of them don't. Regardless, they generally find their classroom experience with me to be unique.

I basically come out during the first class session of each course by explaining my background and interest in gay studies, and I let them put the pieces together. I am amazed, though, how many students fail to make the obvious connection that I am gay. I include at least one gay/lesbian title in every course. We discuss homosexuality during class. I have even lectured once each semester on homophobia to colleagues' classes and will be expanding this work to a campuswide program that addresses violence.

Last spring semester I taught a course on the literature of death and dying. It was an opportunity for me to incorporate personal involvement with AIDS into a larger context. I structured the course in three parts: the many aspects of an individual's death, catastrophic death (epidemics, warfare, the Holocaust, "nuclear winter"), and a third part that drew these two facets together under the topic of AIDS and its impact on the gay community. The course epitomizes my current approach to being gay in the workplace and how we are all humans together, yet how we differ as individuals. Mount Ida is still lagging in AIDS education, so I was happy to see a dozen new faces show up for these AIDS lecture/discussions.

Multiculturalism and democratic pluralism, all the rage in academic circles these days, require more than lip service. As a colleague, I can take my place among my professional peers. As a classroom instructor, I can demonstrate how gays and lesbians share equal footing in our society and how to live the principles of humanism on a daily basis. As a long-term survivor of HIV, I am grateful on a daily basis to be given a life to live and to know my purpose in it.

One True Voice

Jim Jenkins

*Jim Jenkins, a native Washingtonian, is currently a
sales manager at AT&T. Jim has been openly gay ever since
he was hired at AT&T in 1985 and has been actively involved
in AIDS work and in AT&T's organization for lesbians and gays.*

I came out to myself at the age of twelve, and it took another ten years
for me to consider myself an openly gay male. To me, coming out simply means accepting one's gayness through a process that is very
much like peeling an onion. The more I come out, the more layers I discover about myself, until finally I reach the very core of my being. In many
ways I think we all need to come out about something in our lives. We all
need to tell the truth about ourselves if we are to be truly free.

I was raised primarily by my grandmother. Both of my parents worked
when I was a child, and I also had a special bond with my grandmother that
went beyond our blood ties. She taught me always to be myself and to be
proud of who I was. I learned at an early age to appreciate the uniqueness of
every living thing and to challenge myself constantly to grow. I think my
grandmother knew I was gay even before I did, but we never spoke about it
until weeks before my grandfather died. I grew up in a very hostile and cold
environment in which I had to rely on my grandmother for support. When I
was growing up she apologized for my parents but assured me that I would
one day amount to something, and I hope I have proved her right.

Unfortunately, with the death of my grandmother and grandfather came a
separation from my mother and stepfather. My parents are people who did
not come to parenthood with adequate child-rearing skills: my mother had
no capacity to love her own family, and my stepfather dealt with this by seeking affection outside his marriage. I have recently made peace with my stepfather and now regret that he spent his life with such a distant and unaffec-
tionate woman as my mother.

Even though I had admitted to myself that I was gay at the age of twelve,
I never did come out to my friends until I was in college. My first brushes
with homophobia occurred in junior high and high school, where I saw a gay

friend physically beaten and verbally abused on a regular basis. To this day I do not know how he endured such brutal attacks, but they frightened me into silence for most of my adolescence. Since I was fairly small for my age, I did not want to attract attention. When I was a teenager, homosexuality was still considered a form of mental illness, and I had no desire to undergo any form of therapy. I knew what and who I was; being with a man felt comfortable. I never forced myself to date women because I never felt attracted to them physically in any way, though emotionally I did and still do find them more appealing than men.

In the early part of my career, I never found it necessary to come out at work. But once I started noticing the discrimination that went on, I decided to come out to a few close friends at the bank where I worked as a teller. Oddly enough, most of the other male bank tellers I met were gay as well. As I began to pay attention to the news and became an avid reader of *The Washington Blade,* Washington, D.C.'s gay newspaper, I felt that I needed to take steps to protect my rights. Until I read that gays were being fired from their jobs simply because they were gay, I had never thought that my sexuality was much of an issue at work.

While I was working for the Navy Federal Credit Union, I came out to one of my peers. At the time we had much in common, for we were both dating married men. I remember telling her one day over lunch that we had something in common, and she was not surprised when I told her what it was. In fact, once I had come out to her, it was easier to talk to other coworkers whom I considered to be my friends. I eventually left Navy Federal because banking had become a dead end for me. I was ready to try something new.

When AT&T hired me, I made a promise to myself that I would always tell the truth about myself. I have lived up to that promise to such an extent that I rarely think about my gayness anymore. In short, I long ago accepted who I am, and that is all that matters to me. I do not suppress myself in any way and refuse to ever be in any environment in which attempts are made to make me feel oppressed. As a consequence, I do not surround myself with many of the blood relatives with whom I grew up. I will not allow anyone to chastise me for being who I am. I learned from my grandmother the importance of self-acceptance and unconditional positive regard for others. I can accept others for who they are only because I have gone through an intensive process of learning to accept myself.

I have been an openly gay employee of AT&T Communications since I was hired in 1985. AT&T is the first place I have ever worked where my sexuality was known from day one. I am proud to say that my gayness has never been a barrier either to my career advancement or to my relationships with my peers.

AT&T has given me a home in corporate America, and I feel proud knowing that I am working for not only the best telecommunications company in the world but also one of the most gay-friendly corporations in this country. Each year, every employee must review AT&T's Code of Conduct, which clearly states that AT&T does not discriminate based on race, creed, color, gender, or sexual orientation. I look forward to that time every year, because it continually validates my work and my presence at AT&T. Knowing that my workplace rights are protected gives me the freedom to be always myself. AT&T has done nothing but provide me with opportunities for growth, both professionally and personally.

I started out as an account representative assigned to handle customer problems and sell long-distance calling plans for the residential marketplace. My first boss, Li Mostofi, called me into her office during my first day on the sales floor and said to me, "You are a neon person." She said that meant I was bright and very boisterous and different from most other people. I realized at that moment that she was acknowledging that she knew I was gay, and I could tell I was going to like working for this woman.

I choose to decorate my desk with such gay-related items as Pride post-cards and pictures taken of me in San Francisco. In this way, I affirm my identity without having to explain myself all the time. Li saw my buttons and cards and concluded that I was gay. Calling me a "neon person" simply allowed her a safe way to signal her acknowledgment and acceptance of my sexual orientation. Li was very supportive from the outset. We would talk outside the office about my being gay, not simply as a subordinate talking to a supervisor but also as friends.

I remember one particular incident, when I had a slight crush on some-one else in the office but was not sure if he was gay. Li and I discussed it over lunch, and she urged me to just ask him outright. "After all," she said, "if he isn't gay, he should be honored that you are interested." I never did get the courage to ask this person out, but talks such as this became the norm with my friends at AT&T.

Shortly after I was hired I began to date Kirt, a result of the military's ban on homosexuals. He had left the Army willingly rather than allow himself to be discharged for being gay. With my encouragement, Kirt found employment as an AT&T account representative. Unfortunately, he chose to hide his sexuality at work. My boss understood my frustration that Kirt did not wish to acknowledge our relationship publicly, but she also encouraged me to try to understand why Kirt found it hard to be so open.

Kirt and I had a few mutual friends at AT&T who eventually figured out that he was my lover. When we moved in together and had people over for dinner, they saw our bedroom with its queen-size bed, confirming their sus-picions. We ended our relationship when Kirt, who was never really happy at AT&T, decided he wanted to return to his roots in Germany. I had no desire to leave the Washington area or a company that offered me such an unparalleled opportunity to be myself.

Shortly before Kirt and I broke up, I learned that a friend of mine had been diagnosed with HIV. Up until that point, I had been aware of AIDS but had never known anyone who had died from it. When my friend announced to his family that he was not only gay but also HIV-positive, they abruptly exiled him from their lives, refusing even to help care for him as his illness progressed. I was shocked. It was at this time that I decided to become a volunteer for the Whitman-Walker Clinic in Washington.

As a buddy I at first took care of a delightful Frenchman named Daniel. He was a very jolly fellow on the surface, but the more time I spent with him, the more I realized how sad he really was. After Daniel's death, the clinic asked me if I would become a volunteer supervisor and handle my own team of buddies. It was a challenge that I accepted with pride.

At AT&T, everyone who knew me was very supportive of my volunteer work. In fact, once it became known that I worked for an AIDS clinic, I became the local expert on AIDS-related issues. I never minded answering my colleagues' questions, because I welcomed the opportunity to teach them about AIDS and also about myself.

An interesting thing I remember is that some of my peers would tell me about their gay relatives and how concerned they were that they might be infected. I always offered to help them get information, thus making it possible for them to come out about their lives and in some cases about their own sexuality. The more I talked to people, the more comfortable I felt about myself and the more proud of the work I was doing.

Sometimes I would hear about people talking behind my back, but I chose never to confront them, because I had learned early on that often the best way to defuse homophobia is simply to be yourself and be proud of that, hoping that people will finally catch on that being gay is just one aspect of being human. In time it became clear that I was respected for this openness.

My boss at the time, Linda Golson, was extremely supportive of my work as a buddy, though at first she was concerned that I might become stressed out in my job as a single point of contact for some of AT&T's largest business customers. However, I felt very secure in working for her because she constantly affirmed who I was and acknowledged the value of the work I was doing. I promised her that I could balance the work at AT&T and still manage the buddy team if she were willing to understand that I would sometimes need time off to handle emergencies involving some of my clients at the clinic. Fortunately for me, Linda was very willing to take a chance on me and was one of my biggest supporters when I endured times of sadness and grief over the next two years of my life.

In January 1989 I was assigned a new client, Larry, who lived near me on

Capitol Hill. When I met Larry he walked with a cane, as he had been diagnosed with a very bad case of Kaposi's sarcoma and had many lesions on his legs. Over a period of about four months, Larry gradually lost the use of his legs and became bedridden. It was at this point that a few members of my team could no longer handle taking care of him. I took over Larry's care myself, and in so doing I learned that I was very skillful at dealing with the afflictions of others.

I would often tell people that it was difficult to talk about Larry not only because it was hard for me to put into words what I was feeling but also because I know that the average person does not like to talk about death. Eventually I started talking about how I felt and spoke not only about death but also about how my work had touched the lives of others in my office.

Larry spent the entire last month of his life at George Washington University Hospital, and in his final weeks I learned a lot about death. To hold on to someone who died in my presence was one of the most amazing gifts I could have ever received. I was given the opportunity to affirm not only my own life but also the life of another. I cannot write in words what I felt that day. All I can tell you is that Larry's death gave me the strength to live a more joyful life and that its impact on my career is evident to this day.

When Larry died, everyone at AT&T knew what I was going through, and when I went to work shell-shocked the following week, my boss allowed me time off to grieve. It was time that I did not ask for but dearly needed. I have friends who lost their lovers and only took one day off for the funeral because they were so afraid to come out at work and give themselves permission to grieve among their professional peers. I am ever so appreciative of the men and women I worked with at AT&T during this time, because they not only gave me the time I needed to get through Larry's death but were also very concerned for my mental state and made sure that I did not wallow in despair.

One woman, Mary Margaret Matthews, pulled me aside after Larry's death and told me how amazing she thought I was. "Not only do you have the courage to face death but you also are always yourself around people and are proud of who you are," she said. She went on to say that I was the one of the few people whom she truly respected at AT&T. I suppose some of my superiors shared this opinion, because shortly after Larry's death I was promoted into a management position at AT&T as an account executive, a promotion that was perfectly timed to my decision to take a leave from my volunteer work at Whitman-Walker. As an account executive I was responsible for selling on the streets of Washington, D.C. Somehow the prospect of getting paid for walking the streets of Washington truly made me laugh!

During 1990 I increased AT&T's revenues by more than $1.2 million and for my efforts received the Circle of Excellence award at a ceremony in

Washington in March 1991. This was a very formal affair to which significant others were invited. I, naturally, brought my lover. AT&T's top executives typically attended these events, which meant that I would have to deal with the good-old-boy network: if you don't play golf, know a lot of sports trivia, or enjoy making sexist remarks, you were out of the loop. I was understandably apprehensive about the event—but what could have been a very embarrassing night turned out to be very rewarding. My boss was proud of me for having the courage to bring a male companion to a dinner where the regional sales vice president was sitting at our table. To my knowledge, no one had ever brought a same-sex companion to such an event. While I was somewhat nervous about arriving with my lover and introducing him to some of the most senior AT&T managers, once we got there and people greeted my lover warmly, I began to feel very much at ease. My lover was more nervous than I was, but it felt great to be given such a prestigious award with someone I cared for deeply looking on with admiration. It is one of the many triumphs I have had at AT&T during the past ten years.

Another significant coming-out event occurred for me in February 1990. AT&T has an official organization called LEAGUE (Lesbian, Bisexual, and Gay United Employees of AT&T). It started out as a social organization for lesbian and gay employees but has since evolved into a public-awareness group with its own set of bylaws and issues. Each year AT&T's lesbian and gay employees hold a national conference to discuss work issues and to network. For those members who remain closeted, LEAGUE gives them the chance to network and learn about those places at AT&T that are more gay-friendly than others.

In February 1991, I volunteered to represent LEAGUE at a regional meeting of the AT&T Employee Assistance Program (EAP) held to discuss homophobia in the workplace and HIV issues. I was asked to address the meeting because the EAP had little information about where to turn for AIDS care outside AT&T and, a more common problem, about how to address problems of those seeking help because they were also dealing with coming-out issues.

I was quite nervous about the event because I had no idea what to expect from the members of the EAP. Many of them had backgrounds and Ph.D.s in psychology, so I assumed they knew something about dealing with gay people. However, I was still afraid that I would find myself in a room full of bigots. I showed an AT&T-produced video featuring Brian McNaught called *Gay and Lesbian People in the Workplace: What Are the Issues?* and then answered questions, most of which dealt with how to find help for HIV patients. Eventually the discussion turned to issues in managing homosexuals in the workplace. I asked everyone if they felt they had any problems in dealing with gay people, and most of them said that they did not. I'm not sure why the others did not respond.

The only time the discussion got heated was when I presented each of the counselors with a "Safe Place" magnet. I am not sure who designed them, but they are small magnets with a pink triangle and a green circle around it. If you place one at your desk, you are acknowledging that you are gay-friendly and are supportive of diversity in general.

One of the counselors said she felt uncomfortable about putting the magnet up at her desk and did not want one. I asked her if she was afraid to put it up because she feared others would think she was gay. When she said yes, I told her that most nongay people did not even know what the pink triangle meant and that if someone were to go to the EAP for help with coming out, that magnet would allow the person to feel more comfortable in talking to a counselor. What really frustrated me was that she was someone who worked to help others and who in front of me and her peers was acknowledging her own homophobia. I finally got the woman to take the magnet, but I wonder if she ever put it on display.

Other than that, my experiences at AT&T have been very positive. As of this writing I am an assistant sales manager for the company, having also been a trainer and promotions manager. There is not one person unaware of the fact that I am gay, because if they don't hear it from somebody else, they can always see my desk with its pictures and buttons.

If I am involved with someone, inevitably his picture ends up on my desk. In the spring of 1993, when I ended a relationship, my boss, now Judi Hangen, asked me if I needed any time off to deal with my "divorce"; this was perhaps the most personally edifying event of my career. I had only started working for Judi in January, and she was giving me the most support I had ever received from a superior in my entire career. This validated my identity a great deal.

Aside from Judi, I also work with one of the best management teams at AT&T. Our branch was the number-one sales branch for 1993 and 1994. I work with three other managers, none of whom has ever had to deal with such an openly gay person. I am out to them and openly discuss my life with them and have never had a problem gaining acceptance as their peer. In fact, as much as they might hate to admit it, I think I have helped them a lot in dealing with their own awareness of diversity in the workplace. If it were not for Judi's consistent support and friendship, I doubt if I would have been as open about my personal life with my colleagues.

I currently supervise eleven sales representatives, and on the whole we are an effective team that is the single most satisfying group of people with whom I could ever have to face each working day. As a manager, my approach involves a lot of humor and good-natured kidding. Not surprising-ly, I get as much kidding as I dish out. My gayness has sometimes been the subject of humor, but I have never once thought that there was any underlying hostility or bigotry to what people were saying. I often will make myself the object of humor first, not only because I am comfortable with myself but also in order to let people know that if I can laugh at myself, I would not do anything to malign them.

I realize that I am walking a fine line, but I often consider these people to be my family—helping me to grow not only as a professional but also as a person. During the summer of 1993, after I started seeing someone new, my team took a sincere interest their boss's happiness, going so far as to hold a dinner party so that they could decide whether this person was worthy of my affections. It was one of the best experiences I have ever had—relaxing and fun to the point that my boyfriend kept his arm around me throughout the entire evening. Even Judi took a supervisor's interest in my boyfriend because she was glad to see me with someone again and thankful to see the more whimsical side of my personality on display. It is highly affirming for me to come into an office each day and be recognized not only for my abilities as a manager but also for my needs as a human being.

To be this free to be myself is very rewarding. I have never had serious repercussions at AT&T from admitting who or what I am. I am most proud of being an openly gay male. It is with great confidence that I will continue my journey up the corporate ladder and beyond.

911 OUT

Margaret McCarthy

*Margaret McCarthy, a police station clerk, has worked
in a variety of law-enforcement environments. She describes
how she has dealt with homophobia from coworkers ranging
from police officers to fundamentalist Christians.*

I am a twenty-nine-year-old out lesbian employed by the Montgomery County Police in Germantown, Md. I am not a police officer; rather, I am a civilian employee currently working as a station clerk. I have worked for the county police, in different jobs and in different stations, for more than five years.

While I can say that I have always been out at work, my early experiences in the private security industry in Washington, D.C., and in Maryland were not as positive as my experience with the county police has been. At my first job as an armed guard in D.C., I worked with several homophobic people. One male coworker would bring in religious writings. He tried to educate me about the Bible and interpret what the Bible says about homosexuality. I had another coworker who made repeated suggestions that I come over to his house with my girlfriend "so that we all could party." His comments offended me somewhat, but he never gave me any real problem.

My second job as a private security officer was at a shopping mall. There I felt that I had better working relationships with my coworkers, though I never felt as if I fit in. I had a sense that my female coworkers felt threatened by me, while the men just didn't know how to relate to me.

My being out during that period never seemed to be much of a problem for me. I never made any formal statement to anyone about being gay, but I never refrained from talking about my girlfriend or about what we did on weekends. People just knew. They were not hostile to me, even if they did try to convert me.

I did not leave the private sector because it was homophobic. I simply decided to make a career move that seemed right for me. And so began my association with the Montgomery County Police. Montgomery County is considered a liberal county, but I did not actually choose to go to work for the Montgomery County Police simply because I lived in the area. The county police has a Human Relations Code that specifically prohibits discrimination on the basis of sexual orientation. Work is easier for me because of the code: I know that I cannot be fired just because I'm gay. I might have chosen to be a bit less open if it weren't for the code—I don't know. I do not actually know any male officers who are out, but I do know a few out female officers, and they seem to be treated well. Sometimes I think it is easier for civilians to be out, but I have to admit that at times I was the only out person in every job I've been in. In fact, some women who I knew were gay chose not to associate with me on the job. Perhaps Montgomery County Police is not as open as I thought. For me there is no choice, however. I do not like to hide, and though I do not believe in outing, I believe that everyone should be out.

My first job for the Montgomery County Police in 1989 was in the communications center as a police dispatcher. I was in a steady relationship when I started working there, and while I didn't go around advertising it, whenever I was asked about my personal life, I told the questioner exactly who I lived with. While there were people who didn't understand or approve of my lifestyle, they were able for the most part to look beyond the label and see me as an individual. Unfortunately, some of my coworkers were jealous because I assisted the supervisor, so they seemed to use my sexual orientation as an excuse to ostracize me. One woman, in fact, tried to undermine my position by making disparaging comments about me.

As a result, I decided to transfer to the Wheaton station as a desk clerk in 1991. At first it was difficult because some folks at the communications center decided to give me a hard time by outing me and alerting Wheaton station personnel that a "raving lesbian" was coming. Being out and having people know that I was gay was not a problem. I am not ashamed, but I would have preferred to have people get to know me first, so that they would see me as a person rather than as a label. It was even difficult for some of the gay officers to talk to me. While Montgomery County is liberal and accepts gays on its police force, gayness is not an issue that is discussed openly. For the first few months, women who I sensed were lesbians distanced themselves from me. Eventually things settled down, and I became close friends with several of them. In fact, I was open with my supervisor when my girlfriend was ill and admitted that she was more than a roommate to me. The information did not seem to matter to my supervisor, who was supportive.

One of my sergeants at the Wheaton station was a devout Christian, with very strong ideas of what is right and wrong. We had several conversations about homosexuality, with each of us trying to convince the other that his or her views were wrong. I truly enjoyed these talks, because we could keep these discussions on a professional level and not get emotional. At the end of each discussion, we were able to walk away with respect for each other, even though we felt the other person was misguided.

Another of my coworkers was an officer who was working the desk until the county retired him on disability. Charlie had a lot of fun with my being gay. We would talk about different people in the county and who we could get interested in if the opportunity arose. He was interested in why I was gay and how I felt about gay-related issues. We shared the same taste in females as far as physical characteristics went, and we were always joking around. As far as Charlie was concerned, I was one of the boys, someone he could pal around with—and that was just fine with me.

In the almost two years that I spent at the Wheaton station, I had only one confrontation with an officer about any gay-related issue. In discussion of the trial of two men accused of murdering a gay man in Montgomery County, an officer kept using the word *faggots*. I started steaming inside but chose to keep quiet for a while. After he had used the word *faggot* about five times, I asked him to refer to the suspects as "gay males." He replied, "Why? That's what they are, faggots. And I think they deserve what they got." I finally got disgusted and left the room. I do not know why I did not confront this officer more strongly or more persistently. Perhaps I just chickened out. He was not someone I had to deal with every day, so maybe I thought that it was not worth the fight. A friend of mine who had been listening to the conversation later said that the officer did not know that I was gay. I found that hard to believe, because I thought I had been very open at the station and that everyone knew. I later heard that the officer felt bad about offending me. However, to this day he has never apologized, and I never brought it up again. Maybe it was a lost opportunity.

In 1993 I became a station clerk in Germantown. The situation here has been pretty much the same. I continue to be out by not playing games with anyone, answering people's questions, and not hiding. I even have a lambda sign on my car. I have been open, for example, when talking to my girlfriend on the phone. My supervisors have always known, and I have suffered no consequences for my openness.

In addition to my work with the Montgomery County Police, I also volunteer with a small fire department in my hometown. I have to admit that I was a bit more cautious at first with the fire department about my personal life, since I found the atmosphere there to be a bit more closed. Gradually, however, people started figuring it out for themselves. When my lover, Darla, and I bought a house in town, for example, I never made any secret of that fact. By then maybe people had gotten to know me as a person first, so that when they realized I was gay, it was not such a big issue.

I decided to come out directly to one person at the fire department, a woman named Theresa. She and I were on call one night, and there was a lot of time to just sit around and wait. We talked about several things, and I had a strong urge to tell her that Darla and I were lesbians and that we were in a committed relationship. She told me she had figured it out much earlier and that she didn't care what I was. At one point, I had developed an infatuation with her. Had she been gay and had I not been in a relationship, I would have jumped at the opportunity. Theresa was in the process of getting divorced and was therefore going through a rough period in her life. I was with her a lot, both on the ambulance calls and just hanging out at her house. I was worried about my friendship with her, afraid that people would assume that something was going on between us. One night I finally told her about my fears and asked her if anyone had ever said anything to her. Without any hesitation, she told me that she didn't give a damn what people thought and that she was my friend and would stay my friend. That was such a wonderful response, the best anyone could have given. She was a true friend.

Looking back at my life, I know I have been gay for a long time. However, I never really acted on my feelings until I met Darla. I was still living with my parents at this time and was still in self-denial. After I found out that Darla was a lesbian, I went home and told my mother that I had met a really neat person at work and that she was gay. Thinking about it later, I realized that I was attracted to Darla but was afraid of beginning a relationship. Later, when I fell in love with her and began to spend a lot of time with her, my parents became somewhat suspicious. My mother even told my sister that while she really liked Darla, she hoped that I wasn't becoming a lesbian. To give my Roman Catholic parents credit, however, they have never treated Darla with anything but respect, and in time they came to love her. I think that my mother saw how happy I was with Darla, and while she didn't understand it, she tried to accept it. I also told my siblings. One of my sisters, who is an actress, is very comfortable with gay people. She was really the easiest to tell. My sister Ellen was the hardest to tell. She is a white-collar professional who has a hard time dealing with things that do not fit into her norm. My brother did not seem to care one way or the other.

Still my parents and I had never talked specifically about my being gay. I never really tried to hide the fact that Darla and I were in a relationship, but it was never openly discussed. Then last year, I went on a Metropolitan Community Church retreat whose theme was coming out. Over the course of the weekend, I did a lot of thinking about why I had never actually said the word *lesbian* to them. I couldn't come up with any valid reason. They live in Florida now, and on different visits I had tried to tell them but never could get the words out. Finally, I wrote a letter in which I told my parents that I am gay. During the two weeks it took to receive a reply, I was a nervous wreck.

This is where being out at work was a great benefit, because all of my coworkers knew that I had written this letter and were constantly offering emotional support. My mother wrote back to tell me she still loved me, and always would. I feel like my two worlds have come together now. I can be as free at home from having to hide or pretend as I generally have been at work. It feels much better that way.

Building Up to Sounding Out
Paul Scarbrough

*Paul Scarbrough is a native of the Philadelphia area
who now lives and works in Norwalk, Conn. His firm
is one of the leading acoustical consulting firms in the
United States. Paul was trained as an architect at
Rensselaer Polytechnic Institute and joined his present firm
directly from school. Paul is very active in Dignity/USA.*

At thirty-three, I am the youngest partner in a small acoustics consulting firm. We specialize in the design of the acoustics and sound
systems for all types of performing-arts buildings: concert halls,
opera houses, drama theaters, amphitheaters, music schools, and
the like. Since we are a small firm and we do work throughout the country
and around the world, we all have to assume multiple roles and travel frequently on company business. With a staff of only fifteen or so, our studio
has always seemed more like an extended family than a stuffy corporate
office. Deciding to come out at work, then, was a lot like when I decided to
tell my parents.

For a long time, I felt there was no good reason to be out at work. I would
rationalize that my private life was not an appropriate subject for discussion
at the office...that it was nobody's business what I did outside office
hours...that my sexuality did not affect the way I performed my job. It did,
however, affect how I perceived myself. Even if I didn't speak about it openly, I felt a sense of shame associated with being in the closet. I also felt as if
there were several different versions of who I was: the Paul who existed in
the closet at the office, the Paul who wasn't out to most of his other friends,
the Paul who wasn't out to his parents, and the rarely seen Paul who was out
almost exclusively to his gay friends. I suffered a tremendous amount of
stress because I was constantly fearful of being found out by parents,
friends, or coworkers.

As I became more comfortable with my sexual identity, however, I
became less tolerant of the divisions within my life. One day a coworker,
whom I will call Tom, attended a meeting with me at an architect's office in
New York City. After the meeting, Tom commented on how the associate

with whom we had met "seemed a little..."—making clear what he meant with a limp-wrist gesture. I looked Tom in the eye and replied that " 'John' is a very good architect." My response made it clear that I would not tolerate that kind of remark and that whether John was gay had no bearing on his abilities as an architect. Even though I felt as though I had handled the situation well, I still had a sense that I hadn't done as much as I could. Would Tom have even thought of making such a comment had he been aware that I am gay? Had my response actually changed Tom's perception of gay people, or had it simply made it clear that he shouldn't use those kinds of slurs in front of me? My encounter with Tom made me increasingly uncomfortable with being in the closet—but I was still at a loss when it came to understanding *how* to be out at work.

Things changed for me when I got involved in Dignity/USA, an organization of lesbian and gay Catholics. Through Dignity I met many people who had integrated their sexuality, their spirituality, and their day-to-day life. It was a powerful and moving experience to know people who were so at peace with who they were. I began to realize how I had segmented my life into neat compartments and how much energy I expended shifting gears as I traveled between compartments.

About the same time, I became more conscious of the battles being waged for lesbian and gay civil rights. I soon understood how the closet helped to perpetuate stereotypes about gay people and allowed so many people to think that they didn't know anyone who was gay or lesbian. I remembered my encounter with Tom and began to realize that being out was essential to confronting antigay prejudice and bigotry. I could no longer be silent.

Having decided that coming out at work was important to me, I still had to resolve the dilemma of how to do it. For me, the topic simply doesn't come up naturally in conversations, and calling a meeting to announce it to everyone didn't seem right either. I put it off simply for lack of an appropriate way to do it.

As the campaign for the 1992 presidential race began to heat up, I became increasingly concerned about the antigay rhetoric spouting from people like Pat Buchanan and Marilyn Quayle. I always knew there were folks out there like that, but like many gay men and lesbian women, I was stunned to see that the Republicans actually ceded control of their national convention to such extremists. Moreover, I was fearful that few people were making an effort to counter their hateful views. While there was probably little I could do to affect the national scene, I knew there was something I could do at a personal level.

I started by coming out to the two other partners in the firm, who didn't know that I am gay. I sat down with Chris, the founding partner, first. His reaction was much as I expected: it really didn't matter to Chris at all. I told him that I would like to let the rest of the staff know; Chris was supportive of my plan. I told him that I would talk to Mark, the second partner, before talking to the staff.

Unfortunately, my travel schedule for the company intervened, and by the time I actually got around to speaking with the second partner, I found out that Chris had spoken with him, thinking that I had already done so. Mark was generally supportive but expressed some concern about how clients might react. By this time I had acquired an earring, and Mark worried about whether it might tip the balance against us in an interview with a potential client. He asked me point-blank if I had considered the impact on the firm when I got the earring. I was sympathetic to his concern but also questioned whether we wanted clients who would make decisions on that basis.

Even though I had hoped to tell the rest of the staff before the 1992 election, the workload in our office ballooned, and I found myself out of the office more than I was in. It just never happened. I had to find another sensible opportunity to tell the staff. As the spring of 1993 approached and with it the March on Washington, time seemed right.

The day I left for the march, I stopped in the office, assembled the staff members who were in that day (about ten), and explained that I was going to Washington for the weekend. I also explained that I was going to join an estimated 1 million people in a march for gay and lesbian civil rights and that they would certainly see reports about the march on local and network news over the weekend. I explained why it was important for gay and lesbian people to come out to friends, families, and coworkers; how many people believed that they did not know any gay people; and how a fear of someone different was at the root of antigay prejudice. I told them that gay and lesbian people taught their children, advised them on legal matters, fixed their plumbing, and yes, even designed the acoustics of concert halls and opera houses. I explained that in Connecticut, antidiscrimination laws protected my job, home, and other basic civil rights, but that gay and lesbian people in most other states could lose their jobs or be kicked out of apartments simply for being gay. Then I held my breath....

The response was incredible. A couple of folks told me they were happy to know that I was going to the march. One staff member, whom I had previously considered to be homophobic, asked if the whole office could contribute toward my expenses for making the trip to Washington. You could have knocked me over with a feather. It was all I could do to keep from bursting into tears. I left for Washington with a terrific feeling of support from my colleagues, and when I came back to the office on Tuesday, people made a point of telling me that they had seen the news reports and asked how the weekend had been for me. It was great to be able to share the experience with them.

One area that remains an open question is being out with clients. Unlike the office, where you are working closely with people on a daily basis and getting to know them on a more personal level, client relationships tend to be more formal, and there aren't always opportunities to get past that formality. In general, I don't make an effort to either reveal or conceal my sexuality to clients. None of my straight clients, however, censor their discussions of their wives or families. Why should I?

Since coming out at work I have realized that it's the small things that matter most to me: joking with our receptionist, Mary, about whether a visitor to the office is good-looking; receiving calls at the office from my gay friends or about Dignity business and leaving my office door open; talking about vacationing "in Provincetown" rather than "on Cape Cod"; or joining friends for Gay Ski Week. It is so much easier not to worry about who is around after hours when I'm editing a Dignity newsletter.

There have been other benefits. We recently conducted interviews for a new administrative assistant in our office. This person would be working closely with the partners to keep their work organized and schedules under control. For me this also means keeping track of my responsibilities as cochair for the 1997 Dignity National Convention. During the interviews I was able to explain these responsibilities to each applicant and to make sure that they would be comfortable receiving or making telephone calls on my behalf representing a gay organization.

Another empowering experience happened in March 1995, when we were approached by two architectural firms pursuing the design commission for a new performing-arts center in Cobb County, Ga. At a meeting with my two partners and our marketing director, I recommended that we turn down the invitation to bid on this project, citing the antigay ordinances that the Cobb County Commission passed in 1993. My partners were initially reluctant to turn the opportunity down, because they had not heard anything about the ordinance. They did ask me, however, to supply some background material so they could be better informed.

I located the article from *The Advocate* that described how the commission had voted to declare county support "for community standards and established state laws regarding gay lifestyles"—a thinly veiled reference to Georgia's sodomy statute, which is still on the books after the U.S. Supreme Court decided to uphold the state in *Bowers* v. *Hardwick*. I also provided them with a second *Advocate* article, which detailed the commission's vote to rescind all county arts funding for fear that some portion might go to gay-themed art projects. I made my partners aware how pressure from gay and lesbian activists had persuaded the Atlanta Olympic Committee to relocate the Olympic volleyball events from Cobb County, the original site, to some other venue. In a cover memo I pointed out to them that if *gay* had been replaced with *black* or *Latino,* there would have been a national uproar.

After reviewing the material I provided, both of my partners and the marketing director agreed to turn down the Cobb County project. They knew how important this issue was to me, and they also saw the larger implications of an antigay ordinance for our society. In addition, they decided to send copies of the articles I had provided to the architects who had invited us to join their team so that they would understand why we had declined to participate.

It was gratifying to me that my partners would be willing to give up a potentially profitable project in order to send a message about the importance of gay and lesbian civil rights. This happened only because I was out at work. Being out gave me the freedom to address the issue directly and forcefully.

Of course, coming out is a never-ending process. Every time we hire a new staff member, I have to find some way to let him or her know. Usually I just arrange for it to come up in some random conversation. The response has always been good, though admittedly being a partner does help: few people would risk reacting badly to such an admission in front of me. However, I do believe that the positive responses have been genuine.

Since my coming-out in the office, the way people treat me hasn't changed, but the way I feel has changed significantly: life is so much less stressful now that I don't have a secret to hide. I now know how satisfying it feels to integrate the various parts of my life.

Sitting in the Middle of the Bus
Michelle V. Porche

*Michelle Porche first began working with lesbian, gay,
and bisexual adolescents as a volunteer at the Gay and
Lesbian Community Services Center in Los Angeles.
While attending the Graduate School of Education at
Harvard University, she took a job as head of house
at Wellesley College. Though mired in controversy during
her first year there, she has witnessed significant progress
toward a safer and more secure environment on
the college campus.*

I n the summer of 1991, I accepted a position as head of house at one of
the top undergraduate colleges—and the most prestigious women's college—in the country. My duties as a live-in professional in charge of
counseling, dorm administration, and programming were designed to
foster community for students at this all-women's institution. This was, on a
personal level, an opportunity for me to use my skills, qualifications, and interests in women's issues in a unique job while pursuing my graduate studies; on
a political level it was an opportunity to respond to a commitment to diversity
and to a policy of nondiscrimination on the part of the institution.

Throughout the application process I had been clear about my identity as
a lesbian. Attached to my résumé was the most straightforward cover letter
I had ever written, detailing my qualifications and experiences and under-
scoring my perspective as an African-American woman and out lesbian. My
message was that not only could I do the job, but in addition I could be an
important resource for lesbian and bisexual students developing their own
sexual identity. In the course of interviews, I discussed these points in depth,
but not out of proportion to other aspects relevant to the head of house position. I was very forthcoming about the fact that if I was hired, my partner
would be moving in along with me. I was aware that benefits were extended
to spouses and dependents, and I made it clear that for all practical purposes my partner is my spouse and was entitled to the same benefits. I was
encouraged by the news that the college had already begun to explore the
issue of benefits for domestic partners. It was important for me to establish

the institution's response to the following questions: Would there be any problem or concerns regarding my sexual identity? Would I have support from my colleagues, and would they offer protection from potential harassment during a difficult transition? The response was simply that the residence department wanted to hire the "most qualified applicant."

I was at first quite relieved when my prospective employer contacted my references, and I thought I had stumbled on a truly safe place for lesbians, gays, and bisexuals. As the months dragged on and I was given neither a job offer nor a rejection, I began to have some doubts. My doubts grew when I was told that the dean of students wanted to interview me—a deviation from the regular hiring process. I was offended by the interview, though at least the questions were direct: "What are your politics?" and "How do you conduct your personal affairs?" She explained that this was a special case, because even though the college did not discriminate, there had never been an out lesbian employee living *with* the students. *Well, not that* she *knew about,* I thought.

When I was finally offered the position, I was told that I would be placed in a residence hall with older students (sophomores, juniors, and seniors) and that the head of house already in that hall would be moved into a hall with mostly first-year students—the position for which I had originally applied. I was told that older students would be more mature and more accepting of a situation that might be quite new to them. I asked whether this would be a problem for the other head of house, and I was told that there was nothing to worry about. When I arrived at the college two weeks later, I found out that the other head of house was very upset at being asked to leave a residence hall where she had been firmly established. She argued that her displacement was based on her heterosexuality as much as mine was based on my homosexuality. I began to see how disruptive my placement and my colleague's displacement were. News of my arrival had already started to spread among alumnae, students, staff, and faculty. From what I heard, there was more concern over the issue of discriminatory placement than over having a lesbian in a live-in position.

During my second week on the job, while student residence staff members were undergoing training to prepare for the coming year, this issue became more volatile. Lesbian and bisexual students confronted the president of the college when she came to welcome residence staff members at the end of their training. "What message was the administration sending them if it proclaimed that entering students needed to be protected from a lesbian employee?" they asked. Clearly, they felt that their own safety was threatened, that they might be denied fair treatment or protection from discrimination based on sexual identity, and that they were less-valued members of a community that espoused a respect for diversity.

These were some of the same issues being discussed among my colleagues in the residence department. Like these students, they were deeply disappointed by actions that went blatantly against the values that they promoted in the residence halls in which they worked. They were also incredibly supportive of me, spoke openly of their opposition to attempts to segregate me from first-year students, and brainstormed about ways to rectify our placements before the rest of the students arrived for the start of the fall semester. In an attempt to implement a change and to curtail what was fast becoming a campus controversy, a meeting with the president of the college was arranged. She informed us in the residence department that she took full responsibility for the decision regarding my placement and that she based her decision on the belief that if the college hired a lesbian head of house who worked with first-year students and it became known, then the college would no longer attract the best students, and therefore wouldn't get the top professors, and subsequently would not get the sorts of alumnae contributions that it had in the past, and would inevitably have to go coed. We all sat in stunned silence on hearing that. At the time I felt the enormous responsibility for the ongoing viability of a 116-year-old institution on my shoulders. And I missed the opportunity to point out that some of the best students and top professors were themselves lesbian, or bisexual, or gay.

During this time it became known that another head of house, hired at the same time, was also a lesbian. This was actually a point that I had been aware of, since I knew her from a graduate course we had both taken the previous year. Despite everything that was happening around me as I began my job, I felt that it was up to her to disclose her sexual identity of her own volition and not up to me to out her. When she explicitly acknowledged that she too was a lesbian, she claimed that it should have been common knowledge since she had been out when she had been a student at the college, even though that was fifteen years ago. In our department, we hoped that this would sway the administration to rethink the placement decision, since this other head of house was already working with first-year students.

Paradoxically, the issue then became redefined as involving objections to a partnered lesbian living and working with first-year students. I, in my third year of a committed relationship, was seen to be more of a threat to students than an unattached lesbian. In a statement to *The Wellesley News* in September 1991, the president of the college and the dean of students responded to student protest:

> *We recognized that it would be hard for some first-year students (and their parents) from backgrounds where homosexuality is still regarded very negatively, to have to confront a situation that would be difficult for them, just at a time when they were also dealing with all the other stresses and challenges of being away from home and adapting to college....We also know that attitudes toward homosexuality in many parts of our country*

and the world are quite different from the inclusiveness of the Wellesley campus. We believe that it is good educational practice to bring people along at a pace they can handle in absorbing new ideas and values, rather than to force them to confront everything novel all at once.

Many of us wanted to know how good is this educational practice would be for the first-year lesbian or bisexual entering the college. As students began to settle in and classes about to start, my colleague who had been displaced decided that the injustice done to her was too great, so she resigned from her position, took an undisclosed settlement, and moved out. This left a group of vulnerable first-year students without any direct professional supervision for one month while a replacement was found.

Soon after the new head of house moved in and took over the residence hall, her students requested a meeting with me so they could discuss what had happened and gain a better understanding of the situation. For me, this was one of the most honest and moving exchanges I've ever had regarding issues of homophobia and sexual identity, and it was by far the most hopeful.

About forty students squeezed into a small living room, almost all of them meeting an out lesbian for the first time. They talked about their painful introduction to college, away from home for the first time with only one another, a handful of older student residence staff members, and limited contact with professional staff to guide them through their first month. Residence staff spoke of the overwhelming responsibility they faced in a confusing situation without enough professional supervision. The students wanted to know about my aspirations for working at the college and asked about the details leading to the events that followed my hire. Some of them stated very clearly, "We don't care what your sexual identity is—all we care about is that we were denied a professional staff to support us during this transition into college."

For many of them, not having me there in the first place or not having the displaced head of house there because she quit was much more of a problem to them and to their parents than having a lesbian and her partner in this live-in position. Ironically, the very students the administration had hoped to protect were the ones suffering the most. As we talked, many of the students struggled with language and awkwardly searched for words to express their thoughts and frame their questions. In that struggle they reached for an understanding of difference and the meaning of prejudice that is rarely achieved.

After waiting for the rest of the students to file out, a sophomore came up to me and tearfully revealed that she was also a lesbian and was deeply hurt by my not being allowed to work in her residence hall. For her, the implication was that she was deviant rather than simply different. All the lessons on diversity and acceptance that she had heard in her previous year at the college now seemed to ring false. Perhaps she began to question whether there really was a place for her there.

This was a pivotal point in the college's implementation of its policy of non-discrimination. Lesbian and bisexual students now had the attention of an administration reaching for justifications of its contradictions and inconsistencies. Moreover, the story had come to the attention of *The New York Times, The Boston Globe,* and the Associated Press. The very public attention that the administration had hoped to avoid was now magnified. Attempting to avoid being labeled as an institution that hires lesbians, they instead were labeled by the press as an institution that discriminated against the lesbians they hired—which led in turn to an inundation of letters from alumnae, both for and against my hire, that were subsequently printed in the Wellesley alumnae magazine. This particularly poignant statement in defense of my hire was written by a Wellesley alumna, class of 1938, and appeared in a number of publications:

> When I was in college, two of my classmates vanished from campus overnight. We learned via the rumor mill that they had been expelled because they were lesbians. Now, fifty-four years later, a qualified head of house at Wellesley—a Harvard graduate student—is a lesbian. Homosexuality is an issue on campuses everywhere. The issue is old but openness about it is new. Many in the younger generation will no longer tolerate the treatment of homosexuals as pariahs. If honesty is the best policy, this has to be progress....Most people agree that an honest acceptance of others is essential in our increasingly diverse world. To get beyond prejudice I realize I must try to take account of my own fear of difference. For me, the whole topic touches on a broader question: what is moral? The best definition I ever heard was given by a Tongan [who] said, "In the U.S., morality is mostly about sex. In Tonga, morality is about how you treat people. If you are kind and loving to them, that is moral. If you are mean and abusive, that is immoral." Wellesley's new openness toward homosexuality seems to me highly moral.

Another response was the formation of an ultraconservative group of alumnae from Texas. They gave a number of interviews about what they perceived as a "dangerous radicalism" on campus.

As the events of the year progressed, it became apparent that whatever meaning my employment had for me, it had become a lightning rod for the projections of a number of individuals and groups on campus. Students and administrators had various expectations about what my response should be, based on their level of comfort with their own coming-out processes. Discussion of the "controversy," in open meetings and in the press, became a forum for education about homophobia as well as an opportunity to condemn homosexuals. There was a tremendous amount of thought and energy from both sides put into public debates of lesbian, bisexual, and gay issues, as well as how sexual orientation fits under the umbrella of multiculturalism and the effectiveness of multiculturalism itself.

By taking the middle ground of hiring me yet limiting my contact with first-year students, the college effectively confused students on all sides during a time when they could have been provided a clear and powerful practical lesson on multiculturalism and the importance of a diverse and inclusive community, which they had promoted so actively on paper. Despite its best intentions, the college through its actions had given license to those who would engage in a dialogue of prejudice. As one lesbian student put it, "The president's argument is based on one assumption that is particularly weak, and that is the expectation that a multicultural experience is achieved in a phased and distanced way."

Before I arrived on campus, I had thought quite a lot about the stresses that this very visible position would mean for me and my partner. I know that the more I felt put off during the hiring process, the more adamantly I wanted the job, lest anyone think that they had the right to discriminate against me. Once hired, I expected some difficult conflicts with students—I feared that they would meet me and demand to be moved from my residence hall in vast numbers. While that never happened, what did become apparent was how unsuspecting I was about the turmoil that ensued for many students as a result of my placement. I believe it would have made a big difference for students if the network of lesbian, gay, and bisexual staff and faculty (which seemed quite underground at that time, except for the few individuals who extended a warm welcome and support and who personally appealed to the president of the college) had organized quickly in a united and collaborative effort. Over the next few years I saw this network growing in numbers, in visibility, and in its interactions and contacts with students, which is a benefit to all members of the lesbian, bisexual, and gay community.

But that fall, my first reaction to the lesbian and bisexual students was an attempt to direct their reaction of pain and anger into a proactive and positive response. Although there would be no change in the administration's decision regarding my placement, at least there could be some evidence that the inclusion of lesbians, gays, and bisexuals within the umbrella of the college's multicultural initiatives was not just an empty promise. I talked with a number of students individually and suggested that they get together and write up a list of recommendations to take to the administration, to think of ways that the administration could show good faith. Most importantly, I wanted to help encourage a feeling of empowerment in their taking some action. I met with a group of about ten students during their first meeting to draw up the proposal. I helped them think carefully about language and tone, made some modest suggestions about money for programming and invited speakers, and left once they had gotten started. So I was quite surprised—and quite proud of them—when I later read their letter to the president of the college, which also included the signatures of many heterosexual students, demanding an adviser for lesbian and bisexual students. Students also called for a more inclusive curriculum, for a more inclusive admissions office, and for assurances of job security and equal opportunity for lesbian, bisexual, and gay employees.

During a year in which hundreds of positions had been eliminated in a plan of downsizing, the president did respond by creating a new position with the title of director of programming for lesbian and bisexual students. Granted, it is only part-time, but it has been the hub of tremendous activity at the college, as this director creates a space for support, dialogue, education, and programming and has even added a "lesbigay" information superhighway. All of her efforts are meant to reach the entire lesbian, bisexual, and gay community who might be at various stages of their coming-out process. Although I was given a number of opportunities to take the position when it was created, I refused because I didn't want to become the "Big Lesbian on Campus," or BLOC, as my students referred to me. If we really are everywhere, I wanted there to be more evidence of it, thereby helping to take away the stigma and giving students more choices in terms of resources.

During my first year at the college, an out lesbian was hired from among a competitive field to become Protestant chaplain. Highly regarded by other members of the chaplaincy and by members of the administration, she also had hopes, like my own, that she was entering a community that was truly inclusive.

Troubled by the institution's sanctioning of discrimination through my placement, and with the goal of extending herself as a resource to help the administration rethink its decision, she offered a sermon early in the year that pushed my hiring controversy to new heights. The college has a tradition known as Flower Sunday, in which a special multifaith service is conducted to welcome everyone back to school in a spiritual expression of love and hope. This day the chaplain caught everyone off guard, from the president to myself. In a sermon that inspired in me a renewed faith and sense of spirituality, she gave an incredibly moving call for love and acceptance in response to homophobia, telling a story of individual struggle and going on to discuss my hire and placement. She ended with a revivalist zeal, asking all those to stand who were willing to join me and the president "out on a limb" in the fight to end homophobia.

There was a confusing rustling of seats, and even more confused students standing who weren't quite sure of the difference between being homosexual and taking a stand against homophobia. On the one hand, this was the first time since the controversy started that I was able to see the lesbian and bisexual students proudly and joyfully identify themselves. On the other hand, I was bitterly hurt by a group of African-American students who got up in the middle of the sermon and left in angry protest. Afterward, there was a very vocal response from students, some in support and others asking for the chaplain's resignation while organizing around-the-clock prayer vigils to pray for our damned souls.

In 1994, my partner became eligible for full benefits extended to domestic partners as per a newly implemented college policy. At that same time, we also moved into a residence hall in which one third of the students are first-year. Nothing terrible has happened, no parents have removed their daughters from my hall, no student has been traumatized. In my fourth year of this job, I believe that by just living in the same building with us, students have probably learned a lot more about tolerance than they could have in any organized program. They get to know my partner and me as people who are different from them but not deviant from them. If they feel bold enough, they ask us about what it means for us to be lesbians.

During the fall of 1993, I was interviewed by a first-year student who had to write a paper on women's considerations of motherhood. She wanted to get the perspective of a lesbian. I have met many of the parents of my students, and I've even been introduced to a few boyfriends so that I could give approval. But what I am most proud of is the space I have made for lesbian and bisexual students in my home, offering them a place to talk about problems and a place to celebrate who they are. Although I miss seeing the many students who used to come to talk with me from all over campus, I'm happy that there are now so many more resources for them to turn to.

This is not the end of the story of lesbians, bisexuals, and gays at the college; it's just the middle. Despite our best efforts to move toward a truly inclusive community, we are still brutally reminded of the long way we have to go. Most recently, the college community has been tested by a hate incident against a lesbian student and a bomb-threat hoax at a Susie Bright lecture—both symbols of death threats against lesbians, bisexuals, and gays on campus. While no one was physically injured, there has been a rallying of the lesbian, bisexual, and gay community in protest. Despite the upsetting hate incident, the lesbian student refuses to hide or be silenced. The bomb threat, however, successfully drove away a large portion of the audience, closing off potential discussion. It disrupted an event that two students had spent months planning.

Students who are relatively new to the college can sometimes be very vocal in condemning the institution's lack of action. Veteran staff, by contrast, gauge the situation against recent history and are very encouraged. But those student voices are probably the most important ones I listen to. Because they continue to have a vision that goes beyond what I might have thought possible, and they have the energy and drive to achieve that vision.

Science = Death?
Will I. Johnston

Will Johnston is a thirty-year-old editor of high school
mathematics textbooks. He lives in Watertown, Mass.

In 1987 I had been out of college for two years and was looking for a job
when I saw an advertisement in *The Boston Globe* for a substitute
teacher in the Weston public school system. I grew up in Weston, an
affluent suburb of Boston, and went to school there from kindergarten
through twelfth grade, graduating in 1981. The idea of teaching in the school
system where I had been a student was appealing.

I had considered a career in teaching but had never gone to graduate school
for certification. Substitute teaching would allow me to try out teaching without going through the certification process. I welcomed the opportunity to
return to my old school. It was a fine school system, one of the best in
Massachusetts. I knew most of the teachers there already. I also had a secret
dream: I might be able to make the high school experience of the gay, lesbian,
and bisexual students there more livable than it had been for me.

Soon after I sent out my résumé, the chairman of the high school mathematics department telephoned me. He needed a long-term substitute for the
entire year to replace a teacher who was out because of a neck injury. Since
the department chairman had been my calculus teacher in high school, he
was convinced that I would be an excellent candidate for the position. I
would be teaching first-year algebra to freshmen, geometry to sophomores,
and second-year algebra to juniors.

As part of the interview process, I spoke with the principal, a man who
had been a curriculum specialist while I was in school. We met in his large
office and sat in comfortable chairs. This charming mustachioed gentleman
was quite at ease chatting with me, clearly pleased that I was available for the
job. After about twenty minutes he said quite casually, "So, Will, I hear you
are out of the closet." I was stunned. This was not something I had included
on my résumé. How did he know?

The only explanation I could think of was a postcard I had sent from Paris
to my former English teacher almost two years earlier on which I had come

out to her by mentioning that I had just been to a production of Jean Genet's play *Le Balcon* at—of all places—the Comédie Française. I had written a paper for her in high school discussing this play, a paper that had completely ignored the exploration of sex and power implicit in the drama. I told her that my understanding of the work was now quite different because I had come out of the closet as a gay man in college and had read other works by Genet. Had my English teacher shared my news with others? It seemed the only explanation. I had come out to my parents several years earlier, but this was not something they would ever have mentioned to the high school principal if they had happened to run into him.

I told the principal that I was indeed an openly gay man. He asked, a bit gingerly, how I expected to deal with this issue in school. I told him that I would not lie about my sexual orientation if a student asked, but that I didn't expect to make a big deal about being gay while I was teaching. If the issue arose in class, I would handle it as best I could and then continue with the lesson. I had been a member of the Boston Gay and Lesbian Speakers Bureau for a year and was accustomed to speaking to high school students about sexual orientation. My answer seemed to satisfy him.

"I hope you're not offended by my raising this issue," he said, somewhat apologetically.

"No," I replied. "In fact, I'm glad you brought it up. I want to be clear about it."

I *was* glad, in fact. I wanted to clarify the issue before taking the job, because I did not want to feel constrained to be in the closet. Later that day, though, I got angry. Would he have asked a heterosexual candidate about discussing issues related to his sexuality in class? I don't think so. I did understand his motivation, however: he wanted to know what kind of behavior to expect from me, so he could be prepared for any adverse reactions there might be from parents. I understood his caution, but I was also disappointed. His question seemed discriminatory, the kind of question that should be prohibited by law, just as questions about marital status are prohibited. (This happened before Massachusetts had a law prohibiting job discrimination based on sexual orientation. I wonder, though, whether our antidiscrimination legislation has had any effect on the kinds of questions that are asked in job interviews in Massachusetts. I doubt it.)

I got the job and was soon immersed in teaching for the first time. Any teacher will tell you that the first year of teaching is probably the most difficult. You are learning how to deliver to students complicated material that is familiar to you but new to them. You are also learning how to interact with students and how to manage the classroom. It was the most exhausting job I've ever had. After spending the day on my feet, I would return home and lie down on my living-room couch. One of my housemates, whose father is a mathematics teacher, walked in one day and said, "My father does that too."

One thing I was not prepared for was the name-calling that I heard in the hallways every day. Boys called each other "faggot" routinely, and every time I heard it I cringed. I was not out of the closet to my students right away, so I asked my students not to call each other names while they were in my class, but I didn't focus specifically on the word *faggot*.

Name-calling became so much of an issue in one of my freshman classes that I spent an entire period using a technique I had learned at my speakers bureau training. I asked my students to call out some of the names that hurt them most. I wrote them all down on the chalkboard, completely filling it. My students' list included *stupid, loser, bastard, asshole, wench, faggot, whore, slut, hooker, wimp, scum, zit-face, chunky-ass, penis, pussy, gook, schmuck, fuck-hole, nigger, honky, JAP, kike, bitch, cow, pencilneck, basketnose, queer, wuss, coward, baby, pygmy, dickhead, bubble-butt, shithead, cocksucker, moron, dummy, monkey, pothead, jew.*

I then led my students in a discussion of how it feels to be called names, what might prompt people to use name-calling, and why words can be so powerful in wounding others. I ended by asking the students to suggest why it might be important to refrain from name-calling. "Respect" was the one-word answer that a young black girl offered.

After the class was over, I copied down all the words I had written on the board. One student rushed up, hoping to take a photograph of the board for the school yearbook, but I asked him not to, fearing that the photograph without any context would give a bad impression. I erased the board and delivered the list of words to the principal. I wanted him to be forewarned in case students spoke to their parents about the activity and their parents complained. I think he appreciated my letting him know that I had taken time during math class to do the activity. If there was any backlash, I never heard from him about it.

The name-calling problem was reduced in that freshman class but remained a problem with another class of sophomores and juniors, where one student repeatedly taunted another by calling him "faggot." He said it was just a joke. I asked him many times not to use the word. He continued, and one day I could tolerate it no longer. I assigned him detention, citing his disrespectful attitude. He was furious. He came back after class to complain, trying to get out of having to stay after school. He asked me why I was so bothered. "I would understand if I was saying it to you," he said, "or if I said something bad about your mother." Because I was not out, I had to hide behind a screen of generalizations about name-calling. I wanted to say simply that as a gay man I found the word *faggot* offensive. But I couldn't say that without coming out directly, and I was not ready to do that. I guess I was not really as much of an "openly gay man" as I had told the principal at my job interview.

The student whined that this detention was going to ruin his record, that he would never get into Princeton because of it, and that it was all my fault. I did not relent. In retrospect, I feel I was not fair to him, because I was dishonest about my motives for assigning the detention. I suspect that part of my visceral reaction stemmed from experiences I had had in high school.

When I was in high school, I was only dimly aware of being gay. I knew that I found men attractive, but I figured it was a form of envy. I expected that eventually I would go "girl crazy," just as I was supposed to. I certainly didn't think of myself as being gay. I remember one day having a confrontation with another student. Like me, he was a violinist in the school orchestra, and I resented that he played better than I did. I was cold and spiteful to him as a result, and in reaction one day he walked away from me and my best friend muttering "Faggot." I yelled back the first thing that popped into my head, which was "You wish." My best friend laughed. Walking away with my friend, I had a sinking feeling. I had gained points with my friend for the wit of my rejoinder, but at what expense? Deep down I knew that I had betrayed myself and wounded someone else. I was ashamed.

Seven years later, I wondered whether my reaction to the student who called another one "faggot" was my way of atoning.

In school, I didn't completely disguise the fact that I was gay, however. I used to do campy things like bring my lunch to school in a *Masters of the Universe* lunch box my housemates had given me. "Do you really have a *Masters of the Universe* lunch box?" one boy asked me. "Sure," I said. A girl, coming to my rescue, interrupted and said, "What's wrong with that? I have a *Strawberry Shortcake* lunch box."

I also left subtle clues about my involvement with AIDS activism. In the car I drove to work, I left a hat with the NAMES Project logo emblazoned on it visible through the rear window. I pinned an ACT UP button that said SILENCE=DEATH on my book bag. One of the students in the front row of my class squinted at it one day. The sans-serif typeface was tall and hard to read from a distance. "Science equals death?" she asked quizzically. She hated biology class and supported animal rights; maybe she thought I agreed with her.

During the spring term we had a schoolwide "diversity day" aimed at appreciating human differences. One of the guest speakers was a lawyer from Gay and Lesbian Advocates and Defenders. He engaged the audience by starting off his speech saying that perhaps 10 percent of the people in the auditorium were gay, lesbian, or bisexual. This raised giggles throughout the hall and lots of finger-pointing. He went on to say that he really couldn't tell which 10 percent it was.

After the presentation, I learned that it was not only the students who needed information, but some of the faculty as well. Sitting in the faculty lounge at lunch, I spoke with my former geometry teacher. He cited the speaker's strategy as an example of the way statistics can be misleading. He implied that in Weston, of course, the 10-percent figure would not hold. I looked at him and cited some statistics of my own, based on conversations with my high school classmates in the years since our graduation. "I happen to know that in my homeroom when I was here as a student, at least four of us were gay, lesbian, or bisexual," I told him. "Four out of about twenty-five students. That's 16 percent. And that was just the kids with names from Harris to Jones." He was quiet after that.

Not all the math teachers were ignorant about gay issues. I will never forget how pleased I was when one of the teachers invited us to a party at her home and asked that we bring our spouses "or significant others." She aimed that at me, and rather than being offended I felt included. My boyfriend at the time was a lawyer who often worked late, so he couldn't come to the party, but I appreciated the invitation. I don't really like the term "significant other," because it's cumbersome and I feel silly saying it. Maybe she felt that way too, but it didn't stop her from welcoming my partner. I appreciated that.

Near the end of the school year, I felt that I should come out to my students. I knew that my job was over, that I was not going to be teaching the next year, because the woman I had been substituting for was ready to come back. I was applying for a job as an editor of mathematics textbooks with a Boston publisher, the job I currently hold. I had little to lose by coming out, since I didn't have to worry about repercussions for my career. As it turned out, my students found out I was gay in an interesting way.

I marched in the Pride parade in early June, just a month before school was over. I went with my housemates, who were straight, and my boyfriend. A camera crew from one of the Boston television stations walked by as I was standing on the sidelines with my boyfriend. I watched the news that evening and saw that for a split second we were shown on the air.

The next day, one of the girls in my freshman class asked coyly, "Mr. Johnston, why were you on TV last night?" I couldn't ignore the question. I said, "I was marching in the gay pride parade. Did you see me on the news?" That got the attention of the class. "It doesn't mean he's gay," said another girl. "It could just mean that he supports gay rights." I turned to her and said, "That's right. But I *am* gay."

This was too much for one boy in the class. It was the beginning of the class period, and I was taking attendance. He came up to the front of the room and stood by my desk. "You mean to say that you're a practicing homosexual?" he sputtered. I couldn't resist answering him with, "Actually, I don't have to practice. I'm quite good at it." Not the kind of answer that is most appropriate for a ninth grader, I suppose; but this was an honors class.

He couldn't believe it. He asked me if the department chairman knew. Then he had to leave the room, ostensibly to use the bathroom. I suspect it was to alert anyone he could find in the halls about my revelation. A few days later he came into the mathematics office and loitered around. I sensed he wanted to ask me questions but didn't know how. I wondered if he was gay. Maybe. Certainly there were others in the class that I suspected might be. I hope that by coming out I helped them just a little bit, even if they were as dimly aware of their sexuality as I was when I was in high school.

Because it was the end of the year when I officially came out to my students, I did not get much of a chance to discuss sexuality issues with them. I didn't get any feedback from parents or teachers about my coming out; perhaps they never knew. But the students certainly spread the information around. I know that some of the students in my study halls, particularly the boys who were known as troublemakers, were fascinated. They asked me questions about what it was like to be gay. I answered honestly and concisely. I think it disturbed some of them. I hope it helped more of them, whether they were straight or gay.

It's hard to know when you are a teacher whether you have much of an influence on your students. I was there primarily to teach them mathematics, but I hope I taught them more.

Build Visibility
Camille Victour

*Camille Victour is an architect who founded Boston
Gay and Lesbian Architects and Designers (BGLAD)
as a way of creating a community of gays and lesbians
within the design professions. Her coming out was the
catalyst for change in the antidiscrimination policy of one
firm at which she worked. Camille says being an architect
is a great way to impress potential dates.*

I am an architect. I am a lesbian. Pretty much in that order. And maybe a few other things in between; however, I feel that being a lesbian profoundly affects my professional life. My lesbianism has an impact on how I carry myself among my peers and my clients, and it shapes what I choose to spend my energy on. I am very conscious of being a lesbian, and it is my frame of reference for interacting with others I may come into contact with, straight or gay. I therefore find it very hard to pretend I am not a lesbian, though it's generally not something I announce when I first meet someone.

Coming out to myself was a two- or three-year process (or a fifteen-year process, depending on how you count). As I was discovering this new twist in my life's path, I could find no professional role models. I knew very few lesbians or bisexual women at all, and I didn't know of any in my workplace. I was hungry for that connection in my life because I had so many questions. My primary question was, Is it safe to be myself here? Only one gay man was publicly (but discreetly) "out" at my workplace at the time.

I later found out that several lesbians and gay men were working alongside me. It would have been enormously helpful, and saved me from a couple of disastrous heterosexual relationships, had I known that a woman from work with whom I was friends was a lesbian. I was dying to talk with her about what I was going through, but I just wasn't sure if she would be the friend I needed. I was afraid to ask her point-blank if she was a lesbian or even just get her to understand my own confused and curious feelings. My gut feeling was that she was a lesbian, but I didn't want to offend her by being wrong. We even went together to see the Olivia Records Fifteenth Anniversary Concert featuring Cris Williamson, Tret Fure, and Lucie Blue

Tremblay. I still couldn't be sure, though it didn't help that she basically lied when any open-ended queries arose about her life, such as "Are you seeing any*one?*" She was a little surprised to see me, of course, when I bumped into her at Gay Pride a couple of years later, with my first woman lover in tow. Needless to say, I was not at all surprised to see her.

After I had been dating women for a couple of years, I decided there ought to be a gay, lesbian, and bisexual component to the Boston Society of Architects (BSA), the local chapter of the American Institute of Architects (AIA). It seemed to me that if *I* needed such an organization to help me make the connection between my personal life and my professional life, there must be others like me. I had actually wanted to start the group during my own coming-out process, but I decided I had enough to handle as it was. I waited until I felt more sure of my place in the gay community, and in October 1991, I gathered up all my courage and phoned the executive director of the BSA and told him I wanted to start a new committee. I was very surprised by his response: he said he'd been waiting for someone to come forward and start the committee, because he thought it was definitely needed.

That very day the Gay, Lesbian, and Bisexual Architects Network was begun, later to be called Boston Gay and Lesbian Architects and Designers (BGLAD). Being chair of the group for the first two years of its existence required me to be out. I didn't exactly jump out of the closet, however: I stuck my big toe out first by allowing my first name and home phone number to be used for the regular column I wrote for BGLAD in the BSA newsletter. I figured that those who knew me well enough to know my home phone number had probably figured it out anyway. I was also well aware of the fact that there aren't too many architects in the Boston area named Camille.

The next step was to allow my last name to be used on a list of committee chairs that every BSA member receives. Keep in mind here that most of the other committee chairs, and many other regular members, are principals or senior associates in Boston's major firms—my potential employers. This was a big, scary step. I prepared for the worst: harassing phone calls, no job offers, being snubbed by my peers at the Boston Architectural Center, an accredited architecture school at which students work full-time during the day and go to school at night. (I was doing my thesis there when I started BGLAD.) However, I really felt that it was vitally important that someone—and "by Goddess," if it had to be me, then so be it—had to make a visibility statement so that gays and lesbians in the architectural community could find one another.

I was happily surprised when not only did nothing disastrous happen, but people told me they supported the group's mission and thought it was great that I had started it. Nevertheless, even now I am still a little nervous about outing myself by admitting my involvement with BGLAD to straight people whom I know professionally but have not come out to personally. I have always been pleasantly surprised by their nonchalant attitudes and often positive responses.

At the time I started BGLAD, very few architects were truly out in the workplace. Many were out to a few selected peers; a few were not out at all. Many of the members today are sole practitioners; others are young professionals, and still others are students. There are, unfortunately, no principals from the major firms in the area who feel they can be out enough to join us—or else they are not interested in participating for some other reason. I wish very much that they would participate: I feel that their mentorship would be invaluable to young architects like me. In turn, I think we could teach them how attitudes about gays and lesbians in the workplace are changing. For all of us, but especially for me, getting to know one another and hearing other people's stories has helped tremendously. We have given each other the support we need to come out at work. We have found a sense of community, solidarity, and visibility within the profession that was sorely lacking before.

BGLAD has made a difference on a local as well as a national level. The members of BGLAD, along with other gay architects across the nation, have lobbied the AIA for our concerns, and the AIA is (finally) listening. The AIA is mostly known as an old boy network, but with the demographics of the profession changing rapidly, it has discovered that valuing diversity is the key to its continued existence. When the AIA decided to hold its quarterly national meeting in Aspen in October 1993, despite a boycott of Colorado for passage of Amendment 2—which sought to disallow equal-rights protection for gays and lesbians—we and our contacts across the country vigorously lobbied the leadership of the AIA in an attempt to change the location. I was appalled to learn that AIA leaders were actually worried about offending AIA members in Colorado who supported Amendment 2. After we made our presence and our position known, they said they sympathized with our case but had decided to go ahead and hold the conference as planned. However, they promised to make a statement on our behalf while they were there. They felt that since Aspen was one of the more progressive towns in Colorado and had actually passed an antidiscrimination ordinance that included sexual orientation, it would not be fair to penalize the town by moving the conference. While in Colorado, the AIA did hold a press conference to present plaques to the mayors of Denver, Aspen, and Boulder in recognition of their support of equal rights for gays. The AIA also gave a sizable donation to the political action group that was fighting Amendment 2. So while we didn't get them to boycott Colorado, you can be sure that none of the AIA's support for gay and lesbian equal rights in Colorado would have happened without our collective lobbying efforts.

Some of the gay and lesbian architects and their supporters who had lobbied the AIA felt that we had been betrayed and lost the battle once the AIA decided to hold the conference in Colorado despite the boycott. I was actually pleased with the outcome, however. We had succeeded in convincing a relatively conservative and well-respected national professional association to make a positive and public stand in support of equal rights for gay and lesbian people. I felt that the AIA made a fairly valiant attempt to uphold its new nondiscrimination policy by its actions in Colorado.

As for my own experiences in the workplace, in the spring of 1992 I started a new job with a medium-size architectural firm of about fifty employees based in Boston. As part of my initiation to the firm, I received the employee handbook. Upon reading it, I found that the nondiscrimination statement did not include sexual orientation, though every conceivable category besides this particular one was included. Hmph. It really did bug me, and I just couldn't forget about it. I stewed about it for the next three weeks or so before I decided what to do. I approached the office manager in a private meeting and asked him what the story was. He said he'd check with the principals and get back to me. He apparently didn't see any need for discretion, as he hollered out across the lobby to one of the principals as he was getting into the elevator on Friday afternoon, "Camille wants to know why sexual preference is not listed in the antidiscrimination clause." The principal replied, "Have her come to my office Monday morning." Luckily, I did not find out about this scene until Monday morning, so I only had one anxious hour to wait before I was called into his office. I had no idea what to expect. I could only hope that he was a decent, fair person and would see that I was right.

Once I was in the principal's office, he asked me to explain what it was I wanted. I knew I was already out of the closet: after all, why would a straight person risk a confrontation with her new boss over gay rights? I decided that the best way to deal with this situation was to look him in the eye and be as brave as I could. I acted as if it were really no big deal, took a deep breath, and blurted it out. I don't remember exactly what I said, but he politely replied that they'd "just forgotten" to include sexuality in the policy and went on to tell me about the one or two other gay people he knows, one of whom had been an associate who had recently left the company. He felt that the firm would never think of discriminating for that reason and said he'd talk with the other partners and get back to me. Within an hour, there was a new nondiscrimination policy in my in-box that now included me! I was elated.

As time went by, however, I couldn't help but notice that I was the only out queer person in the office. Following my normal style of coming out, I never did make an announcement to the office; but on the other hand, I didn't hide who I was, and I did talk openly to my cubicle mates about my life as though nothing were unusual about it—and, to my surprise, they reacted as if nothing were unusual too. I am sure everyone around heard me conducting

BGLAD business, though I tried to be discreet about it. While people were friendly enough to me, I felt very alone there. I can't help but wonder if my activism played some part in my layoff six months later. Given the state of the architectural business today, there is very little job security, so it is hard to know.

The next firm I worked for was even more conservative than the previous one. This firm didn't even bother to publish a nondiscrimination policy. It did have a monthly newsletter and a "face book," which included every employee ever hired. New employees were interviewed briefly and introduced to the rest of the company in this way. Through this format you could offer a little personal information about your interests, hobbies, and professional accomplishments. Had I been chair of any other committee of the BSA, you can bet I would have tooted my horn about it. I discussed my dilemma about coming out in this forum with a trusted straight friend from college, who had been working at the firm for almost a year before I joined it. He advised against outing myself in this manner. No one else in the firm was openly gay. We agreed that the principals probably already knew that I was gay—and seemed to be fine about it—but the project managers with whom I would be working more directly were more conservative and might request that I not be assigned to them. Without any work to do, I could look forward to another layoff. I decided neither to hide my sexual preference nor to declare it openly.

I do regret not taking the opportunity to come out to the entire firm. I think it would have done that stodgy old place some good to shake people up a little bit. There were quite a number of other gays and lesbians there, which I discovered as they each discreetly came out to me. I could not take the liberty of outing them to one another, so I was the only queer employee who knew I was not as alone as I had first thought I was.

I continued to work at the firm for the project manager who had hired me. When I needed time off to go to the 1993 March on Washington for gay, lesbian, and bisexual rights, I told him where I was going and why. Even though I had never so bluntly come out to him, I was pretty sure he knew me well enough by this time that he would not be surprised or offended by my announcement. He—a middle-aged, straight, white, liberal man—said, "Give 'em hell for me too!" I thought that was very nice of him.

As part of my personal and professional development, I decided that I wanted to find a job where I could do work I believed in, in a place that shared my values. This is probably something we all want, but with the recession making it hard to stay employed, I didn't feel I had much mobility. It has been estimated that the unemployment rate for architects in Massachusetts reached 50 percent during the worst of the recession, between 1989 and 1992. By 1992, however, the economy was looking up, firms were beginning to hire again, and I finally decided I was sick of working for conservative architectural firms doing corporate architecture for even more conservative law firms, banks, and investment firms. I was tired of designing executive dining rooms and VIP teller desks for unsympathetic wealthy people.

It took some patience and some effort, but I now work for a very small, lesbian-owned firm that does work mostly for nonprofit organizations. We design day-care, youth, and elderly centers and work with other types of nonprofit groups. We are also part of a very strong good-old-gals network, from which a lot of our work comes. I am sure there are firms around here run by straight, white males who do this kind of work, and I suppose I could be working for them, but I really wanted to work for a woman; lesbian or not, it didn't matter. I was looking for a mentor as well as an employer.

I love my job, even though I make about 20 percent less than I would if I were working for a larger firm doing work for profit-motivated organizations. I feel very at home here. I can be my whole self, and I don't have to watch what I say about what I do in my free time. My BGLAD friends are all quite jealous.

In working with day-care centers and youth centers, our firm comes across those who still think that lesbians and gays are child molesters. While we would generally choose not to work with anyone who is bigoted in any way, reality dictates that we work with a broad range of clients with large boards of directors. By and large, our clients are fairly progressive people, and many of the key personnel are gay, lesbian, or gay-friendly. So of course, it's fine to be completely out with them.

For many people, being queer is incidental to their work life. They just want to be left alone and not have to talk about their personal life with anyone they work with. In their mind, it's nobody's business. I don't want to maintain two completely separate lives and personae. I'm afraid I just couldn't keep it all straight—pardon the pun. I prefer to have a strong connection between two important parts of my life: my personal life and my work life. I couldn't exist in the closet now if my life depended on it. Being a lesbian and being out and proud about it have been for the most part positive experiences for me. I also hope I can be a positive role model for others, in the way that I needed someone to be there for me. I feel a sense of strength and power in being a lesbian. I love women. Why should I have to hide that?

Some Things Take Time
Bill Elliott

*Bill Elliott, former overachiever, is beginning his second
coming-out process—this time as a gay Republican.
He is a member of the board of directors of Boston's
AIDS Action Committee and of the Log Cabin Federation.
In his spare time, he is a vice president of a significant,
but somewhat socially conservative, high-technology company.*

I've been in the computer business for twenty-seven years, and I've been gay for all of those years. I certainly didn't always know that I was gay, and my process of being out at the workplace started with coming out to myself. My process didn't start with a plan or even a conscious thought. Of course, there had been all that experimentation with boys my own age, but I had given that up when I reached eighteen. Time to stop those things. Time to be a man. For most of those twenty-seven years, being out at work wasn't even a glimmer of an issue to me. There was that one little slip just after graduation at my college roommate's wedding. It wasn't my fault that he had me sharing a room with a high school friend of his who hadn't given up his experimentation. It was easy to view this as just an aberration. Nothing serious. Really. I was straight then, for sure. I graduated from college and went directly to work for IBM. I had fifteen good years there, starting as a programmer, moving on to sales, and eventually management. I met my first and only wife there. She and I were on parallel career tracks and doing well. We both "looked good in a suit"—perhaps the highest IBM accolade.

It's interesting to me, certainly, to look back on this time and the impact it had on my own personal development. "Looking good in a suit" defined success. You learned to wear the right clothes, speak professionally, demonstrate sincerity, and play the game. Being gay wasn't part of the game. It certainly wasn't part of my game. I had given it up, remember? Blocking my own awareness of being gay was not very different from all of the other things I blocked in order to fit in.

I knew, or suspected I knew, a few gay men at IBM during those days, and they were always in jobs a little out of the direct line of fire. Technical instructor. Order entry clerk. But they all looked like IBMers. Why did I think they were gay? And why was I so interested? As far as the women went, I don't think I even had a stray thought that any of those hundreds of brisk, clean-cut, aggressive female salespeople could have been lesbians. It wasn't part of the picture. It would be years before I learned that IBM had a well-earned reputation for exceeding its natural 10 percent share, and in fact was considered in some places a hotbed of homosexuals. I never had any thoughts of anyone being *out* at work. I was so busy making sure I conformed to the image that I had little time even to ask myself what I wanted. But there were these little thoughts that wouldn't go away.

Since my job gave me the kind of schedule flexibility that didn't require accounting for my time every hour of the day, I started dropping by the Art Cinema, a double theater of gay flicks, at lunchtime. I'm not sure who I expected to find there, if I even thought about it, but I was certainly surprised to see it filled with a lot of other blue-suit-and-white-shirt types, looking for something more compelling than lunch. I never saw another person there I knew, but for me, in the late 1970s, this was as close to being out at the workplace as I was going to get. I never even talked with another person there. I certainly never followed anyone into the room off to the right at the front of the theater.

These theatrical experiences, tame as they were, did carry me to the next step, however. Seeing apparently normal men, both on-screen and off, absorbed in this sexual world gave me the first inkling of an idea that my feelings might be okay, somehow.

So there I was: thirtysomething, married, apparently happy, with those little sexual thoughts that wouldn't go away. When I did think about my status—a subject I tried to avoid—I decided I must be bisexual. Bisexuality seemed acceptable to me and seemed to fit the situation. But this bisexuality thing had captured my attention. It was only a small step from accepting the concept to trying it out sexually. So I did.

Wow! What an experience! Or series of experiences, to be more precise. It didn't take me long to figure out that I was far out on the edge of bisexuality—the gay edge, that is. I began to think of myself as gay. Fortunately, before I spent too much time trying to reconcile being gay while being married to a woman, my wife left me. A lucky break. I didn't have to deal with reconciling anything. It took several more years and a couple of years of therapy to understand that I had a lot to reconcile. But that's another story.

Work now began to play a role in my sex life, however, and it wasn't a helpful one. I was beginning to meet other gay men, date, and create relationships. Guys were calling me at work and leaving messages—what was my secretary thinking or saying to the other secretaries?

For example, a man whose personal ad I had answered sent me a letter at work. He hadn't marked it "personal," so my secretary opened it. Inside was a photo of him, shirtless, sitting on a bicycle. My secretary left the photo and the letter in the opened envelope and never mentioned it to me. I was embarrassed for months, even though I've never known if anyone else ever saw it.

I did come out to one friend at IBM. Jessica and her husband were both stereotypical Minnesotans: white blond hair, bright blue eyes, and translucent pale skin. Jessica had confessed to me that she had sexual longings for dark, hairy, Italian men, so I felt comfortable telling her I had the same feelings. Telling her was a spur-of-the-moment thing; I trusted her and never thought there would be any negative consequences. She thought my news was fascinating, and also terrific. Her support at that crucial time in my life was very important to me. I don't know why this positive experience with Jessica didn't translate into my being more open with my coworkers, but it didn't, and I left IBM with no one the wiser. At least, that was my perception. I found out about ten years later from a former colleague that my sexuality was not exactly a secret in the halls of IBM.

Outside the office, my personal life was going well. Eight months after my wife moved out, I met the love of my life. I never thought much about integrating my lover with my work life then. He was a part of my life that was separate from work. My career was progressing nicely. Why would I consider adding coming out at work to my agenda?

I managed to figure out that I was going to have to make some choices about coming out to friends and family, even if I could avoid it in the workplace. I did what I think a lot of us do: I procrastinated a bit, then slowly began to tell my closest friends. It wasn't always a positive experience, but it generally went well. No one seemed too surprised. There were a few people who told me they were okay with my being gay but then were clearly uncomfortable with any further references to it. After a while I realized that these friends weren't very important to me anyway and in time I drifted away from them.

My family was a different story. I wasn't ready to face coming out to them, so I didn't. I introduced my lover to my family. After we had lived in five different places over the next few years, I suppose they decided he was some kind of unusually faithful roommate, or they figured out the score. If they have, we don't talk about it. All that good WASP training about avoiding feelings and difficult topics keeps paying off.

After leaving IBM, I moved to a small but growing high-tech company. The company has prospered, and so have I. I'm a member of the senior management team, one of ten who manage a company of more than 2,000 employees. When I joined the company, I didn't really think that coming out was an issue I'd ever need to face. Why would I? I believed I had successfully managed my sexuality status at IBM; this didn't need to be different from that situation. It was also 1982 and a long way from where gay liberation has taken us today.

I established a pattern of behavior then that really isn't very different from how I operate today. I never deliberately misled anyone about my sexuality. I couldn't manage the intellectual dishonesty of making up stories of female dates. I wouldn't participate in typical male office discussions—"What a pair of maracas on her!" I wouldn't accept put-down humor about anyone. This was conscious strategic choice on my part that allowed me to handle antigay jokes or remarks in the same fashion that I dealt with anti-Polish or black or female comments or bigotry in general. I realized that in so doing I was aligning myself with other minorities—quite a revelation to this WASP male. I was changing, though probably only slightly faster than the world around me.

On the other hand, I was never completely open, and I often changed my pronouns from plural to singular. So it was "*I was* in Provincetown this weekend," not "*We were.*" Notice, I included "Provincetown," so I must have been at least somewhat willing to associate myself with the gay image of this resort, but I also knew that plenty of straight people managed to make it that far out on Cape Cod as well. I suppose there was some unconscious part of me that really wanted people to know.

During my first few years with the company, I concentrated so heavily on managing the company's growth and my own career that I don't recall having any issues with coming out at work. It was much more important to me to go from manager to director to vice president than to go from straight or unknown to gay. The atmosphere wasn't exactly conducive to coming out, either. It wasn't exactly hostile, but it certainly wasn't friendly. For example, an incident indicative of the company atmosphere involved a young engineer named "Jerry," who was gay and quite open about it. He frequently mentioned his "lover" and had a Chippendales calendar above his desk. It seems pretty tame now, but it seemed daring to me in those days. He never suffered consequences that we could point to—after all, he was in a highly individualistic profession, where what you produce is very visible and just about the only measure of success. However, in a senior management meeting, we were discussing the accommodations for an upcoming out-of-town planning meeting, and the company president said, "That's okay as long as you don't put 'Jerry' in my room." There was much laughter at this remark, and the meeting continued. I hope that "Jerry" never heard about this, but it certainly remained with me. If I had any thoughts about coming out, this incident pushed me firmly back in the closet. It clearly was a joking matter to be gay. I wasn't ready to take on the company's president on this issue.

As the company grew, I began to think more and more about being out at work. I felt some sort of obligation to make it somehow safe for others to be openly gay. After all, I was a vice president. These feelings, however, were balanced with my concerns about being effective in my job. If I were openly gay, I might have less influence with my peers and even with my direct reports. Although the company was not highly political, there are politics in all organizations. Being out certainly didn't seem to be an asset politically, and I felt it could be a great liability.

So I did nothing about it. In my first four years with the company, I had one employee tell me that he was gay and that he figured I was too. In this situation, it didn't require a lot of effort for me to come out to him. I never could figure out why this didn't happen more often. It was impossible for me to imagine that my sexuality wasn't somewhat obvious, at least to other gay people. I was aware that it might be more difficult for lower-ranked employees to come out to me in my position as a high-level manager. I didn't like the feeling that I might somehow be intimidating people into staying in the closet. Still, I wasn't ready to do anything overt about it until AIDS became a coming-out issue for me.

Seven years ago, I volunteered as a fund-raiser for an AIDS services organization. It was only a short step from there to leading the annual effort at my company to raise funds for the organization through a pledge walk. In a short time, I managed to get a lot of visibility for the fund-raising and incidentally found myself as something of a spokesman for AIDS at my company. It was a very empowering feeling because I was unconsciously using the epidemic as a metaphor for my being gay.

Two incidents occurred in short order that signaled just how right this activity was for me. One of the company's departments had decided to hold its own lunchtime barbecue, partially as a team-building exercise and partially just to have fun. I had been invited and was sitting at a picnic table talking with people as they passed. A member of the department whom I had never met came up somewhat tentatively and sat next to me. While everyone else at the table was engaged in some conversation, he quietly said to me, "You know, I really appreciate what you're doing to raise money for AIDS. It means a lot to us." I said something vapid like "Gee, it's important to me too," and that was that. He didn't sit there long, and nothing more was said. I've never had another conversation with him on this or any other topic, but I still think about that day.

The second incident was much more significant. One of my direct reports, an excellent manager I'll call Kent, was in my office for a meeting. We had scheduled an hour together, and we had a lot to discuss. As the hour was coming to an end, Kent said, "There's something else I'd like to talk about that no one here knows about." Kent told me that his younger brother, who lived in Florida, had AIDS and would soon be coming home to live with his parents. In effect, he was coming home to die. Without mentioning it directly, Kent made it clear that his brother was gay. It was clear to me that Kent didn't have anyone, other than his family, with whom he felt he could talk about this. It was obviously a big relief to be able to discuss it with someone at work and, I believe, especially with his manager. Over the next few months, Kent kept me updated on his brother's status and eventually told me of his death. I felt very privileged to become a part of Kent's life in a way that wouldn't have been open to me unless I had taken what was another step on the road to being out.

This experience always makes me think of the artificial barriers we establish for ourselves. Kent's barrier was his concern for what people would think about him having a brother with the "gay plague." Mine was the invisible shield—somewhat like those old Colgate toothpaste commercials—that I had erected to separate the parts of my life. I often wonder whether, if I had been completely out, I would have had an even greater impact on others.

Years passed without much change in my level of openness at work. I continued to promote AIDS fund-raising efforts visibly, and I spoke more often about my lover, Max, without stating what his relationship was. "Max and I were at the movies" or "Max is going to come by for lunch." It seemed impossible to me for anyone to have any doubts about my sexuality, but I could never be sure. A lot of people don't really pay a great deal of attention; and maybe what I considered to be such a major issue ("Oh, my God, did you know he was gay!") is likely to be a real yawner ("He is? Who cares.")

I found it very strange, however, that no one ever mentioned my sexuality to me in any way. Surely, some of my work friends would inquire about my personal life, or they'd give some hint that they knew I was gay and it was okay—but that never happened. Was I being too subtle?

Meanwhile, work life rolled on. At one point our company bulletin board announced the formation of a gay employees group to go along with the sixty or seventy other employee special-interest groups. Unlike the others, however, this was a "confidential" group, and contact was to be made through the personnel department. I interpreted that as a signal from the company that "If you're gay, we don't want to hear about it."

Then a seemingly small incident proved to be a turning point. I was on a business trip in Singapore with another of my direct reports—I'll call him Tim. We had finished our work for the day and had a few hours to kill before we caught a plane to our next stop, so we dropped in to a famous local bar. I suspect the distance from home and the exotic locale had some effect on me.

I was telling Tim a funny story that a lesbian friend had told me, and it enhanced the story to know that she was gay. It struck me as completely unfair to mention that my friend was a lesbian and not to mention that I too was gay, so I interrupted my story and said, "You know I'm gay, don't you?" This wasn't a terrific stretch, by the way. Tim and his wife had each met Max, though not socially, and Tim and I had known each other for fourteen years. So Tim answered, "Sure, and I'm glad you finally mentioned it to me." And that was that. I was out at work.

I asked Tim questions that I had been living with for years. "Do other people know I'm gay?" Yes, Tim thought probably everybody did. "Do the other people who report to me know I'm gay?" Tim thought so, though he had never discussed it with them. He told me that he had never mentioned my sexuality to anyone because he respected me and thought that it would seem disloyal somehow to talk about it. I did ask him why he'd never said anything to me, and his answer was very enlightening. He believed that since I never discussed it, I preferred not to. Tim said that he and his wife had discussed inviting Max and me to dinner on several occasions, but he hadn't been exactly sure how to go about it. I had obviously been sitting around thinking I was dropping such broad hints that anyone would feel comfortable discussing this with me, and Tim was clearly indicating he needed more permission before it was okay with him to talk about it with me.

I won't say that this conversation with Tim opened the floodgates, but it did create a change. It also gave me a comfortable way to broach the subject. Since that time, I've said "You know I'm gay, don't you?" to three other people at work. The answer has always been some variant of "Sure." It's interesting to me that all it takes, at this point, is just that simple question. I'm not exactly on a rampage, asking it of everyone, but I'm much more comfortable knowing that I can. And that the answer will likely be okay. I'm sure it's not okay with everyone, but I've learned that it isn't everyone I'm concerned about.

I used to feel that being out at work meant being all the way out, that everybody had to know and everybody had to acknowledge knowing. I want to be out enough that the people I like and respect know who I really am and how important Max is to me. I want them to know it's possible to be gay and a good businessperson.

The process isn't over, however. I think I've learned another truth for me. Coming out isn't an event; it is a process that doesn't appear to have an end. In spite of the fact that I like to finish things, I can live with that.

Without Apology
Eve Diana

*Eve Diana is a passionate writer-dreamer-fighter-
nerd-activist who is employed as a secretary at the
Massachusetts Institute of Technology (MIT).*

In the twenty years since I recognized that I'm bisexual, I've had plenty of practice coming out. The process has become *very* familiar, but it has never become easy. I resent the fact that the coming-out process never ends. I can come out to one individual at a time, to a roomful of people, or on national TV. It doesn't matter: with every new job or person in my life, it's back to square one. It's liberating, even exhilarating at times. I've generously provided my employers and coworkers with free education and consciousness-raising. I tell myself I'm helping to ensure a better life for queers everywhere—but no one's awarding me "tenure" for years of dedicated service. Coming out is an ongoing process, and there are always more doors to open and more thresholds to cross.

I define my bisexuality by who attracts me, romantically and sexually. It reflects my fantasies as well as my past, present, and future. It includes my community, my culture, and my politics. It's about potential, and most of all, it's about choices. I'm not a watered-down lesbian. I'm sure I've been bisexual all my life. Being involved with a man doesn't make me heterosexual, nor does it invalidate my feelings for women—and vice versa. I refer to myself as "queer" because I prefer a label that does not focus on my sexuality. I like that it has become an inclusive term to define anyone who is not heterosexual.

I've been a professional queer at various times in my career. I've considered myself fortunate that I could be part of the gay community on a professional as well as a personal level. When I was employed by gay organizations, however, I found that there was no easy way to tell my colleagues that I am bisexual. Each time I faced my worst fears: the specter of censure, animosity, and judgment. Those fears kept me closeted at one job and drove me to seek clearance from my supervisors to be out on the next. In later jobs I came out swinging with defiance. I no longer shove my queerness in people's faces, but I also no longer ask permission to be who I am. I am simply bisexual without apology.

Being bisexual colors me an odd shade of gray on the sexual-identity spectrum. Daytime talk shows love us, but I'm told we don't really exist. I've been accused of exploiting lesbians, of being promiscuous and untrustworthy and responsible for the spread of STDs. It's all bullshit, though, because I *do* exist, I exploit no one, I'm monogamous *and* a First-Class Girl Scout, and I practice safe sex.

My motives for coming out tend to be more personal than altruistic. Because my bisexuality is such a vital part of who I am, acceptance of that fact by the people in my life is very significant to me. I refuse to treat my orientation as though it were a dirty little secret. I refuse to have my identity reduced simply to whom I fuck. My coming-out makes bisexuals *real* by putting a human face on the issue and helps break down those barbed-wire barriers between "us" and "them."

Another compelling reason for coming out is that my best friend and partner is a man, so I do have the option of pretending I'm straight. I could easily keep my mouth shut and let coworkers assume I'm heterosexual. To allow that assumption to stand, however, would be deliberately dishonest. I am not heterosexual, and I have no desire to be presumed heterosexual. My silence would allow that lie to continue. If I don't speak up, I am invisible as a bisexual, and that invisibility is deadly to me. Why? On a personal level, being dishonest makes me physically and emotionally ill. I have worked for years to be proud of who I am, and being dishonest undermines my hard-won self-esteem. On a political level, if I don't speak up, every myth about bisexuals continues to be perpetuated.

So that's the "why" of my coming-out. Now the "how." At a straight job, I've learned to psych out the level of tolerance first. Coming out as bisexual at a gay job has been awkward and frightening for me because I have absolutely no instinct for sniffing out biphobia ahead of time.

In 1983 I accepted a full-time job as an administrative assistant at Senior Action in a Gay Environment (SAGE), which provides services for gay and lesbian senior citizens. I remember thinking that at last I had a job in which I could truly be myself and could put my energy into work I believed in. It seemed like I'd found heaven, or at least a home.

During interviews, no one at SAGE asked me if I was gay; they simply assumed that I was. During my first week on the job, my boss asked me, over lunch, how my family felt about my being a lesbian. I could have used this opening to tell him I am bisexual, but I didn't. I couldn't face any ambivalence or hostility over my bisexuality; I also didn't want to risk losing a job I already loved. I answered the question about my family truthfully, but without clarifying my orientation. At that point, I had decided that being closeted was preferable to the risks of coming out as bisexual.

I hadn't anticipated how fearful I would be of my colleagues' disapproval. Like many gay men and lesbians before me, I had internalized the idea that there was something shameful about me that I needed to hide. In the midst of the gay community, I came to believe that being bisexual was a flaw I had to conceal, a moral failing on my part.

Being closeted in a gay setting was far more painful for me than being closeted in the wider world. I had a job at which bigotry simply wasn't supposed to exist. SAGE's office was located in the Lesbian and Gay Community Services Center building in New York City, and daily I observed others experiencing the joy of being among their own. The tenants of the center were all nonprofit gay and lesbian organizations; while the employees and volunteers worked long, hard hours, there was an air of great freedom and celebration throughout. I was right in the middle of it, an outsider looking in. I felt like an outsider not because I was bisexual but because I felt I couldn't *reveal* that I was bisexual.

My deception continued for almost a year, the strain only increasing over time. After a particularly trying day at the office, I finally broke down in tears and told my boss the truth. After I calmed down, I asked if he was going to fire me. To my surprise, he said he already knew and was simply waiting for *me* to tell *him*. He gave me a teddy bear he'd been saving for my Christmas gift and told me to stop worrying and take the next day off to get some rest. The only time he brought up the subject again was during my exit interview, before I moved to Boston. He said he valued the integrity I'd shown by telling him the truth about my bisexuality despite my fears.

By hiding my bisexuality, I had treated it as a private disgrace. What I learned from the experience is that I have no stomach for secrets. I felt I was living a lie, with a constant fear of discovery and reprisals. I was burdened with the sheer mental bookkeeping it required. Keeping the secret put up barriers to intimacy and friendships and threw a shadow over my identity that made me feel dead inside, as though I truly did not exist.

My first full-time job after I arrived in Boston was as office manager for the Gay and Lesbian Counseling Service (GLCS). I resolved to handle the issue differently than I had at SAGE by being candid about my bisexuality from the start. Before I accepted their job offer, I came out to both the executive director and the director of services. Both said it was not a problem and agreed to leave it up to me whether to share this information with other employees. I felt comfortable that I was starting out on the correct foot, the honest one.

I tried to appraise the situation by casually asking a gay coworker's opinion of bisexuality without revealing that I was bisexual myself. After he made some unenlightened comments on the subject, including his belief that bisexuals don't really exist, I told him that I was one. He insisted that I was mistaken; *he* knew better. He eventually did take my word for it but was furious with me for trying to make him look foolish. I still think the best approach for challenging a stereotype is by presenting the facts, but I realize I shouldn't have made a game of it at his expense. I never attempted that technique again.

I did not have occasion to come out to any other staff members. The counseling service was having serious financial difficulties, and this made it a tense and anxious place to work. I gave notice after working there for only four months.

On my last day at GLCS, the woman who supervised the staff therapists asked if she could speak with me privately. We found an unoccupied office, and she closed the door. She immediately began to berate me with an intensity that stunned me. She had just learned that I was bisexual, and she was appalled that I had been so dishonest as to "deceive" people into thinking I was a lesbian. She criticized me for taking a job away from a "legitimate" gay person. She denounced my gestures of friendship toward her (which had been welcome when she thought I was a lesbian). She went so far as to condemn what she saw as my inappropriate behavior on the job, at staff meetings, and at the office holiday party. These last objections seemed gratuitous, but since my bisexuality had given her an opening to voice criticisms, she steamrolled on, growing louder and more vehement all the time.

Her words felt like a physical assault; I thought I might pass out from the force of them. I attempted to explain to her why I had chosen to handle the issue the way I had; I tried to convey my years of commitment to and work in the gay community. Her fury would not be appeased. I gave up trying to speak and took deep breaths through the rest of her tirade, feeling seared. I don't remember how I finally escaped the room or pulled myself together enough to get home. My self-esteem and dignity were blasted to shreds. I remember looking in the mirror and being surprised to see my face—not the monstrous person she'd described, just me.

It was my worst nightmare come to life. I thought I had assured safe passage for myself by coming out to my bosses right from the start, but of course their acceptance had no bearing on others' reaction to my bisexuality. The fear of precisely this kind of backlash was what had made me hesitate to come out to my other colleagues in the first place.

I tried to understand why she felt betrayed, which I somehow felt was my responsibility. We hadn't been friends, but we'd shared some enjoyable conversations and office banter, even swapped tattoo stories. It took me a long time to realize that I was being held to a different standard of behavior because I was bisexual. She'd made assumptions about who I was because I worked there and blamed me when she was wrong. It was her problem and her responsibility, not mine.

I was emotionally worn out from the entire GLCS experience, so I decided to look for a job with few demands or complications and found a position as a secretary in the chemistry department at MIT. The low-key work environment I found there was a welcome haven and, except for a few friends I made among coworkers, I took a hiatus from being out.

After three peaceful years on that job, I felt ready for a challenge and took a professional leap to become an administrative officer for MIT's literature section. I already knew the section had a radical political presence because one of the faculty had founded the women's studies program and another ran the gay and lesbian studies program. I made no announcements about my orientation, though my résumé clearly detailed my work experience at SAGE, which I freely discussed during my interviews.

As I got to know people, I slowly revealed my bisexuality as it felt safe enough and/or appropriate to do so. One faculty member didn't mince words: "I'm confused. You look like a lesbian, but you live with a man. What's the story?" He has my eternal gratitude for his candor and directness: it was completely without malice—he simply wanted to know. No one else in the section ever asked to my face, out of either politeness, apathy, respect for privacy, or fear of how I'd answer.

I decided to treat my bisexuality matter-of-factly. I wanted to experience the same sense of comfort and pride my coworkers did in wearing religious symbols and wedding rings, mentioning their spouses and children in conversation, and freely displaying family photos. I felt entitled to that same sense of freedom. I decorated *my* office with family photos, Mapplethorpe prints, ACT UP posters, cartoons, and buttons that expressed my political inclinations. My favorite poster pictured James Baldwin, Eleanor Roosevelt, Walt Whitman, Virginia Woolf, and others not generally known to be gay, and stated in large letters, UNFORTUNATELY, HISTORY HAS SET THE RECORD A LITTLE TOO STRAIGHT. I've learned that this method delivers my message in a quieter way than direct conversation because it lets the observer decide whether, when, and how to bring up the issue.

I was very excited in early 1992 when a queer employees group formed at MIT—and even more thrilled that the word "bisexual" was included from the outset. The name GABLES (Gay, Bisexual, and Lesbian Employees and Supporters) was chosen unanimously. I became an active member, delighted to find other queer allies at work. I didn't declare my bisexuality to the group, but I felt relatively safe that I could do so when I felt ready.

My coming-out at work got a huge shove in January 1993, when my partner and I were invited to be part of a televised panel on bisexuality on the *Donahue* show. The producer of the show wanted a monogamous couple in which one partner was heterosexual and the other bisexual, and we fit the bill. Phil provided his usual mix of ignorance and outrageousness, but the panel of guests was strong and articulate and refused to allow him to turn the show into a circus. Not surprisingly, the toughest concept for the audience to grasp was that a person could be bisexual and monogamous at the same time. It was a little jarring to see how deeply ingrained are people's ideas that bisexuality and homosexuality are about sex, rather than people. With good humor and charm, however, I think we managed to educate a few people. The feedback I received from coworkers who saw the show was wonderfully positive. People who'd previously been silent on the issue went out of their way to compliment me. I learned that the dean of my school and his entire staff watched the show in his office. Although he pretended to be working, he was caught watching several times. He mentioned to me that he'd seen the show but voiced no opinion on the content. I'm told he did express relief that I hadn't mentioned where I worked on national television. His reaction didn't surprise me, but I worried only briefly about the implications for my career. I'd gained far more by doing *Donahue* than I would ever get from my job.

I had my moment of truth when a GABLES member suggested I show the video of the *Donahue* show at a future meeting as part of a program on bisexuality. I began to panic, because I cared very much about how GABLES members would react to my coming out as bisexual to them. I consulted several trusted friends before I took the plunge. When I announced the program at the next meeting, I could barely look up, I was so paralyzed with terror. But when I did, I saw only friendly, interested faces. The program took place a month later and was well received. It didn't erase all my fears about a backlash, but it went a long way toward quieting them.

MIT's weekly newspaper often highlights accomplishments and items of interest about employees. Riding my wave of success, I encouraged the staff to do a short piece about our appearance on *Donahue* (my partner is also an MIT alumnus). I lent them a video of the show and wrote a stirring letter encouraging a write-up, citing MIT's policy of nondiscrimination and new domestic-partner benefits. I curbed all my sarcasm when I pointed out that the paper had done a front-page article (with photos) a year earlier when an employee won the Miss Massachusetts beauty pageant. I suggested a similar article and even offered to provide them a photo of us with Phil Donahue.

I had been warned of the conservatism of the editorial staff at the paper, but I optimistically hoped for fair coverage. Eventually the editor gave me a draft copy of the *very* brief article he had written. It was trite, uninspired, and so misleading that I barely recognized myself. I said I would get back to him about printing it and never did. I let the matter drop because I realized that coming out to the greater MIT community was no longer a priority for me and was certainly not worth having to do battle with the paper.

This experience helped me finally realize that I have choices in the matter. I'm never going to earn "coming-out tenure," but I am entitled to take a sabbatical when I feel like it. I don't have to come out to everyone I encounter, particularly if it doesn't feel safe or worth the effort. I've also learned that *how* I come out often affects how the information is received, so I present my bisexuality as great news and a source of pride and satisfaction.

After years of sweating my way through the process, I'm happy with the direction I've chosen. I realize that there will always be people—queer or otherwise—who feel threatened by me, but I refuse to apologize for challenging their cherished status quo by my visibility. I will not pretend that I secretly desire to be a lesbian rather than bisexual for the sake of someone else's comfort. I don't believe that my bisexuality fragments the gay and lesbian community or that there is a limited amount of equality and justice to go around. My definition of a queer community is one that supports our right to love anyone we choose, and I stand by that right, without apology.

Unfounded Fears
Pat Roche

SEATTLE MAN HEADS NATIONAL GAY GROUP
—*Headline,* Seattle Times, *September 2, 1989. At the
time of the* Seattle Times *headline, which was accompanied
by a lengthy article and a picture, Pat Roche worked at
the largest financial institution headquartered in the Pacific
Northwest. He wondered what impact his outing would
have on his twenty-year career in banking. Many of his
worst fears proved to be entirely unfounded.*

I was born the second of six children in an Irish Catholic family on
March 27, 1944. When I was born, God gave me two gifts: my Catholic
faith and my gay sexual orientation. I like to say that it was kind of like
getting a microwave oven and aluminum cookware. I tried a couple of
strategies to reconcile the two gifts—but sparks continued to fly. One strategy was to pursue my faith and suppress my sexual orientation. This led me
into a seminary in high school. As if that were not enough, I entered a
monastery after I graduated from college. I eventually abandoned these pursuits. I would have made a terrible monk because I didn't like any of the
monastic vows. I didn't like poverty or obedience; I wasn't good at being
silent, and I certainly didn't cherish chastity.

My next strategy was the reverse of the first. That is, I honored my sexual orientation and suppressed my faith. This was equally disastrous, because
I missed my religion. I continued to feel that there must be a way to be who
God made me and still practice my religion. I found a way out of my dilemma when I attended a Dignity mass at St. Joseph's Catholic Church in Seattle
in 1982. (Dignity is a nationwide ministry to gay, lesbian, bisexual, and trans-
gender Catholics.) I encountered many warm and caring people there who
had found a way to integrate their sexual orientation with their religious
faith. I immediately became active with the group. For the first time, I felt
truly whole.

Dignity's national convention was held in Seattle in 1983, and I was asked
to emcee the event. I agreed to do so, but only on the condition that I use
just my first name. I had a lot of fun during the weeklong convention, my first

real taste of gay pride. The experience also planted in me a longing to be who I am in settings other than Dignity, including with my family and at my workplace.

Over the next several years, I gradually shared the fact that I am gay with family and friends. I remained, however, extremely closeted and guarded in my workplace, a Seattle bank.

My first assignment at that bank was as a teller. The personnel director assured me that I would make a good teller. I asked: "Pray tell, what would make you think that?" He responded by saying that monks and bankers had one important virtue in common: honesty. In point of fact, I was no better at being a teller than I was at being a monk. I was friendly to the customers, but I was also forever out of balance.

Happily, the Peter Principle came to my aid. Following my unsuccessful career as a teller, my next job (incongruously) was writing a training text for bank tellers. As the saying goes, "those who can, do; those who can't, teach."

I eventually parlayed my three-volume teller training text into a full-fledged writing career at the bank. Over the next twenty years, I wrote policy and procedure manuals, annual reports, executive speeches, marketing brochures, and news releases. As improbable as it may seem, my monk-to-mogul career led me to the lofty position of vice president and manager of Washington State communications for the bank.

I loved my work. Over the course of my career, my job had exposed me to people in all areas of the company. I was on a first-name basis with all of the senior management and, as far as I knew, was the highest-ranking gay or lesbian among the bank's twelve thousand employees. I, however, had a philosophical debate with myself about the appropriateness of making my sexual orientation an issue at work. Fear of coming out was not the only reason I avoided telling my colleagues at work that I am gay; I also strongly felt that sexual orientation shouldn't play any role in hiring, pay, promotion, or any other aspect of my employment. By not coming out, I made sure it didn't. I wanted to be judged solely on my ability to do my job and on the quality of work I performed. My silence was, in effect, my way of protecting my equality.

The September 2, 1989 headline in the *Seattle Times* shattered the long silence. I had spent the better part of four decades going to any lengths to stay hidden in the closet, so I was as surprised as anyone to see the story. I could hardly believe that after all these years of secrecy I had, for all intents and purposes, publicly outed myself in my hometown newspaper.

I was very concerned when I noted that the article referred to me as a "financial institution official." Even though I was prepared to be a media spokesperson for Dignity, I did not want to mix my volunteer work for Dignity with my real job. I didn't feel that this was fair to my company. I felt especially strongly about this as I had, on occasion, been in the media as a company spokesperson.

My decision to run for Dignity president was, in fact, made only after a great deal of agonized consideration about all kinds of job-related issues. Throughout the year before I decided to run, I was frequently paralyzed with fear and worry. What impact would coming out after all these years have on my future assignments? How would my colleagues, for whom I had a great deal of respect and admiration, relate to me after they found out I was gay? I even consulted a lawyer friend to make sure that if worse came to worst I would be covered by the Seattle ordinance prohibiting discrimination on the basis of sexual orientation. (I wanted to make sure that even though I lived outside the city limits, the law was based on where you *work* rather than on where you *live*. I discovered that it is based on where you *work*.)

It was, therefore, with a great deal of trepidation that I headed to my office on the first workday after the story appeared in the *Seattle Times*. It was Tuesday morning after the three-day Labor Day weekend—a laboriously anxious weekend for me.

I walked into the lobby of the bank's downtown high-rise headquarters and stepped onto a crowded elevator. Just as the door shut, someone said, "Hi, Pat. Saw your picture in the paper." I thought to myself, *People aren't supposed to talk in elevators*. But to my chagrin, the conversation continued when someone else asked, "Why was his picture in the paper?" The original informer said, "He's going to be president of this national organization." A third party then asked, "What kind of an organization?" The gossip said, "A gay organization."

There was then an incredibly long silence until someone finally said, "Oh." At that moment, the elevator arrived at my floor, and I got off. As I stood there dazed, I could hear the elevator slowly close on the startled group behind me. To this day, I would pay almost anything to hear what—if anything—was said for the remainder of their ride.

Having survived this initial reaction to my news, I walked into the area where my office was located. Although I fully expected acceptance from the employees in my own department, as some of them knew in advance of my plans and all of us were friends, I was truly unprepared for what I encountered when I walked through the door. All of my colleagues were gathered in the conference room around a cake with "Congratulations, Pat" on it.

The cake was but the first of many pleasant surprises following my coming-out in the workplace. Several months later, I was nominated by a coworker for a companywide community involvement award for my work with Dignity. Employees from around the company who did volunteer work in their communities were eligible for these awards, which included travel to company headquarters to receive a plaque at a luncheon with the chief executive officer and a day off with pay.

I was all but certain that the fact that Dignity was a gay and lesbian organization—whereas all of the other nominees worked with the Red Cross, Girl Scouts, Cancer Society, or other "mainstream" organizations—would prevent me from receiving an award. Wrong again. Much to my surprise, I was notified that the selection committee had chosen me for an award, that "my work with Dignity was truly exceptional," and that the company was "very proud" to have me as an employee.

Another important result of my coming-out occurred the following year when I successfully urged the bank to officially include sexual orientation as a part of their equal employment opportunity (EEO) policy. I was able to provide the bank's human resources group with information on how other large companies were handling sexual-orientation issues after contacting the National Gay and Lesbian Task Force and the Human Rights Campaign Fund. Shortly thereafter, the company amended its EEO policy to include sexual orientation.

Yet another highlight was being asked by the Seattle chamber of commerce to help conduct a workshop on sexual-orientation issues in the workplace for up-and-coming business executives and community leaders in Seattle. Even my fear about future assignments turned out to be unwarranted. In the middle of my two-year term as president of Dignity, I was promoted to be in charge of corporate communications, not only for the state of Washington but for the entire five-state region the company served.

There were only a couple of negative things that happened after I came out. They occurred in the month immediately following my coming-out. The first instance involved my attendance at a management forum the company held on the first Monday of every month, attended by about fifty managers from around the state. I was responsible for coordinating the meeting, setting the agenda, and recommending speakers, among other related duties. Because Labor Day was the first Monday in September and a bank holiday, the meeting was held on the second Monday, just a few workdays after my election. I remember walking into the meeting with a great deal of apprehension. This would be the first time I encountered many of the managers since the article in the *Seattle Times* appeared. I don't know whether I expected contempt or congratulations. I wasn't prepared, however, for what met me: complete and utter silence. Not one of the managers even mentioned seeing the article or hearing about the election. I knew that many of them were aware of it, and I found their silence both awkward and annoying.

I later heard from a colleague that at least one of the managers thought the whole thing was "stupid." He later elaborated by saying that his employees were concerned about sharing a company bathroom with me. When asked why, he explained that it was obvious that I had AIDS, since I had lost twenty pounds in recent months. (In point of fact, the weight loss was the result of strenuous workouts at the gym.)

Notwithstanding these two minor incidents, my overall experience of being out at work has convinced me that the only way gays and lesbians can make progress is to be a visible presence in the workplace. Even one person can make a significant difference. My years of fear and worry turned out to be totally unfounded. Polls have repeatedly shown that if people know someone who is gay, their tolerance level increases. If gays and lesbians want conditions on the job to change and personnel policies and practices to be nondiscriminatory, we have to make our presence known.

I also believe today that my failure to come out earlier in my career led to some important personal losses. It unnecessarily separated me from my supervisors, my colleagues, and my employees. My narrow-minded insistence on separating work and private life made me a virtual stranger. A number of specific instances come to mind.

My partner and I met on July 20, 1975; we celebrated our twentieth anniversary together this year. Meeting him was the most important thing that has ever happened in my life. Yet because of my secrecy at work, I didn't share my joy at the time or subsequent anniversaries with anyone at the office. Furthermore, before I finally came out at work, I didn't share with them many of the other day-to-day joys and sorrows we experienced as a couple for the years we were together. I feared that my colleagues would view this as "flaunting" my sexual orientation. I somehow downplayed in my mind the fact that my heterosexual counterparts had pictures of their spouses on their desks and invited their coworkers to their showers and weddings. By refusing to let others know about my own loving relationship, I am convinced that I needlessly deprived myself of valuable human connections that could have been forged at the office with people I truly cared about and who, I now know, truly cared—and still care—about me.

Throughout my career, I was also particularly cautious when filling out personnel forms because, as communications manager, I worked on a close professional basis with the managers in the human resources group. Out of a false fear that they would be reading my personnel file, I always listed a brother or sister as "next of kin," "beneficiary," or "person to notify in case of an emergency" instead of my partner. I told myself at the time that it didn't matter. I now believe that it *did* matter. It mattered a lot. By denying our relationship in this way, I feel that I was at some level saying even to myself that our bond was somehow not as important as the loving relationships my heterosexual coworkers had.

I think it is important to emphasize that the good things that have happened to me since I came out on my job are my own unique experiences. I am not naive. There are no doubt many workplaces where it is not safe to come out in the way I did. I respect whatever individual decisions my friends make in this regard. I do know, however, that my own reading of the climate at the bank regarding gay and lesbian issues was way off-base. I very much regret the price I paid for being closeted. I am sorry that I didn't trust in the basic goodness, common sense, and understanding of those around me.

Finally, I hope in the years ahead that countless others will have the positive experiences with coming out on the job that I have enjoyed. I hope that they can be who they are in all aspects of their life and share the gift of their gayness with their coworkers as well as with their families and friends.

The Truth at Work
Grietje Wijbenga

Grietje Wijbenga is a staff scientist with a Ph.D. in physical chemistry employed by a large pharmaceutical company. She immigrated to this country in 1982 from Amsterdam and currently lives in West Orange, N.J., with her partner of eight years. Wijbenga's willingness to take risks at work has led to significant change in the company's attitudes and policies regarding gay, lesbian, and bisexual employees.

To me, coming out means doing what it takes to feel fully integrated into society, confronting my own fears (including homophobia) as honestly as I can, making decisions that will ultimately make me feel safer, and respecting other people's family structures as much as my own. Coming out also means feeling that I can reach my potential, raise children, and be a valued member of society, not a victim. As a gay person I deserve love, happiness, and prosperity, just as others do.

My emphasis on integration influences both my personal and my professional lives. On the personal side, for example, when my partner and I moved to New Jersey four years ago, we hired a gay realtor and a gay attorney to help us find a safe area to live in and buy a house as a gay couple. We are not out to our neighbors—perhaps because we don't spend a lot of time with them, even though we are friendly and helpful, as they are. We live in a mixed suburban neighborhood with Italian, Jewish, African-American, and Asian-American neighbors. We participate in the neighborhood crime-watch system and, like everyone else, take good care of our lawns and our animals.

In my personal life, I am almost fully out. My parents and sister know of my sexual orientation and are as supportive as they can be. All my American friends know that I am a lesbian; I feel more and more that it becomes too cumbersome over the long run to maintain a friendship if you are hiding a large secret. Because I have lived in the United States for the past twelve years, my most recent friendships are with Americans. Because I immigrated from Europe at the time my coming-out process started, some of my older friends don't know that I am gay.

My activism has mostly focused on the work environment—somewhat logically, because that is where I spend a large amount of my waking hours.

In the winter of 1989, I started working for a midsize chemical-pharmaceutical company in New Jersey. I am a staff scientist with a Ph.D. in physical chemistry. Currently I am a member of an Advanced Technology Group with the mission of being "a business-focused technology center." While about five hundred people work at my site, the entire company is the offspring of a larger German company with about two hundred thousand employees. I am a member of two new product development high-performance teams.

While I have had successes with gay activism in the workplace and plenty of positive interactions, I would still have to say that my work environment is generally hostile toward gay people. Homophobia is heavily ingrained at the institutional level. While I have several friends and colleagues at work who are supportive of me and know my family structure, there are currently no formal company policies protecting gay and lesbian rights at my company. I have actively worked over the past four years to change this situation.

My efforts began in the fall of 1991 when I joined a Gestalt psychology training group to learn more about myself and my effectiveness in the organizational development efforts I am a part of at work. I learned from organizational development professionals, who were participants in this three-year Gestalt training program, that AT&T has had a nondiscrimination policy with respect to sexual orientation since 1975. I remember asking an AT&T employee, "You have a *what?*" and her answer was, "We have a nondiscrimination policy that prohibits discrimination based on sexual orientation. We also have an employee resource group called LEAGUE."

Since the summer of 1992, I have been in continual dialogue with activists and members of AT&T's LEAGUE (Lesbian, Bisexual, and Gay United Employees of AT&T). I have admired their courage and strength and appreciated their ongoing support. With the support of a professional organization in another company and the arrival of an antidiscrimination law in New Jersey in January 1992, I felt strong enough to come out at work to some people who mattered most to me. I started with my boss, my colleague Jenny, and a manager I'll call "John."

First I found the courage to tell my boss. For weeks before taking the big step, I remember being on an emotional roller coaster. My rationale for my daring behavior (which at the time felt like stupidity) was that my boss, who is a kind and sensitive person, had never said anything unsupportive to me. When I walked into his office with my knees shaking, he was on the phone making arrangements for his twenty-fifth wedding anniversary. I simply said, "Congratulations on your wedding anniversary. Being in a relationship for such a long time is clearly an accomplishment in this day and age. I'd like to tell you something I've been afraid to tell you for a long time. I am gay, and I have been in a relationship for about six years."

He answered with honesty, "I have wondered about your relationships; this explains it. You don't hear a lot about it around here. I personally do not believe in jokes." This comment made me think that I had been right to trust my boss. Since that time I have never felt that my boss liked me less because I am gay. He even said that he saw my confiding in him as a sign of personal growth. In my later attempts to change my company's policies regarding gay rights—by writing letters to senior management, for example—I have always felt I had his support.

As for my colleague Jenny, I decided to wait until I had told my boss. I walked into Jenny's office and asked if I could talk to her. I said, "You probably already know this, but I am gay, and of course you know my partner because you have met her several times." Jenny responded like an angel. She said she had other friends who are gay and that she had known for a long time because I did not try to hide my relationship with my partner. She also told me that she had asked a gay friend for advice on how to make me feel more comfortable. When I reflect on the conversation we had, I feel warm and safe and blessed that I personally happened to luck out with Jenny. I work with a good friend, and I didn't even know it until I had enough courage to be vulnerable.

My interaction with my manager, John, went somewhat differently. I spoke with him about my decision to bring up gay issues during the company's "equality forum" with the hope of implementing changes in our business conduct policy (BCP). John believed, however, that I should not use the issue of being gay in the equality forum because, in his opinion, being gay is nothing special and because he thinks that I am too aggressive and negative. I don't feel I am too negative. Gay people are still being murdered as a result of homophobic hatred, just as African-Americans and Asian-Americans are still being murdered because of racial hatred. Despite our differences of opinion, I respect John as a sensible and disciplined person. I have simply learned that I am not going to get his support on this issue. Another one of my managers also told me that although a change in the BCP was needed, it would be hard to change the ingrained culture of a chemical company.

In spite of this feedback, I decided to forge ahead, and in October 1992 I became a member of the equality forum at the suggestion of our human resources manager. For the first two months, I did not come out to anyone in the forum. In January 1993, however, I decided to have a talk with George, chairperson of the equality forum. George is not the average confrontation-avoiding, straight, white male in our division. He is, in fact, African-American and sensitive to civil-rights issues and concerns. I told him that I am gay and that being gay creates issues for me in the workplace that have traditionally not been addressed by the organization. George responded that he would like to see dialogue occur among the forum members and that maybe we could get a representative from AT&T to talk to us about gay issues in their workplace. Although George admitted that the issue of sexual orientation had come up a few years ago, he added that nothing had been discussed at that time.

In February 1993, the members of the equality forum decided as a group to become educated about gay and lesbian issues in the workplace. We asked Peter, a representative from AT&T's LEAGUE, to come talk to us. The visit took place that spring and proved to be an overwhelming success. Group members had a dialogue with Peter for about an hour, then we watched the videotape *Gay Issues in the Workplace* by Brian McNaught. Peter and I had previously agreed that both of us would come out to the forum members, but I was feeling pretty scared because there were fifteen people in the room. Fortunately, Peter acknowledged my fear and courage by describing to the audience how he himself had felt many years ago at AT&T. After my own presentation, I told the members of the equality forum that I had received a gift from all of them: the gift of acknowledgment and compassion.

In spite of the success of the equality forum, dialogue with the chief executive officer of my corporation regarding sexual orientation did not begin until our first equality/diversity conference, which was held in June 1993. I came ready to raise the issue. I also came willing to lose my job—not actively looking to lose my job, but willing to. I was fully aware of what could happen and felt full-blown fear.

My chance came when the CEO asked the audience if there were any questions. From experience I know that when dialogue is needed about sensitive or controversial issues, questions generally don't work. Questions avoid meaningful interaction. So I said, "Actually, this is not a question; I'd like to have a dialogue with you about a specific issue. Our company does not have a policy prohibiting discrimination based on marital status or sexual orientation. I would like you to explain the company's resistance to this issue." He explained that the company believed it was inappropriate to have sexual orientation spelled out in the BCP. "However," he added, "the absence of any specific mention of sexual orientation in the BCP should in no way be interpreted as creating tolerance for sexual-orientation discrimination."

I did not allow his statement to put an end to the conversation. I insisted, saying, "I am here to tell you that discrimination based on sexual orientation does exist in this company. I am a lesbian employee of this company, and I feel exactly like the woman in the videotape *A Winning Balance* that we just saw. I feel rejected and isolated.

"Let me tell you about some of the things that have happened to me at work. A few months ago I heard a rumor, initiated by someone at the management level, that I should not be going to a training course in North Carolina because I might want to talk about my gay lover. I felt absolutely devastated when I heard this rumor. Fortunately, my boss was very supportive, and I did go to the training. Some time ago I was in the cafeteria and heard one person say to another, 'You are not gay, are you? Yuck!' I stood up from the table because I lost my appetite. These types of comments and harassment take a toll on me as a gay person. I am interested in hearing your response."

Everything I said or did was part of me. When I said "Yuck," I felt a pull in my stomach. I was talking about the reality of being a lesbian in a company where homophobia and heterosexism have never been openly discussed and where many people continue to believe in myths and seriously outdated information. At times it felt that the risk I was taking was a leap rather than a small step. There were more than one hundred people in the room, and I can remember where each person was sitting. I felt hot. At one point I thought I was going to take off like a rocket. I still gave myself permission to communicate my nightmare. The CEO responded, "I have no objections to changing things." I stood up again to ask, "How are we going to go about changing the situation and when?" The CEO realized that I was pushing.

I received a somewhat confusing response: "Please sit down and give me a chance to answer this. I do not believe in jokes; they are inappropriate in the workplace. But sometimes the sexual behavior that you are referring to is not tolerated by some because of a religious belief. I believe there should be trust and feedback from management without it being threatening. One of my issues is how to deal with complaints, and I believe the equality groups are not for that purpose. I also don't believe that this company has to be socially correct. 'Coming out' is clearly not for everyone, and I don't think that you always have to do it, only when you are comfortable. I believe that we need to work together productively and that business is the bottom line."

Since that exchange with the CEO, I have continued to communicate extensively with the top management of the corporation, with the objective of educating them about gay and lesbian rights. I have received generous support from activists at other companies and organizations, including AT&T, Digital Equipment Corp., Nabisco, DuPont, and Rutgers University.

I've let senior management know in a letter that within the state of New Jersey and in several other states and municipalities, it is against the law to discriminate against employees because of sexual orientation. Companies can be held liable for the misguided actions of their employees if they have not taken reasonable steps to preclude such discrimination. I have also pointed out that if they fear backlash for the simple act of explicitly prohibiting discrimination and harassment of gay and lesbian employees, then that alone is an indication of a hostile environment that can adversely affect the productivity of these employees, to the detriment of the company. Experience has shown that backlash is usually brief and, if the company holds firm in its commitment to true equality of opportunity, quickly dissipates. I know from numerous personal interviews that many companies, including DuPont and Digital Equipment Corp., have recognized that a work environment in which all employees are treated with dignity and respect is a more productive environment. Yet fair and equal treatment of all employees rarely happens without clear and consistent guidance from corporate management. That is why AT&T added sexual orientation to its nondiscrimination clause almost twenty years ago, and that is why many other companies and institutions have added this clause since then.

In August 1993, I wrote a letter on this issue to our CEO and the vice presidents of corporate general counsel and human resources in which I expressed my concern about the continuing exclusion of sexual orientation and marital status from company policy. In my letter I thanked management for agreeing to consider adding marital status and sexual orientation to our corporate nondiscrimination policy.

I remember vividly the conversations I had with my friends about the content of this letter as I was writing it. I told them how angry I felt about the negative and appeasing attitudes of my managers and how sometimes my anger and fear about bringing up the gay issue again and again played tricks with my sanity. I am learning more and more, as time goes on and my story develops, that anger is a wonderful fuel for creativity and that self-expression lets me live with my anger and not be eaten alive by it.

On September 17, 1993, I received this phone message from the vice president of corporate general counsel: "I am calling to give you a progress report. We are planning to amend the business conduct policy booklet the next time it is circulated to make it clear that we will comply with all federal, state, and local laws that forbid discrimination based on sexual orientation. We are also going to make it clear that it is our goal, as part of our diversity effort, to make sure that we have a working environment that is free of harassment for all employees."

I remember that I was in the library when I received the message on my voice mail. I was actually glad that I was not there in person to answer the call, because I would not have known what to say. The protection policy is something I very badly wanted and needed. I even recorded the message on my tape recorder, because I could not believe it was true. My respect for the vice president of corporate general counsel has grown quite a bit since then.

I feel that the change in the nondiscrimination policy is going to help us reduce homophobia, but it will be an ongoing and very slow process. On a personal level I believe I have made solid connections and that many of my heterosexual friends within the company have been caring and consistent with their support. Negativity, roadblocks, and harassment have come almost entirely from middle- and higher-level management. This certainly does not make my company an employer of choice. The collective belief system of the corporate structure that surrounds me is still extremely homophobic. Extensive education will be needed to remedy this situation.

In October 1993, an officer in my company with direct access to the CEO said to me, "You have done a most outstanding job communicating the civil rights of gay and lesbian people within this corporation. I have chosen to let only a few friends know about my sexual orientation. I absolutely do not want the CEO to know. Because of my visibility I fear for my job, regardless of what the business conduct policy says. You are fortunate to be in a different position; you are a scientist."

I had previously commented to this individual about my own fear for my job as well as for future opportunities in my career. I had added that I had the strong feeling that the company would like to get rid of me because I stir things up. To my surprise he answered, "Don't ever think that they will get rid of you. You will be the last one to go. Tony [the VP of my division] will first get rid of the Advanced Technology Group, then walk out the door with you and ask you to turn off the lights. Our CEO will go directly to prison if they fire you. I highly encourage you to stay."

For me personally, this has been a challenging journey, and it continues to be. The biggest challenge clearly was to stand up in front of a group of a hundred people, including the CEO of our corporation, and come out. It was a very scary and emotionally draining and at the same time a very rewarding experience. I am determined to do it again. I am aware that timing, the level of potential hostility in the audience, the size of the audience, and available support afterward are all factors that need to be taken into account when planning educational efforts on gay and lesbian issues.

A Dyke's-Eye View of Corporate Law
Sandra E. Lundy

*Sandra ("Sandy") Lundy is a Boston-based lawyer, writer, and
lesbian activist who has worked extensively with gay, lesbian,
and straight victims of domestic violence. In her story, she
examines the often crazy-making tensions—and sometimes
surprising advantages—of being an out lesbian in the
highly conservative and intolerant atmosphere of big-firm
corporate law. She also talks about exploiting her privileged
position and its material advantages to subvert the most
cherished values of her employers. Since writing this essay,
she has established her own practice, concentrating in
litigation, business law, and advocacy for victims of violence.*

I am a lesbian, a feminist, and an attorney in a large corporate law firm
in Boston. I mainly work for artificial entities such as corporations, limited partnerships, and joint ventures that are run by rich white men.
My job is to help these corporate clients obtain the best possible result
in their disputes and negotiations with other organizations, individuals, or
the government. I work in a world that ignores the larger questions of morality and politics and that has very little respect for difference. In the three corporate law firms I've worked in since entering law school, I have been out as
a lesbian.

Let me say something about my choice of workplaces. I graduated from law
school at the age of thirty-six, after many years of teaching college English and
of active involvement in the women's and lesbian rights movements. I chose
to enter a corporate law firm primarily because I needed money, but also
because I thought "big-firm" practice would give me great training in the handling of complex, intellectually challenging work. Still, I had serious reservations about whether my choice meant that I was selling out and entering the
thickets of moral relativism—law's worst occupational hazard.

So I set some boundaries for myself. One resolve I made was that I would
find a way to do good progressive work. I targeted law firms that had some
demonstrated commitment to public-interest (pro bono) work within the

structure. I was very fortunate because I graduated from a "name" law school at a time when jobs were plentiful, so I had a choice of several good firms that seemed, at least on the outside, to fit the bill.

Most importantly, I decided that I would never be in the closet as a lawyer. It had taken me twenty-seven years of feeling uncomfortable in my own skin (including four years as a wife) for me to understand the fundamental fact that I'm a dyke. I came out publicly very shortly after I came out to myself, because I found the thought of being in the closet for the sake of peaceful coexistence with homophobes to be both morally and politically unacceptable. I'd lost some friends, I'd had a rough time with my family, and one of my erstwhile academic mentors had told me I'd never get a job (and he wouldn't help me get one) unless I went back into the closet. But I never doubted my decision always to be out.

No job, no matter how lucrative or interesting, was worth the compromise of the closet. I came out in my résumé because I knew that any firm that would reject me for being a lesbian was a place I didn't need to be.

So, what's it been like being a dyke in the belly of the beast? Actually, it has been a very mixed bag. On the positive side, I think that being out as a lesbian has, albeit indirectly, helped me to be a good lawyer. As a lesbian, I feel right at home in the adversary mode of the American legal system. In this world, you simply don't get to be a lesbian without the strength to push back against formidable opposing forces.

This lesbian will/power has helped me be a strong advocate. To a greater extent than many straight female colleagues I know, I don't shrink from confrontation or automatically equate being forceful with being "unwomanly" or "undignified." Because I have a very low tolerance for being condescended to or bullied, I can generally hold my own against those ever-present obnoxious male attorneys who try to gain some tactical advantage by playing the gender card. In one deposition I took, for instance, a male attorney and his male client kept referring to me by made-up nicknames and deliberately mispronouncing my name—games they never played with the male attorney with whom I was working. The antics stopped when I prepared to move for court sanctions against both of them. I'm not suggesting that a straight female attorney wouldn't have done the same thing. Based on conversations with female lawyers both gay and straight, however, I think it's easier for out lesbians to assert ourselves in these kinds of situations without second-guessing ourselves or feeling guilty. I think this is because we fight back against the norm that says we should always defer to men.

Another plus of being an out lesbian lawyer is that it frees me to be more creative. Lesbians question authority. We're bold, irreverent. We know that very few boundaries are indelibly fixed. We have learned to continually make and remake ourselves, taking bits and pieces from the culture and combining them in startling new ways. My innovativeness as a lawyer has much to do, I think, with the creativity that is the essence of lesbian identity.

Yet what good is it to have these nice lesbian/litigation skills and use them in the service of masculinist enterprises and the rich white men who run them? This is not a question that I've avoided. I see the lesbian part of myself as the part that passionately opposes the norms of patriarchal culture, particularly as these norms pertain to identity stereotypes (gender, class, race, and so on). While being a lesbian, so defined, may make some of the technical aspects of my job easier, it also intensifies my alienation from my work. Sometimes it takes a superhuman effort for me to engage myself in the details of trading bull-sperm futures or the manufacture of microchip packets. To in any way help the powerful become more powerful and the capitalist more capitalist is for me, as a lesbian and a feminist, deeply troubling. Yet the more I see and understand how power works, the more I am convinced that it's important for progressive lesbians and gay men to insert ourselves into the center of it.

One of the ways I try to address the dilemma of working for "the Man" is to exploit the status of my position to do good progressive work. Since graduating from law school six years ago, I've maintained an active pro bono practice, mainly in the areas of domestic violence (heterosexual and lesbian/gay/bisexual) and political asylum. I have also worked with the Lambda Legal Defense and Education Fund and the National Center for Lesbian Rights on a major gay and lesbian rights case. I am currently representing a battered lesbian imprisoned for killing her abusive partner. I work with the Boston lesbian and gay community, the Boston Police Department, and several district attorneys' offices to improve services for victims of same-sex domestic violence. These pro bono activities are a central part of my legal practice.

For all of these positives of my position, however, there are also many negatives. My experience is that success within the corporate legal world is very much predicated on my ability to fit in. In Anglo corporate legal culture, the more one behaves like a straight white male from the privileged class, the more one fits in—and this goes for white women, for people of color, for people from working-class backgrounds, and for lesbians. Now to behave like the quintessential white male means this: to accept and obey hierarchy, bowing to the power of those above you and flexing your muscles toward those below you; it means to be married and to focus the bulk of your social conversation on your spouse, your kids, and your other possessions; it means an overemphasis on aggression and rationality and a near obliviousness, while one is in the office, to social, emotional, moral, or spiritual issues. It means an impressive tolerance for alienating work; and it means a wariness and competitiveness in one's relations to others.

As a woman and a lesbian I am disadvantaged in this environment. On the one hand I am supposed to act, dress, speak, and perform my job in ways that do not threaten my male colleagues' traditional notions of who a woman should be. Yet women who behave "like women" are often criticized for not being as competent as the men. I see this most clearly in corporate discourse about aggressiveness. For instance, a partner once told me I wasn't aggressive enough before a certain judge, even though I won the motion. That same partner told me that I was too aggressive (toward him!) when I asked him if I could have more contact with a particular client. Other women attorneys I know receive similarly mixed messages. *Aggressive* is simply a code word to tell women that we are inappropriate in the corporate setting, that we do not fit in.

As an open lesbian, I am both well and poorly positioned within this "jock-ocracy." On the one hand, my male colleagues do not expect me to "fem up" to them, to flirt with them and act girlish, as they tacitly demand of straight women. As a result, it's somewhat easier for me to have my work taken seriously; I am not burdened by the presumption of ditziness.

On the other hand, I am correspondingly more threatening to the men—or at least to the ones who are most insecure about themselves. These men express their disapproval in many ways. They may give me unchallenging tasks to do, such as ordering lunch for a meeting; they may give me the silent treatment, withholding any positive feedback even when I do really good work, while praising male associates for the most trivial accomplishments. In other words, being an out lesbian doesn't make me immune to the double standard—I just get hit with it from a different angle.

Another area where things get really difficult is the social isolation. People *never* ask me about my personal life, not even the all-purpose "Got any plans this weekend?" One afternoon, for instance, a male partner invited a few associates, including me, to a lunch to welcome a new associate to the firm. Somewhere about dessert time, the partner asked each person at the table what they were planning to do for vacation—each person, that is, except me. When I brought up a vacation my partner and I were planning, no one at the table followed up on anything I said or showed interest in it, as they had done with one another. I felt like a social pariah—and I was!

I often find that when I mention anything at work about my social life to many of my straight colleagues (though by no means all of them), the conversation dries up pretty quickly. While most of my coworkers seem almost driven to know as much as they can about a heterosexual colleague's spouse or partner, they seem to want to know as little as possible about my same-sex social life. And I'm not alone. A lesbian lawyer friend of mine tried to tell a male partner in her firm that she wasn't feeling well because she and her partner of many years were breaking up. The partner harshly told her that he didn't want to hear about her personal problems. I can't imagine him giving the same response to a straight person.

In other words, many people I have worked with, who talk endlessly about their spouses or their dates or their kids, simply cannot bring themselves to acknowledge that my life has a social dimension. Like so many of my relatives, they can accept my lesbianism as long as I don't talk about it—which means that they can't accept it at all. The result is that I often feel isolated and alienated in the workplace, excluded from the casual social talk through which coworkers build personal relationships and partners and associates find common ground.

A corollary to my invisibility as a lesbian is my apparent interchangeability with other lesbians. In one firm I worked at, for example, I was the only out lesbian for several years. Then along came "Janet," another out lesbian who was about fifteen years younger than I, shorter, slimmer, and not a glasses-wearer (which I am). Shortly after her arrival, people (mostly men) with whom I had worked closely for years started calling me "Janet" and calling Janet "Sandy." Then along came "Mary," another out lesbian who looked nothing like either Janet or me. Once again, several attorneys (mostly men) called Mary either "Sandy" or "Janet," called Janet "Mary" or Sandy." One of the low points of my life at the firm is when I was called "Janet" and "Mary" in the same day. It's as if our lesbianism was a generic category that completely wiped out our individuality and made us all similarly invisible.

Again, I've tried to cope with this situation in the only way I know how, which is to keep being out. When I was in a "married" couple, I kept a picture of me and my partner on my desk. I took my lover to firm functions and made sure to mention her in my small talk. I make sure to mention my gay bar association activities to colleagues. I actively recruit lesbian and gay law students, and I have taken on many gay-related legal projects. I am determined not to let other lawyers neutralize me by erasing my lesbianism, however uncomfortable I make both of us by speaking out. This determination does require extra effort, however, and it can be draining, like talking to someone in a coma.

And professionally dangerous. Recently, I received some media attention for one of my gay-related cases. The publicity freaked out some men at the top of my firm. They became overtly hostile—without, of course, uttering a single direct word of hostility. Suddenly, I was given a slew of "back-room" assignments and found myself excluded from client meetings and courtroom opportunities. All of my corporate legal work was relentlessly scrutinized for mistakes. This corporate chill has happened to other lesbians and gay men I know who have become publicly identified with gay causes. The homophobic worry, I think, is that clients might associate the firm with fags and dykes and, in a whirlwind of rage, take their business elsewhere. Many people I work with are extremely supportive of what I do. The more widely public I am as a lesbian, however, and the closer I get to partnership consideration, the more I'm likely to run up against knee-jerk institutional homophobia.

I've been discussing how lesbianism has affected my lawyering. How has lawyering affected my lesbian identity? Thank Goddess, it hasn't affected my lesbian practices! My experience in law has led me to question certain political assumptions that previously I had associated strongly with my lesbian identity. Most of these assumptions have to do with power, actual and perceived. Before I became a lawyer, for example, I actually did believe in the power of good intentions and hard work to bring about global social change. Now I don't. Maybe I've absorbed the lawyer's ingrained cynicism about motive, but I can no longer envision a world in which one group doesn't try to exercise coercive power over other groups. I've grown to believe that change, when it happens at all, is slow and incremental and in perpetual danger of being erased or creating its own demons. My old political optimism has been displaced by what I'll call a skeptical feminist pragmatism.

I have also come to see that it's possible to work outside specifically lesbian-identified or progressive-identified organizations and still do good lesbian, feminist work in the world. I think that too often, under some misguided notion of political purity, progressive lesbians and gay men tend to ghettoize themselves in certain well-defined "acceptable" areas, leaving closeted and/or conservative lesbians and gay men to the more traditional fields. I wonder now if that ghettoization doesn't contribute to an exaggerated sense of powerlessness. I'm not saying that lesbian and gay people aren't victimized and oppressed. Of course we are. I am saying that we shouldn't let facile notions of righteousness inhibit us from seizing access to status and power and money and all of the other tools that force the world to listen. If my experience as an out lesbian in corporate law has taught me anything, it's that lesbians and gay men can make significant differences in the most orthodox of places, just by being there. We need radical gay people in corporations as much as we need them on gay hot lines.

Unfortunately, those of us who choose to work in traditionally conservative occupations are often ridiculed and censured by others in the lesbian and gay community. Many times, lesbians and gay men have felt entitled to stereotype me as reactionary or elitist when all they know about me is what I do for a living. This is not productive. We can't decry our marginalization and then castigate those who try to work in the places our society defines as "the center." And we can't ever hope to change the social dynamic of our culture without knowing how to dialogue with power.

At some point, I might well find it impossible to continue my adventures in the sanctum sanctorum of corporate law—either because I cannot take it anymore or because "they" cannot. But I think it is worth trying to do what I can while I am here. Thankfully, I have many gay and lesbian friends in similar positions, and we give one another comfort and strength as we negotiate the pitfalls of being out in very conservative environments.

Breaking the Silence
Otis Charles

*Otis Charles is the retired president and dean of the
Episcopal Divinity School and former bishop of the
Episcopal Diocese of Utah. In September 1993, he became
the highest-ranking American church official of any
denomination to come out publicly.*

I am a gay man and a bishop of the Episcopal Church. My perspective is that of a fledgling, self-expressed queer. In the several months since publicly taking a stand for the truth in my life, I have discovered doors opening and closing in patterns both wondrously affirming and sadly disappointing.

Somewhere before adolescence I found myself fascinated with older boys. By the time I got to college, I knew I was attracted to men, was, in fact, turned on by men and wanted to make out with them. It never occurred to me that in the mystery of creation, God had formed me to be a man who loves a man. After all, there was no one to tell me. I didn't think about being different; I simply lived with a continuing compelling attraction to men. At the same time, the last thing I wanted was for anyone to spot that I was queer.

In fact, quite early, I intuited that my attraction to men was not something you talked about. First in high school, then serving as a quartermaster on destroyer mine sweeps in the Pacific during World War II, and later in college, I acted like all the other men I knew. I dated women and talked about getting married. I don't know where I learned to do this. I can only say this attitude was most likely my earliest understanding of survival in the workplace. Little did I know then that my lifelong workplace would be the Church.

My earliest religious experiences were the gift of neighbors who took me to Sunday school with their children. Baptized at seven, I was confirmed two years later on the strength of my own persistence. In the core of my being, where years later I would discover my gayness, the Church and I became one. My enrollment at General Theological Seminary in New York City, therefore, hard on the heels of graduation from Trinity College, came as no surprise to my Trinity friends. The chapel was where I spent my time. The chaplain's house was my haven. Friends had dubbed me "Deacon." It was only in the midst of my senior year that the possibility of being ordained grabbed me. I got myself together and entered seminary in the fall.

Once in New York City, it didn't take me long to learn where to connect with gay men. At a bar in the Village, I met a Harvard law school grad, whom I dated. Being with him was wonderful. I enjoyed him, and although I wanted the relationship, there was this voice inside me saying "It's wrong." No one, not the dean nor any member of the faculty, had explicitly said, "Homosexuality is contrary to God's law." The ways of the seminary were more oblique and more threatening than that: a student would be summoned to the dean's office. Then he would be gone: no public charges, no due process, no official word of explanation to the school community—just silence, but everyone knew the secret. I realized there was no future in the seminary or in ordained ministry for anyone known to be homosexual. So my own struggle with silence began. I believed that my struggle was worthwhile because it was about my vocation and God's call to me. I trusted God to heal me.

I wrestled with myself, pleaded with God, and went about the city with my eyes downcast to avoid temptation. That summer I met the woman who would become my wife. Empowered through the persuasion of prayer with confidence that the Holy Spirit was straightening me out and molding me as I wanted to be, as the Church wanted me to be, I was ready to commit to marriage. Our wedding took place three days following my graduation from the seminary.

Since the time of the Reformation, marriage has been the norm for Protestant clergy. Having a family is clearly a plus, and not just as an empty expression of polite and correct behavior. In any parish calling process, someone invariably says, "It will be so nice to have a family in the rectory." For example, when I interviewed for my first placement as a priest, I was invited to bring my fiancée when I met the selection committee. They paid as much attention to her as to me. When our first child was born, he was showered with gifts. All of our children were the recipients of special educational opportunities. The message was clear.

I enjoyed being married. My wife was a beautiful, passionate woman, a wonderful human being, an incredibly supportive partner, and a devoted, nurturing mother. We were a striking couple and, together with our five children, a handsome family. We loved the Church and the ministry we shared and were mutually committed to having our marriage be grounded, nurtured, and sustained by Christ. I believe these were happy years for both of us. Yet sometimes consciously, and always subconsciously I'm sure, my homosexuality created an emotional barrier in our otherwise fulfilling relationship—something that I'm sure was very obvious to my wife. My desire was to love with my whole being, but I couldn't. Always lurking around in my head was my undisclosed self, tormenting me about the real person I was but didn't want to be. The prayer in my heart was for deliverance from being gay, but I couldn't talk with my wife about it. I turned to my confessor for help. Nothing changed. It seemed hopeless.

God did a marvelous thing in my life by leading me to a school of pastoral care conducted by Agnes Sanford, one of the first in the Episcopal Church to teach the practice of healing prayer. Privately, I opened my heart to her, confessed my homosexuality, and asked for the laying on of hands. I wanted to be healed of my homosexuality. Her response is written indelibly in my memory: "You do realize," she said, "there are many homosexual persons who are priests. Some of the strongest gifts you bring to ministry are direct-ly related to your homosexuality." Then she laid her hands on my head and prayed, calling upon the Holy Spirit to reach into the depths of my being and remove all that was blocking me from knowing the fullness of God's love. It was an ecstatic moment. I left Agnes Sanford's presence absolutely giddy. There was nothing in my priestly training to help me name my experience. I only knew that joy welled up from within me as a mighty torrent, and when the calm returned, I was free, released from the fear of being myself. I knew I was okay just as I was: a man who in the mystery of God's creation is homo-sexual.

I had come out to myself, but I wasn't ready to come out to others. In fact, I didn't return to the group until I got myself "under control." And when I did, I said nothing and continued my life of self-imposed silence. Back home I spoke passionately about the power of the laying on of hands, but I stopped short of revealing my own personal experience. The thought of being homo-sexual had been so painful to me that I couldn't imagine my wife, or anyone else for that matter, being able to handle my saying, "I am a homosexual man." Besides, I told myself, I would lose everything: my wife, my family, my job, respect. I had been freed from the interior heart struggle with my homo-sexuality, but my mind was still held captive by the "truth" learned in semi-nary: one cannot be homosexual and be a priest. I accepted isolation as the cost of having "a place at the table." It would be years before I took to myself the truth proclaimed by an African-American priest, the Reverend Canon Ed Rodman, who concludes every service with the words "Let us not be our own oppressors."

I preserved my equilibrium by throwing myself into my work—taking on all sorts of special projects and maintaining a well-defined circle of friends as a way to avoid thinking about my homosexuality. This approach, though unreal, seemed to work. I sustained my marriage, served effectively as rec-tor of a parish for nine years, was a member of the standing committee of the diocese as well as a deputy to the General Convention of the Episcopal Church, and in 1968 became the executive secretary of a national organiza-tion, Associated Parishes for Liturgy and Mission, while also functioning as a director and staff member of the Roman Catholic Montfort Fathers' ecumenical center in Litchfield, Conn.

In May 1971, I was called by the clergy and people to be bishop of the Episcopal Church in Utah. The consequences of moving out of my dependably predictable world never entered my head during the months of the election process. The Diocese of Utah sent a priest and a layperson to interview me as part of the screening process. They had dinner with me and my family. I know the family setting contributed to their positive impressions. Because I was a married man, no one ever questioned whether I was worthy.

The confirmation procedure in the election of a bishop requires a psychological examination. In this instance, a Rorschach test was included. I took a deep breath and gave my responses to the inkblots, having no doubt the psychiatrist would read me like a book. I thought that would be the end of any possibility of my being a bishop. To this day I have no idea what information the evaluator gave to the search committee. When I queried the psychiatrist about the contents of the evaluation, he simply observed, "It's not your death warrant." Small comfort. I knew I was at risk as a gay man. For twenty years I had lived faithfully within the vows of my marriage. Still, a bishop is a very public person. Once again I faced the question of speaking the truth, at least to my wife and children, and again I opted for my self-imposed silence. In 1971 I became the eighth Episcopal bishop of Utah and one of approximately 450 diocesan bishops of the seventy-million-member worldwide Anglican Communion.

A new set of "tapes" was activated in my head. How would I, a man who knew himself to be gay, exercise power within the Church? What would my response be to gay men and lesbians seeking the Church's acknowledgment and affirmation? How would I interact with openly gay men and lesbians as they sought places for themselves within the Church's ministry? To what extent would I allow myself to be a homophile? How would I respond to individuals who would say to me, "Bishop, we trust you to send us the right priest, just don't give us a homosexual." Where and how would I stand up and be counted? My response to this inner conversation was to be sensitive, notice opportunities to be supportive, exercise leadership, and always act with a compassionate heart. For example, at the General Convention in 1976 and at almost every convention since, I have spoken to the issue of the Church's second-class treatment of lesbians and gay men in general and of those wishing to be ordained in particular. In 1979 I was one of twenty-one bishops who signed a statement affirming their intention to ordain self-affirming homosexual candidates. All the while, of course, I never said out loud what was in my heart: "I stand in solidarity with lesbians and gay men because I am a gay man." I dependably chose the "responsible" safe course: silence.

There is little encouragement for anyone to be out in the Episcopal

Church. More frequently, if you take a stand for the truth, you will be judged negatively. The Church has implicitly, if not explicitly, established silence as the norm. I find myself wondering whether the now-infamous "don't ask, don't tell" policy originated in the military or in the Church. Only through the experience of being fully and publicly out as a gay man have I come to recognize the negative consequences of my complicity in the "don't ask, don't tell" mentality within the Church. I convinced myself that if I "told," everything that I was trying to build, the life that I had, would disappear. I felt like a boil aching to be lanced.

Then it happened. My self-imposed silence ended one summer evening in 1976, five years after I became a bishop. My wife and I, along with several members of my diocese, were gathered at a conference at our diocesan camp high in the majestic Wasatch Mountains. Another bishop and his wife, both friends and colleagues, were leading the conference. We gathered for Compline, the Church's traditional prayers at the close of the day. At this point a man entered the chapel quite agitated, expressing in a loud voice his dissatisfaction with the conference. The bishop suggested that we proceed and after Compline address whatever was troubling him.

About six of us stayed, sitting down in a circle on the chapel floor with the other bishop. The first words out of the man's mouth were "Otis has something he wants to say." I had no idea what he was talking about, yet his words went straight to my heart, neat as a knife. They were the knife that lanced the boil. I was terrified, thinking I was about to be outed. The bishop's immediate response—"We're not here to talk about Otis"—gave me space to breathe. During that time I decided I could no longer remain silent. As soon as the group broke up, I asked the bishop and his wife to wait while I went to get my wife. There was something I needed to say to her. That night in the company of two friends, I came out to my wife.

Her response initially was calm. "Oh, this explains a lot of things," she said. I did not have the self-confidence to ask what. Later, she said, "Your attention has never been with me; it's always with something else." She had experienced me as distant and distracted. Finally, having broken the silence barrier, I would have gladly shouted "I'm gay" from the highest mountaintop so all the world could hear, but I didn't. My wife did not insist on anything changing in our relationship, so I allowed myself to continue to pass as a fifty-year-old straight man.

In 1985, I became dean and president of Episcopal Divinity School (EDS) in Cambridge, Mass. In the course of the exploratory conversations with the search committee, I did not speak nor was I asked about my sexual orientation.

During the interview process, a student member of the search committee, who was gay, called me. He reminded me that numerous openly gay men and lesbians studying at EDS hoped to be ordained. He was concerned that a closeted gay dean might protect himself by aligning with those in the Church who opposed the ordination of lesbians and gay men. Or even more appalling, he might engage in public, self-righteous fag-bashing. Dodging the inference that I was gay, I suggested that he check the record of my support for the ordination of gay people.

While at EDS, I read Paul Monette's autobiographical works, *Becoming a Man: Half a Life Story* and *Borrowed Time*. Through his experiences I began to recognize the tyranny of silence in my own life, and how it had cheated me, my family, friends, colleagues, and the larger gay tribe of which I am a part. No one experienced the true me, not even the few friends to whom I was out. They got the ersatz Otis I constructed for others to see and know. The most difficult truth for me to internalize was the reality that Silence = Death. That was my experience. I knew in my head that Action = Freedom, but for some reason that I don't understand, I resisted until the 1990 General Convention of Episcopal Church.

I sat silently through the convention as the forces against affirming gay and lesbian relationships were hard at work. The debate was acrimonious. I listened in silence as brother bishops debated whether self-affirming, "practicing" gay men and lesbian women could be ordained. Bishops spoke of homosexuality in terms of sin and sickness and challenged the integrity of those who acknowledged ordaining openly gay men and lesbian women. I listened as a brother bishop equated me to an alcoholic. It got so bad that the bishop of Newark called a bishop of Texas "a homophobe."

Profoundly disturbed, I decided to take the next step in ending the tyranny of silence I was living in: I went to my chief pastor, Edmond Browning, presiding bishop of the Episcopal Church, and told him, "I want you to know that I'm a gay man and that I can no longer remain silent." I spoke to him about what my experience was like at the convention. I shared with him my seemingly never-ending coming-out process. He asked me what he could do to be supportive of myself and my wife, and we consulted about the best way to communicate with the bishops. I also consulted with the bishop responsible for pastoral care of bishops, who questioned the wisdom of my making a public statement. Nonetheless, I began actively considering when and under what circumstances I would come out publicly. It wouldn't be until three years later.

One day in January 1993, the chair of the board of EDS was on campus. We walked into my office together. Before we were seated, he said, "There is something I have to ask you. I'm told you are gay. Are you?" "Yes," I responded, "thank you for asking." It felt like a victory. I had promised myself that if asked, I would not lie. But I had never before been asked straight out. We sat down and had a long and good conversation. I shared some of my history and told him that it was my intention to affirm my gayness publicly. The question, I said, was not whether, but when and how. His reaction was to suggest that, should I decide to make a public statement while still dean, it coincide as nearly as possible with the date of my retirement—the month following the close of school.

Still, the precise question of what and when remained unclear to me. There were two opportunities that seemed particularly appropriate. One was at a February meeting of the board of trustees designed to include a special segment on the blessing of same-sex unions. Another possibility was to incorporate my coming-out into a sermon at a post-Easter service, when the entire school would be assembled. Proclaiming the power of Christ's resurrection through the transforming power of God's grace in my life was the most powerful sermon in my heart. Old habits are hard to shake, however, and I decided against both of these possibilities.

Thus winter turned into spring, and spring brought commencement, with its focus on the graduating students. Obviously, this was no time to impose my personal agenda on the life of the school. So I sent a note to the chair of the board saying I would be silent until after my retirement. I left my post as dean and president of EDS in June 1993.

The time to take the final step out was now. After some consultation I decided on my strategy, drafting a coming-out letter addressed to the House of Bishops, due to meet in Panama in September. Mailed just before Labor Day, it said,

For the past several months, I have openly communicated with my family and with growing numbers of my colleagues and friends that I am a gay man. While in many ways I would have preferred that this communication remain a personal and private one, I am well aware that given my vocation and my calling as a bishop, and given the general climate of public speculation so prevalent today, that could not long be the case. Out of respect for the collegiality of the House and for our personal relationship, as well as to avoid conjecture, I want to communicate with you directly.

For forty-five years, I struggled with my sexual identity. In the isolation and darkness, I felt that there must be something wrong with me. I turned to others for help. I prayed with all my heart to be healed. Nothing changed. I was still me, pulled apart inside by feelings I schooled myself to believe were unnatural....

As recently as the summer of 1991, I sat silently through the Phoenix General Convention. I did not join the debate openly and honestly, simply saying, "Hey, you are talking about me. I am a gay man." I allowed myself to be one of "those" spoken about outside the House—the guessed-about number of Bishops who are gay....

My choice to make myself known in this way and at this time is a personal one, whatever motive or meaning others may infer. Sexuality is a

part of the richness, the complexity and mystery of God's creation. It is an essential part of our human experience, and it is a part of the experience of priests and bishops. Indeed it deserves—perhaps even requires—to be dealt with as straightforwardly and sensitively as matters of doctrine and pastoral care.

I have promised myself that I will not remain silent, invisible, unknown. After all is said and done, the choice for me is not whether or not I am a gay man, but whether or not I am honest about who I am with myself and others. It is a choice to take down the wall of silence I have built around an important and vital part of my life, to end the separation and isolation I have imposed on myself all these years. It is a choice to live my life as consistently as I can with my own integrity, a choice to be fully who I am and to be responsible for all that I am.

I am aware that the reactions to my openness about my sexuality will encompass the whole range of emotion and opinion. For those for whom homosexuality is an incomprehensible (or even reprehensible) aspect of human behavior, there may be a sense of shock and perhaps revulsion or sadness. For those for whom the expression of their sexuality as gay and lesbian men and women has long been hidden, suppressed and scorned, there may be a sense of affirmation and perhaps even victory....

For the past twenty years or more, the subject of our diversity— racial, sexual, cultural—has been controversial, painful, and often divisive. Yet something new is being done in our midst—in spite of our reluctance. We now have three black diocesan bishops. Three women have been elected to the episcopate, one a diocesan. The same diocese that elected a woman to be its chief pastor seriously considered a gay man, living in a covenanted relationship. Blacks, women, gays—all have had to struggle and continue to struggle to be visibly present with voice in the exclusive world of white, male, heterosexual dominance.

Because we are a people of faith, our quarrels have at times taken place as theological and moral arguments—often ignoring or even threatening the very ties of brotherly and sisterly love that bind us together as a community of believers....The Spirit is drawing us to a new understanding and experience of inclusion. I also believe God has drawn me to speak the truth of my experience. And I believe that as gay men and lesbians speak openly, telling the stories of their lives, the community of faith is strengthened.

Shortly after this letter went out to all the bishops, some individuals from Bishop Browning's press corps heard about the letter through conversation around the building. They tracked down a person who gave them a copy. When I found out, I quickly became concerned about bad press and decided that I was the best one to represent my story. So I came out to the world.

Since coming out I have had disappointments. Early on, there was the bishop who asked me to spend a month in his diocese assisting with confirmations. I indicated my willingness. Two days after I received his letter confirming the arrangements, he phoned me to tell me that the rector of one of the parishes I was scheduled to visit had contacted him to say that the parish vestry did not wish to have me make the visitation. This event led the bishop to tell me that he should probably contact the clergy of the other parishes about their willingness and then get back to me. I was flabbergasted. This was my first experience of unmasked discrimination.

On the other hand, I have been incredibly affirmed. Many people, including clergy and bishops, have written me letters of encouragement and appreciation. I never imagined the contribution my coming-out would make for others, not to mention the extraordinary sense of wholeness and well-being I experienced from having integrity in my life.

Yes, internalized homophobia and heterosexism linger within me like a virus, nudging me to be "smart" and accept the parameters set by the straight world for me and my kind. I grieve for the suffering that the norm of silence causes young people who are discovering they are gay. By keeping silent in my workplace—the Church and EDS—I have deprived them of an honest role model and an affirming ally.

In spite of my desire to be perceived as a good guy, I am learning to be responsible for my life and to live unashamedly as a gay man. I have had encouragement from some special companions along the way: John Fortunato, author of *Embracing the Exile,* always available to me and my wife when we were married, has been a wonderfully supportive mentor helping me understand the difference between saying "I am gay" and being, living gay. Tom Dobbs, priest and friend, has been a window of self-understanding for me, opening my eyes to the disregard heaped upon openly gay clergy who refuse to choose between the Church and the partner they love. The wisdom, sensitivity, and compassion of James Diamond, rector of Christ Church in Andover, Mass., as my spiritual director during the winter of 1993 allowed me to grasp, at last, what God has been trying to teach me all along—that the only way I can be an authentic human being, a faithful Christian and bishop is by living as the person God created me to be—a joyfully, self-affirming gay man. Ann Overton, chair of the Diocese of California's evangelism committee and longtime colleague, coached me in speaking the truth of my life. And last but certainly not least, the late Paul Monette's courage to be continues to prod me to keep on keeping on, breaking the cords of silence, being a self-disclosing, self-affirming gay man, being accessible to others, and giving the only gift I really have—myself. Finally, I can be an honest and supportive companion for others on the way and for some, perhaps, the only and best opportunity they may have for developing "homo-sensitivity."

Would I have been rector of a parish, elected bishop of Utah, or become dean and president of EDS had I been forthright about my sexual orientation? Probably not. Given prevailing attitudes in the Church's seminaries right up into the 1970s and in some places even today, I would never have been ordained. That's why breaking out of the silence and becoming actively engaged in the movement for gay liberation is so important to me. My commitment is to live my life and encourage others to live their lives so that in days to come lesbians and gay men will only need to remember with dismay how it was for us.

A gay man who is married, a father, a priest, and not out, called me recently from a city on the other side of the country. He asked if coming out had been worth it. "Oh, yes!" was my immediate response. "For the first time since entering seminary, I feel whole." I could tell from the tone in his voice as the conversation continued that I had been the conveyor of courage.

Part III

United We Stand:
A Group Story

United We Stand

Groups of gay, lesbian, and bisexual people can carry a lot of power. Besides the fact that groups can be a testing ground for sharing ideas, communicating successes, taking risks, and challenging thoughts, there is definitely strength in numbers. When the voice that is being raised is not isolated or alone, others seem to pay more attention.

This realization has led to the emergence of gay, lesbian, and bisexual groups in the workplace—and has prompted us to include the stories of members of one such workplace group. For individual members, these workplace groups help make it possible to come out at work. They also provide support, social and work-related contacts, and resources—not only for members but for nonmembers and management.

What follows are the experiences of five founding members of the Bank of Boston's Gay and Lesbian Resource Group. Each of these individuals was grappling with an issue relating to being gay or lesbian at work. Informally, they became aware of one another's existence and struggle. Peter Nee, still in the closet, was working with gay and lesbian youth and being challenged to come out as a role model for them. Paul Bilicki found out that he was the only one out of a group of six friends, including his lover, who was HIV-negative. He felt that he needed to end his silence about being gay. Lee Merkle, whose partner was also employed by the bank, was offered a transfer to California—putting the bank in a position of needing to treat the two of them as a family. Richard Olson was being outed by another employee to his boss. He used this as an opportunity to institute an outreach program to gays and lesbians in the community. Chris Palmer had been speaking with the diversity officer about feeling alone and isolated as a lesbian and wanting to connect with others.

These stories recount the synergy that has resulted from the formation of this group out of the bank's worldwide workforce of sixteen thousand employees. What happened, as you will see, is both encouraging and inspiring. To quote Chris Palmer: "Coming together was like Dorothy and her band of hopefuls from *The Wizard of Oz*. When they were in the wizard's chamber for a second time, standing in fear before this great illusion, Toto pulled back the curtain. Together, they all finally saw that this big, scary thing was just a twerp behind a curtain."

It Happens Here

Peter Hamilton Nee, Assistant Vice President
Real Estate Division, Bank of Boston

I am an assistant vice president in the commercial real estate area, specializing in community-based development initiatives. I have been with the bank since April 1985. I grew up in Natick, a suburb of Boston, and went away to a Canadian military school, where I first started to understand my sexuality. It was a pretty regimented environment, emotionally as well as academically. From there I went to Gordon College in Wenham, Mass., and began my college career thinking that I would be an Episcopal priest. After ninety days in the theology department, I was approached with the strong suggestion that maybe there was another route that my life could take. I think it was not because of my sexuality—I was just beginning to understand it myself—but because of theological differences. Gordon College is a very conservative school, and I was nonconservative and wanting to understand the somewhat radical concept of comparative theologies. (In the late 1970s and early 1980s, no one was into comparative theologies.)

I became an economics and business major and graduated in 1981. I began my career in sales, eventually working at the Ritz-Carlton Hotel, which was a gay-friendly environment. I left that highly service-oriented environment and came to Bank of Boston in 1985. My first position was working in the branches, opening up deposit accounts for businesses and individuals.

Unknown to me at the time, I was outed at the bank before I even started. One of the branch managers, who was gay and out to some people, mentioned to the head of personnel for our area, Anne Filoramo, that he "knew me." That was enough in those days to imply that I was gay. Anne's response was to befriend and support me. I was very successful in retail banking, was a branch manager within two years, and was promoted to the largest domestic branch outside our head office a year after that. At the age of thirty I was running a $100-million operation with a staff of twenty.

At this time, the bank had a quite informal, yet well-informed, network of gay and lesbian employees. We made a deliberate effort to look out for and mentor one another. For example, whenever I had a problem, I felt a lot more secure going to a senior person who was gay or lesbian. My career benefited from the alliances I formed and the advice I received.

In 1989, I left retail banking, an area of the bank where I had a lot of expertise and connections, and entered a rigorous internal training program for commercial lending. I began a three-year process of building new networks in this more conservative world.

Those three years were a difficult period for me because a lot of my friends were dying from AIDS. Although I never encountered any aggressive or overt homophobia, I became less patient with the nonsense I experienced, such as offhand remarks or a lack of sensitivity; I felt that I did not have time to put up with it anymore.

I shared my feelings with Tom Etzel, a vice president in our cash management group. Both of us started to talk about starting an association of gay, lesbian, and bisexual employees. At that time, Tom and I were also developing an interest in working with gay and lesbian youth. A friend of ours challenged us and said, "Look, if you guys don't come out and don't provide role models for kids in the community, they will never know they could do whatever they want with their lives. You said yourself, Peter, 'If they want to be underpaid and overworked, they can be bankers.' If you don't start to provide these role models, then who will?" We decided that we would take a risk by putting together a group to march in the Gay Pride parade. We were apprehensive but knew this was right.

We approached friends in the bank's corporate communications department, who gave us some T-shirts. Because Gay Pride takes place at almost the same time as Boston's AIDS benefit walk, they probably thought that that's what the T-shirts were for. We didn't correct them.

About the same time we put this group together, Chris Palmer, a new manager at the bank, and other friends of hers were exploring—with the same contact people—questions of why sexual orientation was not a part of the bank's antidiscrimination policy and why gay-related issues were not being brought up in our diversity courses. Tom, Paul, Chris, and I, with others, met over coffee. We listened to what each was doing in his or her own area and decided to merge these efforts. Our resource group was off and running.

We had thirty or forty people on a telephone list whom we could call and knew of a hundred more. Today we have about 120 people on various mailing lists—only about 10 percent of what we believe the gay and lesbian bank population to be. We were concerned about how the group would be viewed and did not want it to be seen as confrontational. It was intended mostly as a way for employees to find one another and as a way to provide them some support with AIDS and domestic-partnership issues.

Dani Monroe, who worked in the bank's diversity office, came onboard immediately: she went to Helen Drinan, senior vice president of human resources, and informed her of the group's formation. Helen was excited to learn about several key features we had decided the group would have. First—and this differentiated our group from others of its kind at the bank—from the very beginning our group had a great deal of professional-level diversity. Second, we decided the group would be open to *all* bank employees and retirees, including heterosexuals. We decided that inclusiveness was very important. We could not see how we could operate any other way. Third, we would elect a steering committee from the membership.

We have been very effective as a group in meeting with senior managers throughout the bank. We let them know that we are here and that we are a resource for them and their employees. Because of our group, Bank of Boston's diversity program has been totally revamped to include sexual orientation and many other issues. We have also recently completed a proposal for spousal benefits. At our regular monthly meetings, the president and two vice-chairs have asked to come to speak to the members at large. In all three cases we had strong turnouts for what could have been very scary situations.

The period of the group's formation was a time of great professional change for me. I was out of my area of expertise and on a steep learning curve. I was not and am not in a relationship, and I have so far lost thirty-five friends to AIDS. I was not only grieving but concerned about myself, and I felt that I did not have anyone to turn to. The real-estate department has been very supportive, but I still felt a lot of frustration and anger. The realization that life is short was compounded when I came down with hepatitis A and the doctors did not know what it was for one week. I was a wreck until I found out that I was fine and HIV-negative. It was a huge relief, and it reminded me of the importance of making our workplaces open and accepting. People should not be put in the emotional bind of going through something traumatic while feeling unsafe about telling anyone at work. We spend a lot of time at the office working with our colleagues. When we put all or a portion of our energy into building walls or closets, that's energy that could be better used elsewhere.

There are still people at the bank who will not come out. To some extent it is a generation issue. The only way around the problem is to increase the numbers and shatter the stereotypes so that others can feel safe.

That's why marching in the Gay Pride parade was such an important step. It was a pretty big move, scary yet exciting. I was amazed at the amount of support from the community and from the spectators when they saw the Bank of Boston contingent: they went wild, absolutely wild. Our presence was important in a city dominated by financial services. For the oldest bank in America to march in the Gay Pride parade for the first time was a historic moment. Every time we took a step, Paul Bilicki would look at me and say,

"Okay, we're going to get fired tomorrow, this is it! Enjoy yourself, because it's all over." The second year we had sixty marchers.

We have done a lot in a short time, and I think there is a lot of important work yet to be done. Our effectiveness through educational work never stops, as new managers are always being hired and moving up the the ranks. If we are to turn our organization into the kind that will survive into the next century, we need to be better at training managers and presenting an open and welcoming work environment.

On a final note, it occurs to me that the gay and lesbian movement has focused on legislative change and mandates for equal rights. Although legislative change is important, I believe that the real change is going to come where people work. Attitudes change in the workplace. Segregation changed in the workplace, and when companies started to do the right thing, society changed. Today, when industry leaders like Bank of Boston do the right thing, they are going to change the way America thinks and acts for the better. But if we don't come out, they will never have the chance.

Coming of Age

Paul Bilicki, Senior Manager
Payroll Operations, Bank of Boston

I think I was always gay, though officially I didn't come out till I was thirty-two. I'm now fifty-one. I was brought up in Wakefield, Mass., in a very tight-knit Italian-Polish family and spent much of my childhood and adolescence in and out of the closet. Although I came out when I was thirty-two, I didn't start to experience gay life until I was about thirty-six. I met my current lover, Kevin, when I was thirty-nine, and we've been together for twelve years.

In all the time we have lived together, it wasn't till about four years ago that I decided to come out officially to my family. In fact, the reasons for coming out to my family are probably the same reasons for officially coming out at work. Let me explain.

Kevin and I hung around with four other friends with whom we had been close for about ten years. In 1990, one of the group was taken sick and turned out to be HIV-positive. We were all in shock. As none of us had ever been tested, we all decided to take the big step together.

The results came back four positive, one negative. Me.

When Kevin and my friends tested positive, I felt like a freak for a while. Over and over I still keep asking myself, *How do you live and sleep with someone for twelve years and you be negative while he is positive?* It didn't make sense. It still doesn't make sense to me.

My life suddenly changed as I started to watch my friends die and was forced to face my mortality, Kevin's mortality, and the mortality of our relationship. That's when I decided that I needed to come out to my family.

I always figured that if I were to have a problem with coming out, it would be with my dad. I told my mother first, and she became very quiet. She asked me if I wanted her to tell my father. I told her that I wanted to be the one to tell him. I told my dad, and he never missed a beat. My mom and dad have accepted Kevin as they would any of their other children's spouses. I truly have a wonderful personal support system.

I have been at the Bank of Boston for thirteen years. Until 1990, I was never out, but I was also never in: I was just myself. I have been very fortunate never to have been discriminated against at the bank. I don't think that my career has suffered from my being gay, which is something that I attribute to a work ethic that I learned a long time ago: because I'm different, I felt I always had to be better and try harder. No one would ever get to me because I'm different, because I'm too good at what I do. As a result, I never really paid much attention to being gay.

About the time that Kevin tested positive, I started paying more attention to being gay in general and at work specifically. Now I was beginning to realize that even in taking this work-ethic approach, I was not free. Work has always been my salvation. It has been the place that I could go and lose myself. My newfound sense of mortality made me realize that I had to get my official coming-out at work over with so that I could finally enjoy my life and experience it and share it with other people. Life is so much nicer when you don't have to hide anything.

I told every one of my bosses that I'm gay. They were all fine about it. My staff knows that I'm gay, and it's not an issue for them either. In fact, I am proud to be head of the most diverse department with the lowest turnover of anywhere in the bank.

Then the gay and lesbian group started. While it was in its informal stages, I decided not to be involved. As it became more formalized and more interesting, I decided to run for a position on the steering committee. Because I work in human resources and have worked at the bank a long time, I felt I could make a difference. I also like to consider myself the voice of reason: I was afraid that there might be a radical element present that would want to make the group adversarial. I really like the bank, and I know how the bank works. I felt that I could help hold any radical element in check.

Of course, the more I got involved, the more I needed to come out, and that's exactly what I've done. Shortly after being elected to the steering committee, Peter Nee, Amy Rossiter, Chris Palmer, and I appeared on a panel for senior human resources people. We actually sat in the middle of a room while they asked us all kinds of questions about being gay and lesbian at the Bank of Boston. It was a wonderful experience. I also now teach diversity and of course put a gay and lesbian slant on it. And because of my personal dealings with AIDS, I am part of the AIDS in the workplace task force.

I have to say that one of the most wonderful things that has happened as a result of being in this group (now called the Bank of Boston Gay and Lesbian Employee Resource Group) is that I have met many wonderful lesbians. I had never known many lesbians in my life; for me, they were a whole other world. I had my perceptions of what they were like, and I always thought all lesbians were bull dykes. Joining this group and coming in contact with lesbians like Amy and Chris taught me how wrong I was. Just a few years ago I would have never believed that I could actually be friends with women who are gay.

I have to admit that being a member of the steering committee takes up a lot of my time and energy. Originally I thought, *What do I need it for? It doesn't affect me.* My being gay was someone else's problem. As I've become more and more involved, I have realized that one of the things we have tried to do is make the workplace comfortable for everybody, especially gays and lesbians. I came to the realization that I had managed to make the workplace very comfortable for my own department. Why not do the same for the whole bank? The result of the committee's work is a feeling that we have helped some people. We have taken some people who were totally afraid to come out and reached out to them with the knowledge that there are other people here like them. I realize now that it is important for me to be a role model for other people; I would like to try to encourage more people to come out.

My former boss, the bank's current vice-chairman, Bill Shea, spoke at one of our group meetings. In his remarks he said, "It's not easy, it's never going to be easy. No one is ever going to give you anything. But if you don't come out and stand up, change is never going to happen. I want to encourage you to continue advocating for a comfortable workplace, so that people will feel safe to come out and be who they are."

I am not a spiritual person, but all of this has made me believe in the human spirit. We talk about a lot of things at work, and people ask me about Kevin from time to time. Like my mother, I wear my feelings on my face. Inside myself I want my relationship to go on forever, and I get frightened when I realize that it won't. Often I take the feeling down off the shelf and then put it back up. Each time I put it back, the shelf gets higher and harder to reach. At least, one thing in my life that I don't have to carry anymore is hiding my gayness. Having no more secrets has made me a much better person and made my life a lot less lonely.

Acceptance

Lee Merkle, Assistant Vice President
High Technology Division, Bank of Boston

I joined Bank of Boston in July 1989 as a trainee in the loan-officer development program. I was out in prior jobs and hoped that I would be comfortable enough, in time, to come out to my bank colleagues. I did not know any other lesbians or gay men at the bank my first day, but given sixteen thousand employees I knew I'd find some company eventually. I had no idea how lucky I would be: four of the other fifty trainees were gay or lesbian, including Peter Nee and Kathy Raymond, now my partner of five years.

For me, coming out to colleagues in the training program was uneventful. We spent many hours together in classes, in work groups, and doing team projects, and with certain colleagues, talks about weekend activities easily included my involvement in the gay and lesbian community. Biking with a lesbian biking group and attending political marches and rallies were part of my life, and I did not hide those activities from my colleagues. With others I was less open, changing pronouns, sometimes forgetting who knew whom. As I spent more time at the bank, I met other gays and lesbians in various departments, pretty much as I had expected. I was becoming part of the informal network of known gays and lesbians. There seems to be a strong desire among gays and lesbians to identify others in the community, to feel a sense of belonging and strength in numbers, and I found that desire to be just as strong at a conservative institution such as Bank of Boston as anywhere.

During the first year at the bank, my professional life merged into my personal life as I got closer to Kathy. Although we started dating during the training program, we were not very open about our relationship at the bank until, after the program, we were placed in separate departments. Once placed in lending positions, we each had a new group to come out to, in much the same way as at the beginning of the training program—little by little, one or two people at a time. Because we were out, each of us was invited to and felt welcome at the other's work parties: holiday parties and off-site trips when spouses were included.

In 1992, we had a commitment ceremony, and gay and straight friends from work made up 15 to 20 percent of our guests. After our wedding, when we took three weeks off for our honeymoon, my manager approved the carryover of a week of the previous year's vacation time. When we came back with rings and photos of our wedding, some colleagues who hadn't known about our plans before the event noticed and congratulated us. By this time, we each felt comfortable bringing a photo of the other to put on our desks. Overall, I learned that by talking to colleagues and managers about our life, we were respected and accepted at work. This feeling of acceptance made me more able to participate fully in my job. I was there as a whole person, not leaving parts of me outside, detached.

Because I was comfortable being out at work and had generally good experiences at Bank of Boston, I was glad when Amy Rossiter, a friend from the lesbian biking group, became interested in a position at the bank. I was able to dispel for Amy the myth that this conservative financial institution was unfriendly to gays and lesbians. Speaking from my experience, I encouraged her to join Bank of Boston. In fact, when talking with friends who work in more typically "liberal" settings such as social work, teaching, advertising, and architecture, I've found that the bank is often a better environment for gays and lesbians, as it makes an effort to have employees treat one another as professionals.

The informal gay and lesbian network grew through work and community events. The annual AIDS walk, sponsored by the bank, attracted a large number of gay and lesbian employee participants and provided an opportunity for growing the informal network. The annual Gay Pride parade also served the same purpose and was a catalyst for getting more gay and lesbian employees to identify themselves to one another. Peter Nee, Tom Etzel, Chris Palmer, Amy Rossiter, and Kathy and I were consistent participants and encouraged others to join us. I met people from other departments with whom I had often spoken on the phone. Going back to work afterward was more fun and fulfilling, because I knew the people I was working with and we had established a common bond.

When Peter, Tom, and Chris were deciding to establish a formal employee group, I was interested in participating for several reasons. First, a group would give senior management live examples of gay and lesbian employees willing to represent others. Second, gay and lesbian employees who feared coming out would have positive examples within the bank, which might encourage them to come out and be counted. Third, I just wanted to know more people at the bank. The Gay and Lesbian Resource Group served all three purposes, and I went to meetings as the group started to form and grow in 1992 and 1993.

As a result of a job transfer within the bank, I came out to higher levels of management and also joined the steering committee of the group. When offered a lending position in the bank's office in Palo Alto, Calif., I learned a lot about the bank's awareness and sensitivity to gay and lesbian issues and was generally impressed. While Kathy and I were out to our managers, we had never had a reason to discuss our personal lives with more-senior managers. When my prospective manager asked me if I was willing to move, I said I would have to discuss it with my partner. At first she assumed I was referring to a business partnership, so I clarified: "We're married, but we're both women." The bank does not track significant others, so there was no way of knowing that I was not as single as my legal marital status would imply. Kathy's division tried valiantly to keep her, but we decided to go to California. After the initial surprise, the bank treated us as a "household" for the entire transfer. House-hunting trips and moving expenses for Kathy were reimbursed by the bank, as they would have been for any family member. As a result of the whole process, I was now out to senior management and off to an exciting new opportunity.

As I was getting ready to move from Boston to Palo Alto, the resource group was forming a steering committee. My friendship with the other group leaders and my desire to have a meaningful group organized made me a candidate to be one of the initial steering committee members. My recent exposure to management without losing my job and my desire to stay in touch with Boston were personal reasons that made me interested in taking on the role.

My personal contribution to the group was working on the proposal for parity in benefits, the primary nonsocial objective I have for the group. I attended a National Gay and Lesbian Task Force conference at Stanford University, with my registration fee paid by the bank's diversity office, and networked with other companies that have or are working on parity in benefit programs. Working with a group task force, I wrote the primary draft of the proposal, and I hope to be at the bank when parity in benefits is approved. As part of the group, I have been able to present to senior management a personal view of life as a lesbian at Bank of Boston. I feel that I am more respected as an employee, not less respected, because I'm a lesbian.

When I first came to the bank I felt unsure of how I would be accepted. So in an effort to conceal the "lesbian parts" of myself, I would often withhold my thoughts, ideas, and work-related suggestions, which reduced my overall contribution. Now that I feel able to contribute fully, I give more in all aspects of my work than I did when I felt I needed to work hard at hiding parts of myself. Not being out takes work: changing pronouns, revising events as you tell them, and withholding certain information—all of which detracts from what you can contribute to the job. Being out is better for me as a person *and* as an employee.

As I move forward, one question remains unresolved for me: is the bank willing to take a leadership role and be consistent on every level regarding true acceptance of gays and lesbians and support of diversity? Currently, the Bank of Boston views diversity, and acceptance of gay and lesbian employees, as an internal issue. What about outside the bank? Does the bank's diversity become a business ethic and make the bank willing to lose business with companies or individuals that do not accept or respect the bank's diverse workforce?

Whatever the future holds, I believe that we have made significant inroads from where we were when our resource group began, and our effect on our workplace has been significant. I believe that our accomplishments as a group have made our workplace a safer place for gays and lesbians to be out and a better place for our colleagues, as we feel able to give more fully of ourselves. Sure, there's always more to do, but for now I am proud of my colleagues and proud of the Bank of Boston and how far it has come.

The Outing

Richard D. Olson, Jr., Assistant Vice President
First Community Bank, Bank of Boston

oming out in my personal life was a very positive process. Outside of my workplace I made no secret about being gay. All of my family and friends knew. Work was quite the opposite, however: because of the conservative nature of banking, I maintained a stance of not telling anybody at work about my personal life. It was hard, because I always worked for small, conservative banks where everybody knew everyone else by first name, including the president.

Things began to change when the bank I worked for failed in June 1991 and was acquired by the Bank of Boston. I decided to retain the "don't tell anyone about your life" policy. The day after the bank failed, I received a dozen roses from my then-partner and two arrangements from friends. They were trying to help me feel better because my work life had just been turned upside down. Everyone was asking who they were from. The first phrase out of my mouth was, "I have a very open-minded girlfriend." So one set came from my girlfriend, one from my mother, and another from a customer. I maintained the secret for a while—or so I thought.

One evening I was working out in the bank fitness center near another member of First Community Bank whom I'll call "Tom." Tom had finished and was on his way out the door. I was still on the rowing machine when he turned around, came over to me, and said, "Oh, by the way, someone came out for you to your boss, Gail, and I thought that I would come out and tell you that I am gay." I nearly fell off the rowing machine. It was then that everything started changing for me at work.

All of a sudden my secret had been betrayed, and I was beside myself. I knew I had to be calm and not my classic self and scream *"Whaaat!"* I asked Tom what happened. He said, "I came out to my manager recently because I wanted to know how senior management feels about gay and lesbian employees. What he told me was, 'Gail seems to know that Richard's gay and doesn't have a problem with it, so I don't think that she would have a problem with you.'" The fact that this whole conversation had taken place and I didn't know anything about it just amazed me. (I never found out exactly who had outed me.)

I was devastated. It was like coming out to your parents. On one hand I was relieved, but on the other hand I thought, *Who the hell are these people I hardly know to be having this discussion about me and talking about my personal life?* The funny thing was, the more I thought about it the better I felt. I started thinking, *How many times does so and so come in and talk about his kids, his wife, his life?* I have these conversations with people all the time—but it's always about someone else's life and never about mine, and no one was asking.

About this time I attended diversity training with other employees from First Community Bank in which we talked about all of the standard diversity issues. No one, including the gay and lesbian employees in the meeting, brought up anything about gay and lesbian issues. During a break, I approached two other people at the training whom I knew to be gay, one of whom was Tom. I asked them, "Why isn't anyone bringing up gay and lesbian issues?" They said that they were scared because of who was in the room. When the break ended I asked the trainer, Rosa Hunter, how she saw gay and lesbian issues fitting into our workplace. Rosa stopped and said, "Oh, let me tell you a story." She proceeded to tell us about Chris Palmer, whom I did not know at the time, and her feeling of isolation as a lesbian at the bank. Chris had approached Rosa about wanting to connect with more gays and lesbians here. That was it. Rosa did not ask any questions, and we didn't push the issues, so it died in the training. I believe that we could have communicated our needs a little better.

What did come out of this training session was that I decided I had to express my frustration to my boss about the conversation that took place without my knowing it. I had also decided that I would not take an adversarial approach and that I had an opportunity to turn this into something positive. So I asked to speak with her after a meeting. I began by saying, "Something happened recently that I want to tell you about." I recounted everything that had gone on, and she was as upset as I was.

I told her that I had thought a lot about our division's commitment to address the needs of underserved communities. Because two of the areas we serve have large gay and lesbian constituencies, this was a great opportunity for our bank to reach out to that historically underserved group. This was also an opportunity for me to work with the institution to sensitize it to the needs of the gay community, thus making First Community Bank the bank of choice for gays and lesbians. It just made good business sense.

My boss agreed and said that she would make a proposal to Gail. She suggested that we simply address the business issues as we would in approaching any new market. She went to Gail and explained my proposal without addressing my sexual orientation. Gail's response was phenomenal; she gave the green light.

I was going through a whole new coming-out process, and I was scared. I felt that everything was moving too fast. Up to this point, my experience had told me not to be out, that it could put my whole career in jeopardy. Although I was getting the message that it was okay to be gay at the bank, the problem was that I was scared and very unsure of how to be my gay self in this industry. For the first time I was without gay models to help me negotiate a path through this process.

I decided to start by putting two pictures on my credenza, one of me and friends on the beach in Provincetown, and another with friends sitting in Santa's lap. It was a big step. Then, because the outreach was getting into full swing, in addition to my boss I came out to my business development team and a few other coworkers.

After the outreach began in January 1993, the division president, Gail, was interviewed by one of our local gay newspapers, *Bay Windows*. It was very validating for me. I was being seen in the community not just as a gay man but as a businessman. Shortly after the article appeared, I joined a local gay and lesbian professional networking organization, the Greater Boston Business Council. At their monthly dinners and various networking gatherings, I took the position that "I am from the Bank of Boston First Community Bank, and we want to do business with you." I wanted people to know that they could come in to our offices and feel comfortable.

About this time my whole division went to another off-site diversity training session led by a new person, Dani Monroe. I found myself sitting again in a diversity seminar, with other gays and lesbians, and no one was talking about gay and lesbian issues. I continued to sit there while other coworkers started talking about their diversity issues. That gave me the courage to raise my hand and say I would like to talk about how being a gay employee at the bank has affected me. In doing so I was deciding to come out to all the managers at First Community. We talked about it. (I felt like I wanted to vomit, because of my anxiety.)

Before this, I had been out to people I knew and felt comfortable with. Here I was, sitting with twenty-five people whom I knew only superficially. That is when the old tapes started to play again. I felt scared that word would get around that Richard Olson was a big fairy. It was wasted energy, because that never happened.

At the same time, Gail asked me to participate in a management-training video that she was also going to be in. She gave me the green light to be myself, saying, "I'm choosing you because I want you to talk about how you feel as a gay employee about working here." I still felt scared. I still felt that it was not okay to keep coming out. I was bringing all my old stuff into this new experience. I was insecure, unsafe, and once again all the old tapes were playing in my head. They are like the Energizer bunny: they keep going, and going, and going....

Then I had another experience that helped me quell the old tapes. On the day of the interview—Valentine's Day, as it happened—I got a dozen roses from the man I was seeing at the time. Everyone was around, and I was petrified. Without skipping a beat, Gail asked if they were from my boyfriend, whom she had met at a party, and started looking for a vase for them.

Then I was contacted by a man named Peter Nee, who knew about me and what I was doing in my division through another coworker. Peter asked me if I would be interested in attending an informal gathering of other gays and lesbians from various divisions of the bank. I was very interested, and I went and met a lot of others who believed that a group like this could validate their experience as gay men and lesbian women in the bank.

As we talked with one another, we realized that there was one fundamental belief that was bonding us together: we needed to affirm for the bank that doing outreach to gay and lesbian customers, treating gay and lesbian employees with equal respect, and affording them all the opportunities that you would afford a heterosexual individual were good business. The group began to snowball, and Dani Monroe suggested that we pull together in a more organized way, which we did. At Peter's invitation, I joined the ad hoc steering committee of the group, now called the Bank of Boston Gay and Lesbian Employee Resource Group.

I am more productive today because I don't have to hide any facet of my life. I don't have the fears that I still hear others talk about. I have come to respect other people's processes, realizing that not everyone is where I am now. We all do it in our own way and time. I've been blessed with a great family who is accepting and have a comfortable network of friends and coworkers. The last piece of bringing my life together as a gay man was my work life, and now I have that.

Come Out! Come Out! Wherever You Are!
Chris Palmer, Senior Manager
Employee Communications, Bank of Boston

The two jobs that I had prior to coming to the Bank of Boston laid the groundwork for me to embrace outness at work. I grew up in Bangor, Me., where I was a journalist for ten years, running the features desk of the *Bangor Daily News*. As a journalist, I have always approached my work from an objective perspective. While working there I was not really closeted but had never really said that I am a lesbian. If anyone were to have asked me, I certainly would have confirmed it.

My first coming-out-at-work experience occurred as a result of a tragedy in Bangor. You may have heard about a gay young man named Charlie Howard, who had asthma and was harassed by three teenage boys, who threw him in one of the canals that run through the city of Bangor. As a result, he had an asthma attack and drowned. Like thousands of others, I was outraged. I realized that if I were to edit or write anything about this tragedy, that there was no way that, as a lesbian, I could do so objectively.

The media descended on Bangor to cover the story. I was approached by a man from *The New York Times* who wanted to interview me. I made a decision that I had to tell my bosses that I was going to be interviewed and that because I was a lesbian I could not be objective. I felt that in losing my objectivity I was being dragged out of the closet. One of the hardest things for me in all of this was not being in control of the timing: I wanted to be running the show.

All of this was a catalyst for my then-partner and me to make a move from Bangor to Boston. I decided to go back to graduate school and earned my master's degree in business administration. After graduate school I was hired by Fidelity Investments, a place that I did not experience as gay-friendly.

Nevertheless, I decided that this time I was going to be more proactive about my lesbianism. So after my staff got to know me, I came out to them. Like typical yuppies, they were fine with it—but we never discussed it again. I felt that I had made some progress in coming out, but because it was not discussed, I felt uncomfortable and very alone. I knew of only one other lesbian at Fidelity—and I knew that she was a lesbian only because I had seen her at

Gay Pride. Soon after Pride I tried to approach her at work, but she made it very clear by her behavior that she did not want me anywhere near her.

I was laid off by Fidelity and was hired by the Bank of Boston six months later. I was at the bank for two months when my position was cut; fortunately, I was not. The bank did a great job of placing me at our operations center. It was a very blue-collar environment and very family-oriented, so I was amazed to find how warm a place it was to work. After I was there a while, I began to look around and realized that I was feeling lonely in this, the most diverse workplace in which I had ever been placed. I began asking myself whether, if this place was able to tolerate such a high level of diversity, I had a chance at last to be openly gay at work.

I knew the bank had an office of workforce diversity, which Fidelity and especially the *Bangor Daily News* had never had. Feeling that this was a good place to start, I made an appointment to speak with a woman named Rosa Hunter. I did have a legitimate business reason for talking to her about some training issues, but, as you can imagine, I also had my own personal agenda for this meeting. When we came to the end of our business, I said, "Rosa, I have something else I would like to discuss with you. I'm lesbian, and I want to know how to find other gay and lesbian people at the Bank of Boston." She looked a little stunned and kind of laughed and said, "No one has ever asked me that question before." She was open to learning and talking about it and said, "I'll get back to you."

Meanwhile, a lesbian named Stella Chan, who also worked at the bank and had gone to the same graduate school as I had, received our graduate school's alumnae newsletter. I had put a piece in the class notes about something that my partner and I had done, referring to my partner as "she." Stella immediately picked up the phone and called me. She introduced herself by saying, "Hi, Chris, my name is Stella, and I saw your item in the alumnae class notes. We both work at the bank, and we're both lesbians; let's get together." Stella worked in the same department as Peter Nee, and in fact they sat right next to each other. Soon after this phone call, Stella, Peter, and I got together and started exploring the idea of starting a gay and lesbian support group.

At that meeting I told Stella and Peter of my recent meeting with Rosa Hunter, and we all decided that I should take Stella with me to my next meeting with her. We figured that a place to start addressing gay and lesbian issues with Rosa would be making sure that the language used in the bank's equal employment opportunity statement included sexual orientation.

Through word of mouth and Peter's underground network at the bank, which was quite extensive, a small group of us got together at Peter's house for our first planning meeting. Subsequently we had three other house meetings; people began to bring other people, and this grassroots group mushroomed. It felt wonderful to finally be building a supportive network of gay and lesbian coworkers.

Just as word started getting around that this gay and lesbian resource group had formed, the bank hired a new diversity director, Dani Monroe, a wonderful and enthusiastic straight woman who became very excited about the group and quickly jumped onboard with us. She also made senior management aware of our existence. The group started to attract about sixty people for each meeting. The founders (Peter Nee, Stella Chan, Amy Rossiter, Richard Olson, and I) became the ad hoc steering committee. Because our numbers were becoming so large, we decided it was no longer fair to ask people to host meetings in their homes. So we brought the subject of moving to a larger space up for discussion with the whole group. Space in the Bank of Boston's home office was suggested, but people were scared that someone from human resources would stand outside the door and take down names. We decided to move the meeting to a place that would feel safe and would be gay-supportive.

About the same time, Stella was looking for a new position within the company and felt at some risk about being an open lesbian. She was afraid it might hinder her career options and felt strongly that she did not want to be outed. When she was in fact outed, as the result of a comment made by a steering committee member, her displeasure with the incident created some dissension in the ranks. Stella believed that being out should remain a personal choice and that group members had a responsibility to respect one another's varying comfort levels with the issue. At the same time, the steering committee agreed that none of us could lead the group without being out; we needed to be seen as role models. I felt very sad when Stella chose to withdraw from the steering committee as a result of this controversy.

The steering committee began to take stock of the fact that we were not duly elected from among the membership, and we decided it was time that we become more formalized and elect a steering committee from among the membership. I was one of those elected. The steering committee then decided to set about the task of meeting with senior management. I was frightened, because I had my own images and stereotypes of the Bank of Boston as being a conservative, Yankee, 210-year-old, uptight, three-piece-suit kind of an organization that is still very male-dominated. What I found instead was tolerance and openness.

We were all amazed at the receptiveness, graciousness, and openness with which we were met. In fact, they were complimentary about the way we had gone about organizing and about how inclusive the group was. I was completely blown away.

I have two possible explanations for this receptiveness. First, we are survivors and had just come through a rough economic time as an institution. I believe the bank has survived by including people through rewarding their courage and diversity of ideas. Second, I credit Helen Drinan, our senior vice president of human resources. As the highest-ranking woman in the organization, Helen already worked hard on behalf of minority groups at the bank, and she has done a superb job of sensitizing other senior managers and top executives.

I have to say that I am continually amazed by the effectiveness of our resource group. We have educated and sensitized our workplace in a way that even five years ago I would not have believed—yet it is just a drop in the bucket compared to the work that we still need to do.

Finally, I can't believe how far I have come personally, when I look back to my days at the *Bangor Daily News* and Fidelity Investments, and how alone I felt when I first came to the bank. I went from a place of loneliness to having companions, comrades, and friends who speak my own language at work. It has had an incredibly powerful impact on my self-esteem and sense of personal freedom.

If there is one message you get from all of this, I hope it's "Come out! Come out! Wherever you are!" Just do it! It won't be easy at first, and you may feel a lot of fear. But if you can just grab hold of the sense of pride in yourself, you will live your work life in a whole new way.

Part IV
Know Your Rights

Know Your Rights

Richard P. Branson, Esq.

*Richard Branson is past president of the Boston
Professional Alliance, a gay, lesbian, and bisexual
professional organization. He is a principal in the
law firm of Chin, Wright & Branson, P.C., 155 Federal
Street, Boston, MA 02110. Richard's practice includes
representation of gay and lesbian plaintiffs in
discrimination actions.*[1]

At a monthly meeting of the Boston Professional Alliance in November 1994, the newly reelected Republican governor of Massachusetts, William F. Weld, addressed an audience of 200 gay and lesbian professionals. Governor Weld explained that his policy of hiring people based on their abilities, regardless of their sexual orientation, was "a complete no-brainer. It's just elemental fairness."[2] In the governor's view, it simply does not make sense to deny American business and American government the talents of gay and lesbian people. Governor Weld practices what he preaches by hiring openly gay and lesbian people at all levels of his staff and state agencies as well as by his judicial appointments.[3]

In condemning the antigay referenda proposed in various states, Governor Weld noted how it would be inconceivable today to propose a similar referendum that would prohibit antidiscrimination laws in employment based on race, color, religion, national origin, or sex. Eventually, and with leadership from the public and private sectors, the notion that it is consistent with American values to deny someone employment based on their sexual orientation will become as unacceptable as the blight of legalized racial discrimination, now universally rejected in the American legal system. But the governor's message that night struck one chord in addition to a call for the basic American principles of fundamental fairness and social justice—namely, a call to American pragmatism: discrimination based on sexual orientation is bad for business.

There is a growing recognition in the American business community that it is time to end the foolish practice of hurting itself either by denying itself the full talents of gay and lesbian employees or by stultifying the full expression of those talents by allowing antigay work atmospheres to exist. Through the leadership of courageous and creative individuals, companies have begun to adopt antidiscrimination policies that have a direct effect on the legal status of gay people within those companies. Some companies have gone further to try to create workplace equality by the adoption of employment benefits for the domestic partners of gay and lesbian employees. Although the total number of companies with nondiscriminatory policies is small compared to the size of the American economy, the Chinese adage that the journey of ten thousand miles begins with the first step is appropriate. In fact, we are well on the way, but there is much to accomplish through both private and public law.

Ending sexual-orientation discrimination in the workplace requires a multipronged approach. This chapter explains some of the legal protections that now exist, describes some voluntary efforts in the private sector to create protections by changing the prevailing corporate cultures, and discusses ways in which equality in the workplace for gay and lesbian people can be advanced.

Legal protection against discrimination can be found in both public and private law. Public law includes the United States Constitution, state constitutions, the laws passed by the various legislative bodies and local governments, judicial decisions, as well as executive orders by Presidents and governors. Private law comprises those agreements individuals make among themselves through contracts and self-governing rules and regulations.

The U.S. Constitution

In theory, gay employees are protected by the Fifth and Fourteenth Amendments to the Constitution against discriminatory acts of governmental bodies, but not against the discriminatory acts of individuals or organizations.[4] Governments are constrained to act with a legitimate governmental purpose, not capriciously. The Fifth and Fourteenth Amendments' protection against the denial of "life, liberty, or property" without "due process" and its guarantee of "equal protection" require that governments act rationally in dealing with gay people in public employment. Discriminatory acts in public employment can be justified only if there is a constitutionally supported rationale for the discrimination. Therefore, the rules of the workplace should apply equally to homosexual workers and to heterosexual workers.

History demonstrates that there is a gap between the letter of the law and the personal and political beliefs of the judges applying it. Many courts have not overcome their antigay prejudices and have been unable to think rationally in applying the Constitution to employment discrimination involving sexual orientation. Fortunately, in 1969 a federal appeals court applied the legal principle of due process in the case of *Norton* v. *Macy*.[5] In that case a gay man was ordered reinstated at his position at the National Aeronautics and Space Administration. The government failed to show there was a rational basis for having fired him. The court refused to accept the mere characteristic of his being homosexual, without any history of behavior that was disruptive to the efficient functioning of the civil service, as providing a rational basis for his discharge. The legal principle in the Norton case has been codified into the federal civil-service law. However, it is unclear what level of openness about one's sexual orientation will be considered disruptive of the workplace.[6]

The California supreme court applied the Norton due-process rationale in the 1969 decision *Morrison* v. *State Board of Education*.[7] In that case the court determined that homosexuality and homosexual conduct alone did not constitute unfitness for the job upon grounds of immorality and ordered the teacher reinstated. Other state courts have made decisions contrary to these cases and have been satisfied that homosexuality alone can give the state a rational basis for termination. Not all states have applied the Norton principles in the teacher-related employment cases.[8]

Our Constitution's guarantee of equal protection under the Fifth and Fourteenth Amendments promises equal treatment under the law by our government. The equal-protection clause prohibits illegitimate discriminatory group classifications. Over the past thirty years the Supreme Court has developed an elaborate legal analysis for the application of this paramount American legal principle. The Court has devised a three-tier system for judicial review: strict scrutiny, heightened scrutiny, and rational-basis review.

For example, classifications based on race, religion, or national origin are suspect categories and require strict judicial review. Such classifications will not be upheld unless the government can show that such a classification is "suitably tailored to serve a compelling state interest."[9] For a classification such as sex or illegitimacy, the court will apply a heightened level of review. Such a classification will survive only if it is "substantially related to a sufficiently important governmental interest."[10] Finally, if a classification is not "suspect" or "quasi-suspect," then a discriminatory classification is presumed valid and will be upheld by a court "if there is a rational relationship between the disparity of treatment and some legitimate governmental purpose."[11]

Under this system of equal-protection jurisprudence, the level of scrutiny the court gives to the discriminatory classification tends to determine the success of a plaintiff in a lawsuit. In *Watkins* v. *United States Army*,[12] a three-judge federal court panel did apply the strict-scrutiny test to an Army sergeant dismissed for being gay and found in his favor. The equal-protection argument was later rejected by the full panel of judges for that circuit, but the judges decided that his dismissal was in fact illegal for other reasons. Other cases have applied the rational-basis test and found for military plaintiffs, as in

Meinhold v. *U.S. Department of Defense*[13] and *Cammermeyer* v. *Aspin*.[14] Others have upheld the sexual-orientation discriminatory practices against gay and lesbian military personnel as rational, as in *Woodward* v. *United States*[15] and the security-clearance case of *High Tech Gays* v. *Defense Industry Security Clearance Office*.[16] The ultimate level of scrutiny under the legal doctrine of equal protection applicable to military cases is still uncertain.[17]

State constitutions also have due-process and equal-protection provisions, which are applicable to public-employment situations. In 1979 the California supreme court applied its state equal-protection provision in the case of *Gay Law Students Association* v. *Pacific Telephone and Telegraph Company*,[18] thereby prohibiting the state-protected utility from discriminating on the basis of homosexuality alone. Your state constitution is likely to have similar provisions, even if your state's supreme court has not yet applied them to sexual-orientation discrimination.[19]

Statutory law

Federal law. There is currently no federal statutory law that prohibits employment discrimination based on sexual orientation. Title VII of the Civil Rights Act of 1964 prohibits discrimination in almost all employment, and in private employment where there are fifteen employees or more, based on race, color, religion, sex, and national origin. Since 1978, a bill amending Title VII by adding sexual orientation as a prohibited category of discrimination has been repeatedly proposed. Such an amendment would have universal impact affecting all states because of the priority federal law has over state law. The number of members of Congress who sponsor the amendment each year has come to a static level, and a promising new approach has been taken, by the civil rights movement. The proposed legislation, entitled in the 103d Congress the "Employment Non-Discrimination Act of 1994," would provide full protection against employment discrimination based on sexual orientation, while exempting certain employment-related claims that Title VII permits. The act did not pass the 103d Congress, and essentially the same legislation was proposed in the 104th Congress.[20]

State and local law. There are currently nine states and more than one hundred cities and counties that include sexual orientation as a prohibited category of discrimination in employment.[21] The nine states are Wisconsin, Massachusetts, Hawaii, Connecticut, California, New Jersey, Vermont, Minnesota, and Rhode Island. State laws passed by legislatures have a broader impact than local laws because they usually affect both public and private employees. These laws essentially prohibit employment decisions based solely on a person's sexual orientation. They do not require the hiring of gay people or insulate gay people from ordinary work qualifications. A typical law makes it unlawful for an employer, "because of the race, color, religious creed, national origin, sex, *sexual orientation*...of any individual to refuse to hire or employ or to bar or to discharge from employment such individual or to discriminate against such individual in compensation or in terms, conditions, or privileges of employment unless based upon a bona fide occupational qualification."[22]

Such laws attempt to remedy discriminatory practices in hiring, firing, promotions and demotions, salary and benefits, and prevent harassment[23] or other inequitable treatment based solely on an employee's sexual orientation. Such laws do not always remedy the compensation difference between married heterosexuals and similarly situated gay and lesbian couples that arises from failure to extend family health benefits to gay and lesbian families. Antidiscrimination legislation typically requires a quick response to the discriminatory act by calling on the employee to file a complaint with the state or local agency or administrative body given the jurisdiction to hear discrimination complaints. Failure to file a complaint in a timely fashion will result in loss of the right to pursue the claim of discrimination. Usually the administrative body will perform an investigation, but the employee will have the burden of proving unlawful discrimination. Although the powers of the various agencies differ, possible remedies include reinstatement, back pay, emotional-distress damages, and attorney's fees if a finding of illegal discrimination is made.

Employment contract

When a person enters someone's employ, a contract is formed, the terms and conditions of which are defined through either written terms or oral terms. This contract can be a highly regulated one, as in the case of union contracts, or can be given very little definition, as in the case of the typical verbal hiring of an individual.

Nonunion contracts. The typical nonunion employee's employment is governed by the so-called "at-will" rule. Simply put, one can be terminated at the will of the employer for any reason unless there is some law that prohibits the employer from doing so for an unlawful reason, or because there is a violation of the employment contract. Much of the law that governs the exceptions to the at-will rule is created by judges through their decisions. These legal precedents become binding on employers in those jurisdictions where the cases are decided. Such decisions become part of that state's common law. The scope of these judicial decisions varies from state to state. An attorney familiar with your local laws should evaluate any possible remedy under the local and common law of your state.

In some jurisdictions the courts glean the terms of the employment contract from the contents of employer handbooks, personnel manuals, and other company materials. Employer manuals increasingly include nondiscrimination policies forbidding discrimination on the basis of sexual orientation. This can be construed as part of your employment contract and thus can create a possible argument against a discriminatory termination. Some jurisdictions imply a term of good faith and fair dealing in all employment situations, while other states allow at-will employees to claim that the circumstances of their termination violate public policies of their state. An attorney conversant with the rulings of your local courts will be in a position to determine what contractual or state common-law rights you have.

Union contracts. Some unions provide added protections for their gay and lesbian union members. The collective-bargaining process is governed by federal and state law, which create rules and procedures that bind the employer and union leadership.[24] Union contracts often allow for termination only for "just cause" and provide for grievance procedures for other work-related problems such as harassment. In addition, the labor laws and union contracts provide for grievance procedures that can lead to binding arbitration outside the courtroom context. Union contracts also frequently contain nondiscrimination clauses that give outright protection to gay people. It is important to note that in order to exercise certain remedies, one must respond quickly and assert rights under the collective-bargaining agreement. The grievance procedure can lead to an arbitrator's award, which may include reinstatement and back pay.

Sometimes the hostile attitudes of union officials creates an additional problem. However, unions have a duty of fair representation for all members. Failure to act because of a member's sexual orientation will open the union itself to a discrimination claim by a gay, lesbian, or bisexual union member.

Practical advice

Being open and honest about one's sexual orientation at the workplace often evokes reactions from employers and coworkers. Reactions that result in discriminatory employment decisions by an employer or harassment by coworkers are unacceptable and require statutory or contractual remedies. Some states have provided for protection; most have not. Many cities and counties have prohibited sexual-orientation discrimination, but the remedies provided are diverse and have varying degrees of effectiveness.

Discrimination laws usually have a short statute of limitations. If you feel you have been treated unfairly, consult as early as possible with an attorney familiar with your legal remedies under local civil-rights law, as well as those more traditional rights under tort and contract law. In so doing, you will be able to make an informed decision about a legal challenge. The following suggestions can be helpful in the process of dealing with a discrimination claim.

1. Prepare a written chronology of events and provide a full history of your employment. Include a cast of characters, potential witnesses, circumstances under which your sexual orientation became known, the nature of the unfair treatment, the reasons why you believe your sexual orientation has been the cause of the discrimination, the nature of any homophobic remarks, and the who, what, where, when, and how of all such actions. Early on, get written statements from witnesses who acknowledge the discrimination. Do not share these materials with your employer, and if you have consulted an attorney in advance, prepare them at your attorney's direction to preserve attorney-client privilege.

2. Gather all the papers you have that concern your employment, including correspondence, employee manuals, handbooks, contracts, policy statements, and any communications between you and your employer. Do not copy confidential or restricted documents from your employer's files unless you normally have access to them and unless your employer's policy permits copying.

3. Request in writing from your employer a copy of your employment records. Some states require an employer to give you such copies. If you are allowed only to inspect them, review the file and make a list of all the documents in it. Be sure to keep a copy of the letter you send to your employer.

4. Even if you are unfairly treated, do not act rashly or otherwise give rise to a legitimate reason for termination. Control your anger. Save your energy for the legal battle.

5. Secure the emotional and moral support of friends and professionals. Emotional distress from unlawful discrimination is often compensable. Seeing a professional will help you document that element of your damages. Join a gay professional or social organization. Do not isolate yourself.

6. Be sure to exhaust your remedies within the context of your place of employment. If your employer has a remedial procedure, get your lawyer's advice on following it. Do not sign termination letters, statements of reasons for termination, or anything that would show your agreement to a negative evaluation of your job performance without consulting an attorney.

7. You have a duty to mitigate your back-pay damages by looking for employment if you are fired. Keep copies of all your job-seeking correspondence and responses of potential employers. Save the newspaper advertisements you respond to and keep copies of cover letters sent with résumés, as well as a diary of telephone contacts and job interviews.

8. File for unemployment benefits for practical as well as strate-

gic reasons. If the employer contests the unemployment benefits, he or she may give a clue to what defenses might be raised to your complaint of discrimination.

9. If you are in a union, see the shop steward or other appropriate union official immediately to initiate the remedies available to you under your union contract. If your immediate union representative is unhelpful, go up the chain of command to get help.

In states and cities where there are strong legal protections, it may be strategically advantageous before discrimination occurs to let your employer know that you are gay. This is a very personal choice that only you can make. Speak with a local attorney about this strategy. It is often an employer's retort that "I didn't even know he was gay or she was a lesbian." However, lawyers often say that what is good for your case may be bad for your life and what is bad for your case may be good for your life. Career advice and legal advice are two different matters. Nevertheless, good legal advice can help you evaluate the risks.

Corporate policies and the Wall Street Project

In addition to increasing legal protections, among the most important developments in the advancement of gay equality are the efforts being made to change the corporate culture in America. As the corporate value of diversity in the workplace gains momentum, the gay community has an increasingly effective vehicle to obtain basic human rights for gay people. As coworkers come to value the importance of diversity and understand the dignity of all human beings, they will contribute to the change in societal attitudes that is needed to make legal protections through legislation more likely. Efforts by such groups as the Wall Street Project[25] play an important role in focusing the gay community's energy on corporate change.

The goal of the Wall Street Project is to eliminate discrimination in every American workplace. It encourages gay people and their friends to exercise their prerogatives as stockholders, pension fund participants, insurance policy holders, and contributors to colleges, universities, and foundations, to demand change in the workplace. The tactic includes both careful information-gathering about corporate policies and requests for sexual-orientation nondiscrimination policies. As stockholders or as indirect participants in corporate ownership, we can apply needed pressure to companies to adopt sexual-orientation nondiscrimination policies.

A very positive example of attempts to change corporate sexual-orientation discrimination can be seen in the response to the actions of Cracker Barrel Old Country Store Restaurants in firing eleven gay employees in the summer of 1991. Cracker Barrel is a publicly traded company whose stockholders include pension funds. The Wall Street Project enlisted the support of New York City pension fund officials, who held a significant number of Cracker Barrel shares in the pension portfolio. Although it took a court order to achieve it, eventually these joint efforts succeeded in presenting a resolution calling for the adoption of a sexual nondiscrimination policy and the rehiring of the eleven gay workers at Cracker Barrel's 1993 annual meeting. Although the resolution did not pass, it received 15 percent of the vote—a considerable amount in public-interest proxy fights.

In 1993 the Wall Street Project completed a census of corporate America that provided a comprehensive survey of the employment practices of the *Fortune* 500 service and industrial corporations as related to sexual orientation. The Wall Street Project made the following key findings about the *Fortune* 500:[26]

1. One out of every four employees of the *Fortune* 500 service and industrial corporations works for an employer that has a written sexual-orientation nondiscrimination policy.

2. One hundred thirty-four *Fortune* 500 corporations have written sexual-orientation nondiscrimination policies.

3. Most of these policies have been adopted since 1990.

4. Both large and small corporations have nondiscrimination policies.

5. Corporations in diversified service, financial, or high-tech fields are the predominant companies with nondiscrimination policies.

6. Companies with nondiscrimination polices are found mostly in the Northeast and the West.

7. Companies generally adopt sexual-orientation nondiscrimination policies when employees ask for the policy.

The Wall Street Project has also begun a new endeavor, which may have a major impact on workplace equality. Similar to the Sullivan Principles, which provided a socially responsible guide to doing business with South Africa in the time of apartheid, the Equality Principles on Sexual Orientation proposed by the Wall Street Project will set goals of fairness for corporations by giving them the opportunity to adopt socially responsible principles for the elimination of sexual-orientation discrimination in the workplace.

In the preamble to the Equality Principles their purpose is stated: "To become successful in the ever-competitive world of business, a company must strive to create an environment in which all employees are treated with respect. Through the cultivating of diversity in the workplace, a company can draw fully upon the potential for creativity and commitment represented by all its employees. Implementation of these Equality Principles on Sexual Orientation are an important step in that direction."

The goal is to encourage the adoption by corporate America of the following eight basic principles:[27]

1. Discrimination based on sexual orientation should be explicitly prohibited, such prohibition to be included in each company's written employment policy statement.

2. Discrimination against HIV-positive employees or those with AIDS should be strictly prohibited.

3. All employee groups must be given equal standing regardless of sexual orientation.

4. Diversity training should include sexual-orientation issues.

5. Spousal benefits for domestic partners of employees, regardless of sexual orientation, must be granted on an equal basis with those given married employees.

6. All negative stereotypes concerning sexual orientation should be banned in all company advertising. Media advertising may not discriminate on the basis of sexual orientation.

7. Companies must not discriminate in sale and purchase of goods and services on the basis of sexual orientation.

8. Written nondiscrimination policies on sexual orientation must be disseminated throughout the company.

Starting with the *Fortune* 500 industrial and service corporations, the Wall Street Project will ask those companies to support and implement the Equality Principles. In addition, the Wall Street Project—along with the many public officials, pension fund trustees, socially responsible investment firms, major national lesbian and gay community organizations, international, national, state, and local gay and lesbian political leaders, and numerous community-based professional, political, and AIDS organizations—will urge institutional investors, including pension funds, religious institutions, foundations, unions, colleges, and universities—which control $4 trillion in investments—to ask companies in their portfolios to adopt and implement these principles.

It is incumbent upon us to exercise our economic strength to expand the adoption of corporate nondiscrimination policies. The gay community and our friends can put into action the power of their multitude of corporate and economic relationships to obtain equality for gay people in the workplace by pressuring corporate America for nondiscriminatory policies. Eventually, the business world must recognize that sexual orientation nondiscrimination policies are not only the simplest expressions of human decency and fairness but also the best business choice for the most productive use of a diverse workforce.

Workplace equality

Full workplace equality above and beyond nondiscrimination policies finds its expression in the extension of family health insurance and other benefits to the partners and children of gay and lesbian employees. Domestic-partner benefits are generally provided to straight and gay employees who have a spousal equivalent. Some companies provide domestic-partner benefits only to gay and lesbian employees in established relationships on the theory that straight people have the option of marrying and receiving married-couples benefits.

As part of its survey, the Wall Street Project also identified thirty-two *Fortune* 500 companies that provide further domestic-partner benefits, including bereavement leave, family leave, use of company facilities, health-care coverage, and a variety of other benefits such as relocation benefits, life/travel/accident insurance, tax/stock plans, companion passes for travel, and child care.

Results from litigation in the area of domestic-partner benefits is mixed. However, many state civil rights statutes do not specifically cover such work/family-related benefits. The failure to legalize same-sex marriages continues to be an impediment for gay and lesbian partners to receive equal treatment under a vast number of federal and state laws, not the least of which are pension, death, tax, and other employment-related benefits.

Conclusion

A national civil rights act prohibiting sexual-orientation discrimination is the ultimate legal solution to equality under the law. In the meantime, public and private executive leadership can provide significant cultural change and legal protection by adopting sexual-orientation nondiscrimination policies. Clearly there is no legal justification, consistent with basic American legal principles, that can justify denying hard-working, taxpaying gay American citizens basic human rights. However, we know from the history of the African-American civil rights movement that bringing about true justice and the accompanying legal change requires moral courage. From this same history we also know that recognition of the contribution of gay men and lesbians to our society is essential to the accomplishment of that legal change. The public acknowledgment of gay and lesbian citizens' contribution to American society is well on its way. Eventually, the absurdity of legally sanctioned discrimination on the basis of sexual orientation will be exposed as patently un-American and intolerably unjust.

Notes

1. The contents of this article are the responsibility of the author alone. The author would like to thank Todd Fernandez, Esq., for his helpful suggestions and

Richard Rasi for the opportunity to participate in the project. This article should not be relied upon for specific legal advice. It is not intended to be an analysis of each state's law. Your particular problem should be reviewed by a lawyer familiar with your local laws. Employment-discrimination law is constantly changing and varies widely from jurisdiction to jurisdiction.

2. See "Weld Reiterates His Support for Gay Rights Issues," *Bay Windows* (December 8, 1994): 3.

3. See story about Mitchell Adams, the Massachusetts commissioner of revenue, and Kevin Smith, then-commissioner of the Division of Capital Planning and Operations, now Governor Weld's chief of staff: "Two Male Weld Officials Say They Live as a Couple," *The Boston Globe* (November 13, 1992): 21.

4. The due-process clause of the Fifth Amendment makes the equal-protection clause of the Fourteenth Amendment binding upon the federal government. see *Bolling* v. *Sharpe*, 37 U.S. 497, 498–99, 74 S.Ct. 693, 694 (1954). The Fifth Amendment states, "No person shall be held to answer for a capital, or otherwise infamous crime, unless on a presentment or indictment of a Grand Jury, except in cases arising in the land or naval forces, or in the Militia, when in actual service in time of War or public danger: nor shall any person be subject for the same offense to be twice put in jeopardy of life or limb: nor shall be compelled in any criminal case to be witness against himself, not be deprived of life, liberty, or property, without due process of law; nor shall private property be taken for public use, without just compensation." The Fourteenth Amendment states, "All persons born or naturalized in the United States, and subject to the jurisdiction thereof, are citizens of the United States and of the State wherein they reside. No State shall make or enforce any law which shall abridge the privileges or immunities of citizens of the United States; nor shall any State deprive any person of life, liberty, or property, without due process of law; nor deny to any person within its jurisdiction the equal protection of the laws."

5. *Norton* v. *Macy*, 417 F.2d 1161 (D.C.Cir. 1969).

6. See *Singer* v. *U.S. Civil Service Com'n*, 530 F.2d 247 (9th Cir. 1976), vacated, 429 U.S. 1034 (1977). An employee of the Seattle office of the Equal Employment Opportunity Commission was terminated for being too open about his gayness, including seeking a marriage license. Although his dismissal was upheld by the Ninth Circuit's decision, it was later vacated by the Supreme Court at the request of the Carter administration.

7. *Morrison* v. *State Board of Education*, 82 Cal. Rptr. 175, 461 P.2d 375 (Cal. 1969).

8. For a thorough discussion of teacher's rights see Mary L. Bonauto, "A Legal Overview of the Rights of Gay, Lesbian, and Bisexual Teachers," in *One Teacher in Ten,* ed. Jennings (Alyson Publications, 1994), pp. 257–76.

9. *City of Cleburne* v. *Cleburne Living Center, Inc.,* 473 U.S. 432, 440, 105 S.Ct. 3249, 3254 (1985).

10. *Cleburne,* 473 U.S. at 441, 105 S.Ct. at 3255.

11. *Heller* v. *Doe,* 509 U.S., 113 S.Ct. 2637, 2642 (1993).

12. *Watkins* v. *U.S. Army,* 837 F.2d 1428 (9th Cir. 1988) amended, 847 F.2d 1329, different results reached on reh'g, 875 F.2d 699 (9th Cir. 1989) (en banc), cert. denied, 498 U.S. 957, 111 S.Ct. 384 (1990).

13. *Meinhold* v. *U.S. Dept. of Defense,* 34 F.3d 1469 (9th Cir. 1994).

14. *Cammermeyer* v. *Aspin,* 850 F.Supp. 910 (W.D.Wash. 1994).

15. *Woodward* v. *United States,* 871 F.2d 1068 (Fed.Cir. 1989), cert. denied, 494 U.S. 1003, 110 S.Ct. 1296 (1990).

16. *High Tech Gays* v. *Defense Industry Security Clearance Office*, 895 F.2d 563 (9th Cir 1990).

17. The issue of equal protection and the military service continues to unfold as the Clinton administration's "don't ask, don't tell, don't pursue" policy is litigated. In the federal case of *Able* v. *United States*, no. 94 CV 0974 (E.D. N.Y. March 30, 1995), 1995 WL 149460 (E.D. N.Y.), the district court's decision declared the policy in violation of the First Amendment and the equal-protection clause. The issue of homosexual status versus the propensity for homosexual conduct presents the military with absurd issues relating to proving intent to commit homosexual acts. The court made the following historical reference to the danger of status discrimination: "Hitler taught the world what could happen when the government began to target people not for what they had done but because of their status"; see Memorandum of Decision at p. 6. The court's decision dealt only with the speech aspects of the policy as codified in 10 U.S.C. s 654(b)(2). The lower court's decision will be appealed by the government.

18. *Gay Law Students Association* v. *Pacific Telephone and Telegraph Co.*, 156 Cal. Rptr. 14, 595 P.2d 592 (Cal. 1979).

19. State constitutions contain various provisions that could be applicable. See *Woodward* v. *Gallagher*, 59 Empl. Prac. Dec. P 41,652, 1992 WL 252279 (Fla. Cir.). A homosexual deputy sheriff was reinstated on the grounds that his termination for private sexual conduct prior to his hiring was a violation of the Florida constitution's right to privacy.

20. The "Employment Non-Discrimination Act of 1994," introduced by representatives Barney Frank and Gerry Studds and Sen. Edward Kennedy in the House and Senate, adopts many of the remedies of Title VII but is a separate act similar to the employment provisions of the Americans With Disabilities Act, 42 U.S.C. sec. 12111. The legislation received strong bipartisan support in the 103d Congress, with 32 Senate and 138 House cosponsors. For further information, contact the Human Rights Campaign Fund, 1101 14th Street NW, Suite 200, Washington, D.C. 20005, telephone (202) 332-6483. HRCF is working with the Leadership Conference on Civil Rights, which has made passage of this bill a priority for the 1990s.

21. The National Gay and Lesbian Task Force's Policy Institute offers a publication that lists the states and local governments with antidiscrimination laws. Its address is 2320 17th Street, N.W., Washington, D.C. 20009; telephone (202) 332-6483.

22. Massachusetts General Laws, chap. 151B, sec. 4(1).

23. See *Smith* v. *Brimfield Precision, Inc.*, 90-SEM-0150, for a precedent-setting case in which the Massachusetts Commission Against Discrimination found that a male machinist employee of the defendant had been "constructively discharged" from his employment when the employer permitted same-sex sexual harassment by a male coworker to continue, forcing the employee to leave his job.

24. For federal law see National Labor Relations Act 29 U.S.C., sec. 151 et seq.

25. The Wall Street Project is a program of the Community Lesbian and Gay Rights Institute, located in New York City. The mailing address is Wall Street Project, 82 Wall Street, Suite 1105, New York, NY 10005-3601.

26. See "1993 Census, Sexual Orientation Policies, *Fortune* 500 Service & Industrial Corporations," a Wall Street Project publication. These findings have been generally confirmed by a recent publication, which published the results of a similar census in 1993 and contains valuable information about individual *Fortune* 500 corporations: see D. Baker, S. Strub, and B. Henning, *Cracking the Corporate Closet* (HarperCollins Publishers, 1995).

27. See Wall Street Project, "Equal Principles Set Goals of Fairness for Corporate America," May 4, 1995. Contact Nick Curto, Cochair. Voice/fax (212) 289-1741.

Other references

Harvard Law Review editors, *Sexual Orientation and the Law* (Harvard University Press, 1990).

N. Hunter, S. Michaelson, and T. Stoddard, *The Rights of Lesbians and Gay Men: The Basic ACLU Guide to a Gay Person's Rights*, 3d ed. (Southern Illinois University Press, 1992).

A. Leonard, *Sexuality and the Law: An Encyclopedia of Major Legal Cases* (Garland Publishing, 1993).

W. Rubenstein, ed., *Lesbians, Gay Men, and the Law* (New Press, 1993).

R. Achtenberg, ed., for the National Lawyers Guild, *Sexual Orientation and the Law*, rev. (Clark Boardman Callaghan Publishers, 1994).

Legal organizations dealing with sexual-orientation discrimination

American Civil Liberties Union
National Gay and Lesbian Rights Project
132 West 43rd Street
New York, NY 10036
(212) 944-9800, ext. 545

Gay and Lesbian Advocates and Defenders
P.O. Box 218
Boston, MA 02112
(617) 426-1350

Lambda Legal Defense and Education Fund
666 Broadway, 12th Floor
New York, NY 10012
(212) 995-8585

National Center for Lesbian Rights
870 Market Street, Suite 570
San Francisco, CA 94102
(415) 392-6257

National Lesbian and Gay Law Association
P.O. Box 77130
National Capital Station
Washington, DC 20014
(202) 389-0161

Epilogue

The stories in this book serve as an example of the many different journeys that gay, lesbian, and bisexual people take in their process of coming out. At each turn in the road, a decision between truth and silence is made. Regardless of the choice, there are challenges, rewards, and consequences. These stories have shown us some of the consequences there can be for telling the truth. The experiences of these men and women have also told us of the price that is paid for remaining silent.

There are no right or wrong ways to be out, because the journey for each of us is unique. As these stories have shown us, we each need to do what is right for ourselves. We cannot do it without looking inside to find our true self while looking outside to find the support of others.

We do not have to take the journey alone. There are millions of us out there on that journey. Every once in a while we must stop and share our story with those we meet on the way.

You have your own story to tell. Tell it.

Alyson Publications publishes a wide variety of books with gay and lesbian themes. For a free catalog or to be placed on our mailing list, please write to:
Alyson Publications
P.O. Box 4371
Los Angeles, CA 90078
Indicate whether you are interested in books for gay men, lesbians, or both.